The History of
Israel and Judah

in Old Testament Times

by
Francois Castel

translated by
Matthew J. O'Connell

PAULIST PRESS
New York/Mahwah

Maps and charts by Frank Sabatté, C.S.P.

Drawings and photographs in this book are courtesy of *Le Monde de la Bible; La Bibbia,* published by Civilta Cattolica, editions Ancora 1973, copyrighted by Pietro Vanetti and Denise Castel.

This title was originally published as *L'Histoire d'Israel et de Juda* by Editions du Centurion, Paris.

Biblical translations: Revised Standard Version.

Library of Congress
Catalog Card Number: 85-60294

ISBN: 0-8091-2701-6

Published by Paulist Press
997 Macarthur Boulevard
Mahwah, N.J. 07430

Printed and bound in the United States of America

Contents

Preface	1
General Chronology	2
Introduction	3
The Period Studied	6
Geography	7
The Main Routes	10
1. Prehistory	13
2. History	21
The Amorites	22
The Patriarchal Tradition: Genesis	24
The Patriarchs	26
Abraham	26
Isaac	29
Jacob	30
Israel	30
The Patriarchs and Egypt	31
The Hyksos	33
Joseph	35
Egypt and the Hurrians	35
Canaan	37
The Fourteenth Century	39
Habiru = Hebrews?	41
Oppression in Egypt: Exodus	41
Moses, Exodus, Numbers, Deuteronomy, Leviticus	43
The Exodus from Egypt	45
Sinai and the Law	48

3. **The Age of the Conquest**   51
The Agents of the Conquest   52
The Conquest of the South   55
The Transjordan   58
Central Palestine   59
Jericho   62
Ai   63
Gibeon   63
Dan, an Unusual Tribe   64
The Northern Tribes   66
The Twelve Tribes   67
The Shechem Assembly   68
The Tribal League   68

4. **The Age of the Judges**   71
The Judges   71
The Lesser Judges   72
Jephthah   73
Othniel   75
Deborah   75
Shamgar   77
Ehud   77
Gideon/Jerubbaal   78
Abimelech   79
Samson   80

5. **Samuel and the Establishment of the Monarchy**   81

6. **The Reigns of David and Solomon**   86
David   87
The Succession   91

7. **Schism: 933 B.C. (?). 1 Kings 12**   97
Dating   99
Jeroboam, King of Israel and Rehoboam, King of Judah   100
War between Judah and Israel   102
Israel: The Omrid Dynasty   103
Ahab   104
Jehoshaphat, King of Judah   106
The Battle of Kharkar   106
Elijah   107
From the Death of Ahab to Jehu   109

Elisha   109
Jehu   109
Judah: Athaliah and Joash   112
Kings Jehoahaz and Joash of Israel, King Amaziah of Judah   113
Jeroboam II of Israel and the Prophet Amos   113

8. **Assyrian Domination and the End of Israel**   **117**
Tiglath-pileser III   117
Judah under Uzziah and Jotham   117
Isaiah   119
The Last Years of Israel   120
Micah   123
Judah in the Reign of Hezekiah   124
The Reign of Manasseh   128
Nahum   130
The Reign of Josiah   130

9. **Babylonian Domination and the End of Judah**   **135**
Jeremiah   136
Jehoiakim   137
After the Destruction of Jerusalem   139
The Jews in Egypt   140
The Jews in Mesopotamia   141
Ezekiel   143
Babylonian Judaism   144

10. **Persian Domination and Return from Exile**   **147**
End of the Neobabylonian Empire and
Birth of the Persian Empire   147
Second Isaiah   147
The Persian Period   148
Documentation   150
Return from Exile and Rebuilding   151
Cambyses   153
Darius   154
Xerxes   155
Esther   155
Malachi   156
Artaxerxes I   156
Darius II   158
Artaxerxes II   160
The Samaritans   164

11. **The Period of Hellenistic Domination**   **166**
    The Successors   168
    Seleucid Domination   172
    1 and 2 Maccabees   174
    Daniel   174
    Judith   177

12. **The Maccabean Resistance and the New Hasmonean Kingdom** **178**
    Attempt To Hellenize Jerusalem   178
    The Jewish Revolt   180
    Jonathan Maccabeus   182
    Simon Maccabeus   184
    John Hyrcanus   185
    Aristobulus I   186
    Alexander Janneus   187
    Salome Alexandra   188
    Aristobulus II   189

13. **The Roman Occupation**   **192**
    Herod and the Reconquest of Judea   198
    The Herodian Succession   204
    Archelaus   206
    Herod Antipas   206
    Herod Philip   207
    Judea as a Roman Province   207
    Caligula   212
    Philo   216
    The Embassy to Rome   218
    The Jews under Parthian Domination   219
    Emperor Claudius   221
    Agrippa I   221
    Judea to 66 A.D.   222
    Agrippa II   224
    The First Jewish War   225
    Josephus   226
    Organization of the Rebellion   228
    The Galilean Campaign   230
    Jerusalem   231
    The Capture of Jerusalem   232
    The Final Resistance in Palestine   235
    Qumran   236
    Alexandria   239

From the Destruction of Jerusalem
to the Revolt of Bar Kokhba   239
Christians and Jews   241
The Final Jewish War   242

Notes   **249**

Bibliography   **257**

Index   **262**

Preface

Why a *History of Israel and Judah* in a series of guides for leaders of Bible study groups? Such leaders know the answer from their own experience: groups that study the texts of Scripture over the course of the year as well as readers who study the Bible in greater isolation often want a systematic presentation of the history of Israel for reference use. Unfortunately, aids of this kind are not common.

François Castel's book fills the gap: it is neither overly succinct, as are the historical manuals that form a chapter of the various "Introductions to the Bible," nor esoteric and inaccessible to the ordinary person, as are the histories of Israel (in many cases, remarkable achievements) that are written in the perspectives and language of university scholarship. Castel's book is indeed rather compact and will require some effort from the reader, but the same reader will be quickly won over by the author's clarity and real gifts as a writer.

Michel Cambe

General Chronology

Middle Paleolithic	60000 to 40000
Upper Paleolithic	35000 to 9000
Mesolithic (Natufian culture)	10000 to 7500
Pre-pottery Neolithic	7500 to 6000
Pre-pottery Neolithic A and B	
Lacuna	
Pottery Neolithic	5000 to 4000
Lower Chalcolithic (Wadi Rabah)	4000 to 3600
Upper Chalcolithic (Ghassulian)	3600 to 3200
Pre-urban	3200 to 2900
(Fifty years earlier in northern Syria)	
Early Bronze I	2900 to 2800
II	2800 to 2550
III	2550 to 2300
IV (also: Early Bronze/Middle Bronze	2300 to 2150
Middle Bronze I or: Intermediate Bronze)	2150 to 1950
II A	1950 to 1800
II B	1800 to 1630
II C	1630 to 1550
Late Bronze I	1550 to 1400
II	1400 to 1200
Iron I ⎫ Israelite period	1200 to 900
II ⎭	900 to 539
Persian period	539 to 333
Hellenistic period	333 to 164
(Jewish independence: Hasmonean Dynasty)	164 to 63
Roman period	63 to 350
Byzantine period	350 to 635
Ummayad period (Caliphs at Baghdad)	661 to 750
Abassid period	750 to 1258
Seljuk Turks in Syria-Palestine	1055 to 1250
Crusades	1098 to 1291
Mamluk Turks in Syria-Palestine	1250 to 1517
Mongol invasion	1258 to 1260

(Jean Sapin, *Etudes théologiques et religieuses*)

Introduction

To open the Bible is to discover the history of a people's dealings with God. It is a real history, played out in the heart of the area we know as the Fertile Crescent, a history that will be set down with the help of categories borrowed from the cultures this people encounters.

Events are indeed the source of many of the biblical stories, but the history is narrated for the sake of a lesson to be drawn from it: In the light of this reading of our history, how are we to live, act, hope and struggle today? The history is being told for the redactor's contemporaries; it is history that moves in a certain direction; the telling differs depending on whether the text at hand is a defense of the monarchy, a prophetic discourse, or the work of the priests. This is why in dealing with each text an effort must be made to determine how much is interpretation, or even successive interpretations, and how much is event. The task is always a difficult one, and never finished. It is only possible to offer hypotheses which must then be refined by expanding our knowledge of the history and civilizations of the Near East and by carefully studying the literary history of the texts that have come down to us.

Here are a few examples to illustrate what I mean. At first sight, the story of Cain and Abel may be classified as a mythical narrative, and the historian may believe that the text has nothing for him. In a second phase, he may inquire how this story displays a peculiarly Israelite culture in which God takes up the cudgels in behalf of the weak, the victim. But he can also make contact with the history of a clan of which we know far too little: the clan of Cain's descendants, the Kenites. Living as nomads, they will for a long time enjoy a monopoly as metalworkers; the archeologists are rediscovering them today, and this leads us to reflect on the relation of the Kenites to Moses.[1] The latter's father-in-law is sometimes said to have been a Kenite (Jgs 4:11). As a result, the Kenites seem to enjoy a special status in the midst of Israel.

At the other end of the spectrum, the capture of the town of Ai is told with such a wealth of detail that it seems evident we are dealing with a firm historical tradition. And yet archeology shows us that the town of Ai was a ruin long before the Hebrews entered Canaan. We must therefore ask why the Hebrews wrote such a text. The answer must be looked for not in a history of events but in the history of thought: Where, and in what century, and for what reasons did the Hebrews think they should compose such a passage?

I have already mentioned archeology twice. This discipline is a constant source of material with which to compare the biblical text. In the optimum case, the Bible and archeology say the same thing or else complement one another; thus the prophecy of Jeremiah and the results of the excavations at Lachish are very largely in agreement regarding the siege of Jerusalem in 587 B.C. Too often, however, scholars themselves have attempted to harmonize their discoveries with the most prominent narratives in the Bible. Thus they believe they have rediscovered the mines and stables of Solomon. A better dating and further excavations have yielded quite a different result. The discovery of the mines of the Arabah, between the Dead Sea and the Red Sea, made it possible to write a history of the place going back to the fourth millennium and in particular provided us with information on the mines of Pharaoh Rameses III and on relations between Egypt and the Kenites. It was here that a gold-plated bronze serpent was discovered which strangely resembles the bronze serpent of Moses (Num 21:8).

The stables at Megiddo provided information not on the age of Solomon but on the works carried out a century later by Ahab, king of Israel.

As sites are gradually uncovered, archeology supplies a sizable body of material, but it is material that needs to be dated, classified and carefully deciphered; the labor, which is time-consuming and calls for scrupulous care, has not yet yielded all its results. The present state of knowledge may yet be profoundly altered; thus the discovery of Mari in 1933 (see map, p. 20) gave us a fresh view of the age of the patriarchs; after 1947 the discoveries at Qumran radically changed our understanding of Judaism around the time of Christ (pp. 236-8). In 1975, 15,000 tablets were discovered at Ebla in Syria,[2] which concern a very poorly known period in the history of Palestinian Syria, 2400–2250 B.C. It will be some years yet before we are in a position to make use of this new wealth.

Though some sites have yielded archives, many yield only their ruins; an attempt must be made to date these and then to explain them in function of history as already known to us. Unfortunately, invaders or destroyers do not often sign their handiwork. When archeologists uncover a town in Palestine that was destroyed in the thirteenth or twelfth century B.C., who will tell us whether it was an internal revolution, an Egyptian campaign, a Philistine invasion or a Hebrew invasion that caused the destruction?

The writing of a history of Israel and Judah requires that an attempt be made to unravel the knotted skein of traditions and in this way get back to the facts. The facts must be compared with what archeology and history tell us of the neighboring peoples. In fact, archeology and the history of these peoples must themselves be challenged. Today it is possible to attempt to take our bearings. We can offer hypotheses which are as objective as possible, but the hypotheses must be immediately subjected to the test of literary, historical and archeological research. Each new contribution

Suggested Sources of Reading

Journals on Archaeology
Biblical Archaeologist Review
Biblical Archaeology
Revue Biblique
Bible et Terre Sainte

Journals on the Bible
Bible Today
Biblical Theology Bulletin
Catholic Biblical Quarterly
Journal of Biblical Literature

The History of Israel
John Bright, *A History of Israel* (3rd Edition, Westminster Press, 1981)
S. Herrmann, *A History of Israel in Old Testament Times* (Fortress Press, 1975)
Roland de Vaux, *The Early History of Israel* (Westminster Press, 1978)
Martin Noth, *The History of Israel* (Harper and Row, 1960)
B. K. Rattey, *A Short History of the Hebrews from the Patriarchs to Herod the Great* (Oxford University Press, 1976)

Archaeology
M. Avi-Yonah, editor, *Encyclopedia of Archaeological Excavations in the Holy Land* (4 volumes; Prentice-Hall, 1975)
William F. Albright, *The Archaeology of Palestine* (Penguin Books, 1949)
Y. Aharoni and M. Avi-Yonah, *The Macmillan Bible Atlas* (Macmillan Co., 1977)
H. G. May, *The Oxford Bible Atlas* (Oxford Press, 1974)
Kathleen Kenyon, *Archaeology in the Holy Land* (Praeger, 1960)

will make it possible to focus this work more carefully and will surely lead
to the questioning of many points on which we still have little certainty.

Throughout the present book I run the risk of having ignored or un-
dervalued a document or a piece of research. Even more frequently I will
in good faith have put my trust in a biblical or extrabiblical document without having realized the criticism that needs to be made of it. Each reader
must therefore redo this study for himself with a view to correcting and
improving it.

The Period Studied

The people of Israel and Judah did not make their appearance in a
single place nor at a precise moment in time. They were an entity that took
shape slowly, in the midst of the very ancient civilizations which occupied
the area between Mesopotamia and Egypt. I shall begin, therefore, by
trying to show how they came to birth, how a people was formed which
would attain to full unity only with the coming of David's kingdom, the
establishment of Jerusalem as their capital, and the building of the Solo-
monic temple.

The tribes existed long before the tenth century B.C., and their various histories must be traced prior to the point when they became parts of
a single epic centered on the figures of Abraham and Moses and on the
foundational event: the exodus from Egypt and the experience at Sinai.

The combination "Israel and Judah" was in existence only during the
two reigns of David and Solomon, that is, for less than a century. The two
parts, Israel and Judah, experienced different fates, but their life was always characterized by the hope, the desire, the need of being reunited.

Israel was eventually to disappear under the blows of Assyria in the
eighth century B.C. Judah was to be destroyed by Babylon in the sixth
century B.C. But the destruction of the states did not mean the death of
the people. The Jews continued to live, think and write, both in Palestine
and in Babylon and the diaspora.

On Palestinian soil Jewish entities reappeared in the time of the Persians and under Greek hegemony. A new kingdom came into existence in
the second century B.C. thanks to the Maccabean rebellion, but it would
succumb under the weight of internal oppositions that were manipulated
by the Romans.

The Roman occupation ended in the terrible Jewish wars of 70 and
135 A.D., which put an end to any and every Jewish political entity. Nonetheless Israel lived on in numerous communities both in Palestine and in
Babylon and through the diaspora. A complete history would require fol-

lowing the separate stories of each of these communities as well as the spiritual, cultural and economic bonds uniting the various communities.

I have chosen to stop at the point when the Israelite tribes ceased to be gathered together in a single country and to have a direct consciousness of a common life and common interests.

Geography

The geographical area of which I shall be speaking stretches from Mesopotamia to Egypt and from the Mediterranean to the desert of Arabia. The kingdoms of Israel and Judah were bounded on the north by Lebanon and Syria, and on the south by the "river of Egypt," the identification of which varies.[3] In the east the Jewish tribes attempted with varying degrees of success to settle in the Transjordan on the plateaus of Gilead, Ammon and Moab.

The Mediterranean coast was largely outside the Jewish sphere. It was controlled north of Carmel by the Phoenicians and their two principal cities, Tyre and Sidon. South of Carmel, the Jews were in constant conflict with the Philistines, who in the end gave their name to the country: Palestine.

The country thus bounded was completely lacking in unity from north to south and east to west. If we take as our criteria rainfall and differences in land surface, we can distinguish four parallel areas running north-south: the coastal plain, the hill country, the Jordan depression, and the Transjordanian plateau.

North of Carmel the coastal plain was very narrow but favorable to shipping and trade, which were in the hands of the Phoenicians. South of Carmel, the plain widened and sandhills marked the coast. Only under Herod the Great (22 B.C.) would the Plain of Sharon have its great port of Caesarea.

Before the invasion of "the peoples of the sea" in the twelfth century B.C. Jaffa (Joppa), south of Sharon, was the only port on the coast; it had the advantage of a rich hinterland, was well defended by the fortress of Aphek, and controlled the coastal caravan route. Jaffa was to become important once again only with the Persian invasion; it had been a very important port in the thirteenth century B.C.

South of Jaffa, the plain, or Shephelah, enjoyed a Mediterranean climate which favored the cultivation of fruits and vegetables; it was under the control of the Philistine cities, which were able to carry on trade both via the caravan routes of Arabia and via the Mediterranean and especially Cyprus.

Still further south, the Gaza strip was an inhabited area of great antiquity, and its people profited from their strategic position between Egypt and the Cisjordan.

In the center, starting at the Lebanon mountain range, a region of hills from 1,800 to 3,000 feet in altitude extends south to the Negeb and Sinai. North of this zone and separated from it by the Jezreel depression lay Galilee. It had the advantage of 39 inches of rainfall and was the granary of the country. The Jezreel depression was only 150 feet above sea level and was especially fertile. It possessed, moreover, the only important road crossing the country from west to east. It was therefore a strategic crossroads where stood the very ancient fortified town of Megiddo, a place where influences from the north and from Egypt inevitably met.

South of Jezreel extended the hills of Samaria and Judea, countries that became less and less fertile as one moved southward or turned eastward. These were areas for the breeding of small livestock, for vineyards and fruit orchards; the vegetation was the skimpy vegetation of the steppe.

Nonetheless it was here, away from the main communication arteries, that two kingdoms developed: Israel with its center in Samaria, and Judah with its center at Jerusalem. It was here, too, that all the ancient sanctuaries—Shiloh, Shechem, Bethel, Hebron—were to be found.

The eastern part of Judea was already a wilderness area; further south stretched the Negeb, an area of arid steppe where nonetheless at an early time pioneer farmers, along with numerous craftsmen working with copper, bone and stone, settled in the most fertile sections. The Negeb was a place of passage for caravans traveling from Egypt to the north or to Arabia; but from as early as the fourth millennium it was also a place of significant mining activity in which Egyptians and semi-nomads (probably the Midianite Kenites) joined hands.

Beginning in the tenth century B.C. numerous fortified towns, with their accompanying farms, were established in the Negeb by the kings of Judah, who wished to keep their eye on the caravan traffic; among these towns were Arad and Ezion-Geber.

But the great age of the Negeb came with the Nabateans who, beginning in the third century B.C., took control of all the caravan routes by building such commercial centers as Oboda and Elusa. Though halted in their commercial expansion by the Romans beginning in the first century B.C., they were able to transform the Negeb into cultivable land by controlling the runoff of water.

The third strip of country running north-south comprises the valley of the Jordan which has its source in the Lebanon, on the sides of Mount

Hermon. At Lake Huleh the valley is already 204 feet below sea level; at Lake Tiberias it is −675 feet, at the Dead Sea, −1,274 feet. The northern end of the valley is extremely fertile, and fishing has always been one of its profitable activities. But as one descends further into the valley, it becomes increasingly an unhealthy furnace, with the exception of the very beautiful oasis of Jericho. The Jordan is not navigable, and thus creates a natural frontier. This band of territory continues southward via the depression of the Arabah, in which there were a few watering holes and, most importantly, the mines of Timnah. The Arabah provided a passage between Arabia and the Sinai.

Across the Jordan the Transjordanian plateau arises steeply. It stands from 2,700 feet to 3,600 feet high in the west and then slopes gently to the east. The climate on the plateau is harsh, but once again it has the advantage of rainfall. In the north, the plateau of Bashan, which is crossed by the Yarmuk, is a land of farmers and cattle-herders. Further south, the highlands of Gilead are crossed by two small rivers: in the north the Jabbok, in the south the Arnon which is the frontier between Gilead and Moab. It was here that Gad and Reuben found pastures.

Further eastward lies the land of Ammon, a steppe on which the breeding of small livestock was possible. It was in this area that the kingdom of Ammon developed, with its capital at Rabbah of the Ammonites. Excavations now underway to determine what this kingdom was like have uncovered a small sanctuary of semi-nomads, probably dating from the thirteenth century B.C. It consists of a small courtyard that contains a standing stone and is surrounded by rooms. The sanctuary is identical with the one found at Gerizim, and we may be able to learn something from it regarding the practices of these semi-nomads who were close in character to the clans of Abraham.

South from the Arnon extended the land of Moab with its extensive cultivated plateaus. Moab was a land of stockbreeding and nomadic herding. Its kings, whose capital was Dibon, enjoyed a period of brilliance between the tenth and the eighth centuries B.C.

Finally, in the far south lay the land of Edom, a country of caravaneers. At a very early point in history, the Edomites built small forts to protect the trade routes. The most outstanding period in the country's history was that of the Nabateans, who built the marvelous city of Petra.

Throughout these territories rain falls between November and March; the summer is totally dry. Since the terrain is very undulating, it suffers greatly from the runoff of what water there is, and the moisture does not sink deeply into the soil. Moreover the aridity increases toward the east and the south, where the country turns into wilderness and desert.

We can understand, then, that the Canaanites should have adored Baal as rider of the clouds and giver of spring rains. We can understand, too, the cycle of death and resurrection associated with him: does not the rain that falls from the heavens seem to be swallowed up in the maw of the parched earth? And yet this apparent death portends a victory, for the earth will be rendered fruitful and be covered with greenery. This accounts for the fine representation of Baal with the thunderbolt, the latter being transformed into vegetation.

At all periods the chief problem of the country will be the need of water. If a drought is too intense and prolonged, herdsmen and flock must, like the patriarchs, seek refuge in Egypt.

In building towns, the inhabitants had to learn how to tap subterranean springs and bring the water in through long channels cut in the rock under the fortifications. Such water systems are attested from the time of Solomon at Jerusalem, Hazor, Gibeon, Gezer and Megiddo. Even today, the hydraulic works of Palestine stir our admiration, whether they were the doing of Herod the Great, the Essenes or the Nabateans.

The Main Routes

The land was crossed by three principal routes. The only strategic and easily accessible route, the one followed by all the conquerors, ran from the Nile through Gaza and up the coast to Jaffa, then turned inland toward Megiddo and followed the Jordan valley as far as Lake Huleh, where it crossed the valley and headed for Damascus and Mesopotamia. This route is well known to us from Egyptian, Neobabylonian, Persian, Greek and Roman texts and bas-reliefs. Despite its many fortified places, it was the route taken by all the conquerors, who often did not bother with the little kingdoms situated on the hills to the east. This route was known as the *Via maris* or Sea-road.

The Bible tells us of a second route, known as "the King's Highway" (Num 20:17; 21:22). This ran down from Damascus, skirted the Transjordanian plateau as far as the Dead Sea, followed the Arabah to the Red Sea, and gave access to Arabia. Jews, Moabites, Edomites, Ammonites, Arameans and Nabateans all went to war for control of this route and its trade.

There was a third route that kept to the hilltops. It was a tortuous and difficult route that served the chief cities and towns of Jewish history—Beersheba, Hebron, Bethlehem, Jerusalem, Gibeah, Rama, Mizpah,

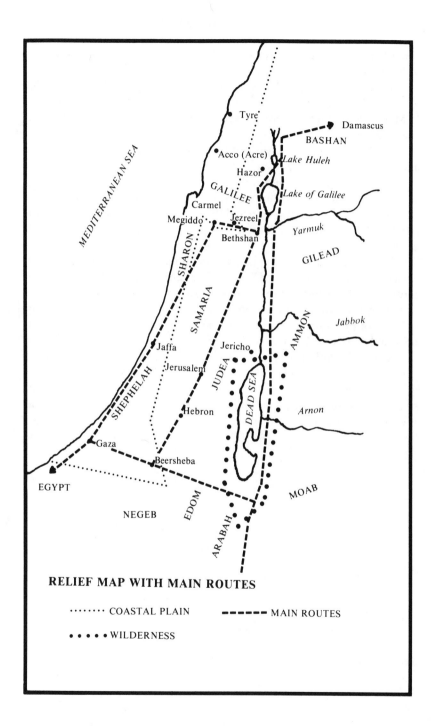

RELIEF MAP WITH MAIN ROUTES

········· COASTAL PLAIN   ------- MAIN ROUTES

• • • • • WILDERNESS

11

Bethel, Shiloh, Shechem, Samaria and Dothan—before reaching the plain of Jezreel.

East-west routes were few and impracticable except for the one that followed the plain of Jezreel and made it possible to go from Acco (Acre) to Megiddo and then to Beth-shean and the plain of the Jordan and on into the Transjordan.

There was another cross-country route from the coast to Jerusalem and giving access to Jericho and the Jordan valley, but it was a quite unsafe route, as the parable of the Good Samaritan attests.

Finally, the site for the city of Samaria was chosen because it gave access to Jerusalem in the south and the territory of the Phoenicians in the north, while at the same time it had easy access to the Mediterranean coast.

This geographical survey helps us to understand why the country was always so difficult to unify. Because of the great conquerors but also because of the Philistines, the coastal plain was rarely controlled by the Jews. Galilee was always somewhat peripheral; in addition, being cut off from the rest of the country by the strategic route via Jezreel, it was an easy prey and a temptation to all conquerors.

The infertile hills of Judah, on the other hand, roused the greed of conquerors less than did the rich land of Samaria. This explains the survival of the influential kingdom of Judah, the importance of which was not so much territorial as national and spiritual, for the temple common to all Jews was at Jerusalem.

Chapter 1
Prehistory

For that time long ago for which we have no written documents and therefore no sure explanation, archeology makes it possible to find traces of life; these are fragmentary in the pre-historic period, but from then on they become increasingly well defined.

In Palestine the first humanoid dates from about 600,000 B.C. The first important known site is Tell 'Ubeidiya, south of Lake Tiberias; roughly chipped pebbles from about 300,000 B.C. have been found there. Chellean picks and sharp pieces of flint have been found from about 130,000 B.C. in the very important cave of Umm Qatafa (south of the Herodion) and in the cave of Tabun at Mount Carmel.

Between 100,000 and 50,000 B.C. the Dead Sea and Lake Tiberias formed a single lake; during this period there was a flourishing industry in flint: points, blades, sharp-edges, awls, scrapers. Like the cave of Tabun, the cave of Sukhul has yielded numerous human remains with surprising characteristics. Was Carmel man a hybrid of Neanderthal and Homo sapiens? Or was he a transitional human type?

The finest flints from this period are undoubtedly the knife-shaped points found in the cave of Abu Sif in the wilderness of Judea.

The period of which I have just been speaking, the Middle Palaeolithic, ended ca. 35,000 B.C. The large animals—elephant, rhinocerus, hippopotamus, buffalo—had disappeared and been replaced by smaller animals. Human beings continued to live in caves but we also see them living in the open on the coastal plain, in the Jordan valley and in the dry areas of the Negeb. They hunted bison, brown bears, bucks, stags and wild boars. This period is characterized by the appearance of the small-flint industry, as seen, for example, in the points found in the cave of Emireh near Lake Tiberias.

The period from 10,000 to 7500 B.C. saw the development of the so-called Natufian culture, which derives its name from a Wadi northeast of Lod. Here, in the cave of Shuqbah crescent-shaped scrapers have been found, but also and above all large-size tools: sickle blades and mattock blades that point to the birth of an agrarian civilization. In the cave of Kebarah, between Caesarea and Dor, four sickle handles made of bone have also been found, along with points, hooks, harpoons, needles and combs of the same material. The use of bone made possible decorative motifs representing the heads of animals, or simply geometrical motifs.

At Ain Mellaha, in the valley of Lake Huleh, remains of dwellings have been found that are round and pit-like. At the center of each is a hearth surrounded by stones. The largest of these houses (22 feet in diameter) also has an interior wall covered with plaster; in a pit traces of red paint have been found.

The site contains numerous graves; most of the skulls are adorned with several rows of shells. In addition to the small flints already familiar, pestles and mortars of stone have been found; these are decorated with geometric motifs or incised with dotted lines. Finally, a human head of flint and a statuette of a headless man, also of flint, have been found.

If the calculations are accurate, 200 to 300 people dwelt here; they lived by hunting, food-gathering and fishing in this especially rich valley.

Ain Mellaha is not an isolated instance. Ca. 9000 B.C. Jericho likewise shows a set of dwellings; burial sites containing necklaces of shells are plentiful in the cave of el-Wad on Carmel.

Ca. 7500 B.C. Jericho makes its appearance as the oldest town known to us. The houses, which are round huts, are protected by a wall that in turn is surrounded by a ditch; to the west stands an imposing round tower 27 feet in diameter. The population may be estimated at 2,000 people living partly by agriculture and partly by hunting and food-gathering.

After a period when the site was abandoned, houses reappear which are rectangular in shape and have brick walls decorated with herring-bone motifs, while around the base runs a frieze painted red.

From the eighth century B.C. on, places of worship can be identified. Some strangely decorated human skulls were certainly part of a cult of the ancestors: the features have been modeled in earth that was probably painted, and shells are used to represent the eyes.

The Mother Goddess of Munhata.

The site at Munhata (9 miles south of Lake Tiberias) shows the same succession of round and square houses, but here baked bricks and rubble are used together for the walls. The floors are covered with pebbles or sometimes with a coat of plaster on a bed of reeds. The importance of agricultural life is emphasized by the number of sickle blades, millstones, basins and plates of stone, and pestles.

This period, Pre-pottery Neolithic, sees the beginning of a more systematic agriculture as men begin to select grains to be cultivated. There is evidence too of the first attempts to domesticate animals, or, according to another theory, people begin to keep close by them the animals required to meet cultic needs.

Ca. 6000 B.C. the climate becomes dry, many villages are abandoned, and sizable villages are found only in northern Syria, around Byblos.

Ca. 5000 B.C. the period known as Pottery Neolithic begins. This phase of civilization can be traced at Jericho or Munhata, but the most important site is undoubtedly Sha'ar ha-Golan, on the right bank of the Yarmuk. Many objects made of flint have been found here: polished axes, hoes, chisels, serrated sickle blades, burins, scrapers, arrow points, javelins. Stone furnishings are abundant: mortars, pestles, basins, handmills, cups carved out of rocks.

What is new, however, is a very sizable collection of pottery decorated with incised herring-bone patterns; these pots would henceforth

Ossuary from Azor from about 3500 B.C.

Skull found buried under the floor of a house in Jericho about 7500 B.C. with a headband of beads.

take the place of stone vessels. In addition to this utilitarian pottery a number of clay statues have also been found; they represent women seated or standing, with arms crossed or bent back to their chests and supporting their breasts. At Munhata one of these statues is of a mother goddess. Other objects, modeled or carved, represent phalluses or vulvas, religious symbols attached to a fertility cult.

The statuary also includes figures cut in small stones. The shapes are schematic and emphasize the eyes, the nose and the sexual parts.

This period extends from 5000 to 4000 B.C.; during it agriculture becomes increasingly important, while stockbreeding also makes progress. Objects from this period are more and more frequently polished by means of sand and water.

The Chalcolithic period is one of intensive agriculture and stockbreeding. As far as monuments are concerned, it is characterized by the

A polychrome fresco from the wall of a chalcolithic house at Ghassul, about 3500 B.C.

erection of numerous megaliths. Thus there are over 200 dolmens in Upper Galilee, while there are over 20,000 in the Transjordan where they often form groups of from 300 to 1000 megaliths. In most instances, the dolmens are surrounded by one or two circles of smaller stones. These high places are not all equally old; the one at Gezer with its ten megaliths probably dates only from 1600 B.C.

At Tell el-Far'ah, northeast of Nablus, a strange type of dwelling has been found. People there lived in pits from 6 to 15 feet in diameter and about 3 feet deep; walls of earth and stone continued aboveground the sides of the pits.

At Teleilat Ghassul, northeast of the Dead Sea, numerous dwellings have been discovered. Rectangular or trapezoidal in form, they are separated each from the others by narrow paved lanes. Most consist of a single large room to which side chambers might be added. The walls are of baked brick on a foundation of stone. The inside of the walls is plastered, whitewashed, and sometimes decorated with polychrome frescoes. Each house has its chests, ovens, brick or stone benches, and in some instances jars set in the floor. In addition to flint tools and objects of stone, there are pottery bowls decorated with a red stripe, cups in the shape of horns, and a receptacle which seems to be a churn. For the first time, points and axes of copper make their appearance.

But in this area the most surprising discoveries were in the "treasure cave" on the slope of Nahal Mishmar on the shore of the Dead Sea between Masada and En-gedi.

In addition to the usual pottery utensils and jewelry the archeologists have discovered wicker baskets and mats, leather sandals, woven cloth and even a loom. While the bones of animals—sheep, gazelles, goats, bears and birds—are numerous there, wheat, barley, lentils, onions, garlic, olives and dates have also been perfectly preserved.

Most extraordinary of all, however, are 429 copper objects displaying remarkable workmanship. The most surprising are "rods" (probably sceptres) topped by heads of birds or animals or even a human face. The best known of them is surmounted by a bush of ibis heads. Of great interest too are the crowns decorated with figurines of birds or stylized representations of temple doors. It is unfortunately still not possible to explain the provenance of these objects, which date from between 3500 and 2800 B.C.

I may also call attention to the sites at Tell Abu Matar and Bir es-Safadi. The dwellings here are underground, with access through wells from 4¹⁄₂ to 6 feet deep. The rooms, which are connected by tunnels, had earthen roofs supported by wooden beams; light came from primitive bowl-shaped lamps. Some rooms even have chimneys, and the floor is hollowed out to make storage-pits that are covered with flat stones. These storage-pits, which point to intense agricultural activity, contain wheat, barley and lentils.

As everywhere else, so here are found objects of flint and stone along with pottery, but also copper weapons: clubs, axes, points. There are traces of primitive metallurgy which was doubtless related to the copper beds at Punon in the Arabah.

The taste for adornment was highly developed, as can be seen from the shell necklaces and pendants, the copper rings, the precious stones. There was also a liking for ivory, and a real workshop has been uncovered at Bir es-Safadi.

Important, too, in this second half of the fourth millennium are the funerary rites discovered at Azor (near Tel Aviv) but also at Benei Baraq, east of Jaffa. About 200 ossuaries have been found. Two represent animals, but the rest are made in the shape of dwellings. The facade and roof are supported by beams. The facades are usually surmounted by a gable. These ossuaries are sometimes decorated with palm-trees and with plaits or trellises of plant-life, but most often with geometrical motifs. Above the opening, which is large enough for the skull to be introduced, stands a stylized human figure, the nose being usually indicated. Some of these house-ossuaries are mounted on piles. Large jars with an opening in the shoulder also served for interment.

We may note, finally, that the discovery has been made at En-gedi of what seems to be the oldest temple in Palestine. At the center of a large enclosure a sanctuary has been discovered containing an altar in the midst of bones, dust and ashes.

The end of the Chalcolithic period brings us into the Bronze age, which approximately coincides with the beginnings of history.

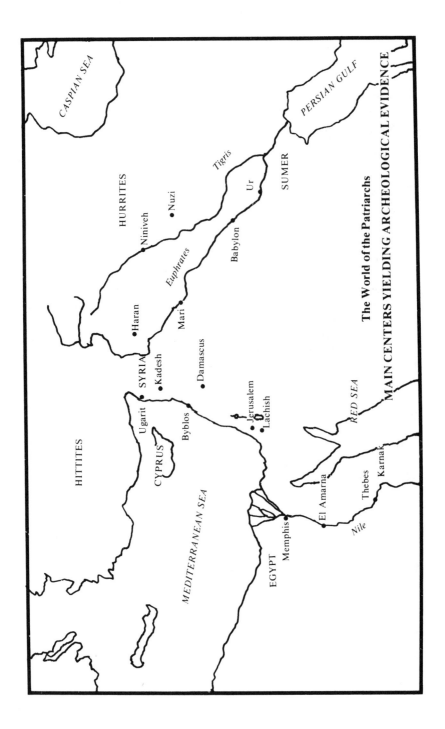

The World of the Patriarchs
MAIN CENTERS YIELDING ARCHEOLOGICAL EVIDENCE

CASPIAN SEA

PERSIAN GULF

HURRITES

Tigris

SUMER

Nuzi

Niniveh

Ur

Babylon

Euphrates

Haran

Mari

Damascus

SYRIA

Kadesh

RED SEA

Ugarit

Jerusalem

Byblos

Lachish

HITTITES

CYPRUS

Karnak

El Amarna

Thebes

MEDITERRANEAN SEA

Memphis

Nile

EGYPT

Chapter 2
History

History begins with the Sumerian civilization at the start of the third millennium.[1] The ancient tablets from Ur make it possible for us to reconstruct the political organization of that city. We should bear in mind, however, that in the eyes of the Sumerians themselves, their civilization was one that had been rebuilt after the deluge, as their cuneiform tablets make clear.

Biblical culture adopted the same scheme; that is, it knew of pre-deluge and post-deluge civilizations. This culture thus had its roots in very ancient visions of the world and became a vehicle for their wisdoms, political ideas, myths, cosmogonies and cults. It did, of course, provide a new reading, a new interpretation of all these, but it remains true that biblical faith and history can be understood only in the light of Israel's encounters with these other great civilizations.

While Sumerian civilization was emerging in the north, in the south Egypt too was entering upon the stage of history. As early as the fourth millennium its art was already remarkable, and its traders had gone as far as Byblos, while by the beginning of the third millennium it had developed hieroglyphic writing. This coincided with the beginning of the Old Kingdom, which, it seems, undertook an expedition into the Sinai.

From this point on, Palestinian Syria, located as it was between these two main centers of civilization, becomes better known to us. In addition to the results of excavations, there are available to us commercial and military data as well as texts both cuneiform and hieroglyphic. Many towns were established in this period: Megiddo and its temple at the end of the second millennium; Beth-shean, Ai and its temple in the middle of the

---

Legend of Sargon the Great

"I am Sargon, the mighty king of Agade. My mother was a poor woman; I never knew my father. My father's brother lived in the hill country. My city was the city of Azupiranu, on the bank of the Euphrates. My mother, a poor woman, conceived me; she bore me in secret; she placed me in a reed-basket, and sealed my lid with pitch. She abandoned me to the river, which did not drown me. The river carried me to Akki, the drawer of water. Akki, the drawer of water, looked upon me with kindness; he drew me out and raised me as his child. Akki, the drawer of water, appointed me to care for his garden. During the time I gardened the goddess Ishtar certainly loved me. I exercised kingship."

---

third millennium. Then, too, the city of Tyre, which was to become the trading center of the Phoenicians, was probably founded ca. 2750 B.C.; but the first texts that tell us of Tyre are from Egypt and date only from the nineteenth century B.C.

We draw even closer to the subject of this book when we take cognizance of the first "Semitic" invaders who superseded the Sumerians ca. 2340 B.C. and established the Akkadian empire. The great king Sargon I founded a Semitic empire that included Babylonia and Sumer and reached as far as Anatolia. From the beginning of the second millennium Sargon's reign became the subject of rereadings. His life and in particular his birth were turned into a legendary exemplar; the story was later to serve the redactor of the Bible as a model for his own telling of the birth of Moses. This brilliant Akkadian civilization was in turn destroyed by the Guti in their invasion ca. 2200 B.C. The latter were replaced by the Sumerians who established a new empire, only to succumb in turn to pressure from the Amorites.

The Amorites

The Amorites made their way into Syria and Mesopotamia beginning in the third millennium. They were nomads, but they cultivated relations with the cities and towns, engaging in trade with them and enjoying an acknowledged status. Gradually the balance changed, and the Amorites came to power in the cities. They established their own dynasty 2300 to 2200 B.C., with Babylon as their capital. The name "Babylon" means "Gate of God," but in the Bible it was interpreted as derived from the root *bll,* "to confuse." Babylon will later be the place of exile and a place cursed by God.

The greatest king of Babylon was Hammurabi, who reigned at the end of the eighteenth and beginning of the seventeenth centuries B.C. He supposedly received from one of his gods a block of basalt on which were incised two hundred and eight-two laws, many of which will reappear in the Jewish legislation associated with Sinai. For example, the law of talion: "An eye for an eye, a tooth for a tooth," is common to the two codes.

Hammurabi was a great conqueror, who in the course of his campaigns captured Mari. The excavations at Mari have proved exceptionally rich, for they uncovered the royal archives, 25,000 cuneiform tablets dealing with economic, juridical and diplomatic matters at the beginning of the second millennium.

These tablets constitute a remarkable witness to life at the crossroads of the Sumerian, Babylonian, Anatolian and Syrian civilizations. They show us the complex relations that existed between the sedentary folk, the semi-nomads and the full nomads. They help us to understand Abraham's relations with the Canaanite cities and towns.

Among the nomads mentioned in the Mari archives we must single out the Benjaminites, a highly mobile and warlike group; these characteristics resemble those of the Israelite tribe later known as Benjamin. The Mari correspondence also speaks of the Habiru, bandits who were known for their raids. Here again the question arises: Was there a connection between the Habiru and the people later called Hebrews?

Extract from the royal archives of Mari on the Benjaminites

"Asidakim and the kings of Zalmakum, on the one side, and the Suqaqu and the elders of Bene Iamine, on the other, have entered into a covenant in the temple of Sin at Haran.

"With regard to the gathering of the shepherds from the towns of the Bene Iamine and to the reprimand to be delivered to them, my lord has written to me. . . . Even before my lord's letter reached me and when I was staying with my lord at Main, I had learned of this affair from my attendants. As a result, I summoned the sheiks of the towns of the Bene Iamine and I reprimanded them as follows. . . .

"They conducted a first raid and captured many sheep. I sent relief troops in pursuit of them, and these troops killed their dawidum.* Not one of them escaped, and they gave back all the sheep they had taken. They began again to conduct numerous raids and they stole sheep, but I sent relief troops after them. . . ."

*Scholars ask whether we have here an explanation of the name of King David.

Code of Hammurabi 145–147

"If a man takes a wife and if she does not bear him a child, and if he decides to take a concubine, he can take a concubine and bring her into his house. He is not to treat this concubine as the equal of the wife.

"If a man takes a wife and if she brings her husband a slave woman who bears him children, and if this slave woman then competes with her mistress because she has borne children, her mistress may no longer sell her. Her mistress may however brand her and count her among the slaves.

"If the slave woman has not borne children, her mistress may sell her."

The Amorites extended their rule far to the west, with Ugarit becoming one of their important trading centers, and advanced as far as the Jordan. Their accession to power in Mesopotamia coincided with the destruction of many cities and towns in Palestine. Did the Amorites drive other peoples before them? Did they themselves enter this new territory? Are the Canaanites of the Bible close relatives of the Amorites? These are all questions which cannot yet be answered. In any case, it is in this period that the patriarchs are to be located.

The Patriarchal Tradition: Genesis[2]

We have no historical document that would inform us about the patriarchs. The book in which we read of them was the result of a lengthy development that reached its conclusion only in the time of Ezra, in the fourth century B.C. Analysis brings to light, behind the final redaction, three earlier phases.

All the writings in the Pentateuch go back to oral traditions which may have been in circulation from the nineteenth century B.C. down to at least the tenth and which then continued to exist side by side with the first written documents. It is impossible to say what these traditions looked like in their early form, especially since, as I indicated earlier, they were at that time embedded in very ancient cultures.

The first written tradition of which we have any trace is known as the "Yahwist" tradition because of the name "Yahweh" which it uses for God. This tradition was probably put in writing during the time of King Solomon, ca. 1000 B.C.

At that time, the writer's purpose was not to compose a strict history but rather to show how the unity of the realm under the king had been willed by God from the beginning, from the days of the first clan chieftains: Abraham, Isaac, Jacob, Israel.

More generally, the writer wishes to show that the salvation offered by God is promised to all nations; this intention is reflected in the picture of Solomon as the wisest of the wise, who draws the other nations to him, as in the case of the Queen of Sheba.

The land promised to the patriarchs is the kingdom of David in its period of splendor, when it reached from the river of Egypt to the river Euphrates (Gen 15:18). The writer is not bothered by seeing a Philistine king living there in the time of Abraham (Gen 26:1), although in fact the Philistines did not gain a foothold in Palestine until the twelfth century B.C.

In like manner, the story of the two brothers Esau and Jacob embodies a theologian's vision of the antagonistic relationship between the agricultural kingdom of Solomon and the nomad kingdom of Edom.

A second tradition goes back to the eighth century B.C., which was the age of the great prophets. The primary concern of this tradition is to defend Israel's faith in its God, who is here called Elohim, against a confusion with the Canaanite religion. Because of the name used for God this source is called the "Elohist" source. Its focus is not on the royal tribe of Judah nor on Abraham but on the northern kingdom and its sanctuaries at Shechem and Bethel, sanctuaries with which the names of the patriarchs Jacob and Israel are connected.

What is important according to this source is not the land but the revelation of the sovereign God to his people through the mediation formerly of the patriarchs and now of the prophets. There is no universalism here but, on the contrary, a forceful condemnation of the Egyptians and the Amorites (Gen 15:13–16). God already tells Abraham of the coming sojourn in Egypt and the condemnation of Pharaoh.

In the seventh century B.C. the Yahwist and Elohist traditions were reorganized as a unit, with a preference given to the Yahwist, unless this latter was only supplemented by the traditions from the north.

In the sixth century B.C. a new need arose. The people had been deported to Babylon; they no longer had a king and they were calling in question the covenant with God. There was need, therefore, of reinterpreting their past history with a view to restoring their confidence; the result was the Priestly history. At the very beginning, in Genesis 1, it states a kind of leitmotif: "Be fruitful, increase and multiply." Life is from God and not from the Babylonian Marduk; the God of Israel is the one and only Creator. God's covenant is an everlasting covenant, but the people, having sinned against God, must annually celebrate the great feast of atonement (Lev 16). The symbol of the permanence of God's promise was Abraham's purchase of the cave at Machpelah as a burial place for Sarah.

This cave, Abraham's sole possession of ground in the promised land, is the equivalent of a pledge; it foretells that the whole land will be given.

The Patriarchs[3]

As the Amorites advanced, a number of semi-nomadic tribes entered Canaan. They did not all enter at the same time, nor did they settle in the same place. These various clans subsequently united to form a single people; in order to give expression to their unity, the clan leaders were represented as members of a single family of which Abraham was the ancestor.

The God worshiped by these various clans was called the God of their fathers (Gen 31:5, 20; Ex 3:6, 16), the God who had promised a land and a posterity. This kind of God is well attested as early as the nineteenth century B.C. among the Assyrian traders of Cappadocia. He was a nomad's God.

When the patriarchs reached Canaan, they found ancient sanctuaries at Shechem, Mamre, Bethel, and Beersheba.[4] At each of these sanctuaries the Canaanites adored El, the father of gods and men, the creator whose wisdom, goodness and justice they lauded. He dwelt in a mysterious place "at the source of the rivers," a mythical place that reminds us of the Garden of Eden. As a result of their contacts with the Canaanites, the patriarchs identified the God of their fathers with the various El figures. He now became a parent who could be addressed as such and with whom they could share communion meals. He was honored by the erection of sacred stones and in meetings under oak and tamarisk. All these were practices that would later be severely condemned by the prophets, but they go back to the initial encounter with Canaan.

The great festival of these stockbreeders was celebrated in the spring when the time came to move the flocks to summer pastures. On this occasion they selected a young lamb without defects for a sacrifice that was intended to ensure the fertility of the flock and protect it from sickness. The time would come when this nomad festival would be reinterpreted in the light of the exodus from Egypt and would become Passover.

Abraham[5]: Genesis 12–25

The name "Abraham" is an Amorite name meaning "My father is exalted." Sarai, Abraham's wife, bears the name of the goddess who was consort of Ningal, the great moon-god worshiped at Ur and Haran.[6] The names of Abraham's relatives—Serug, Terah, Laban—are well attested at

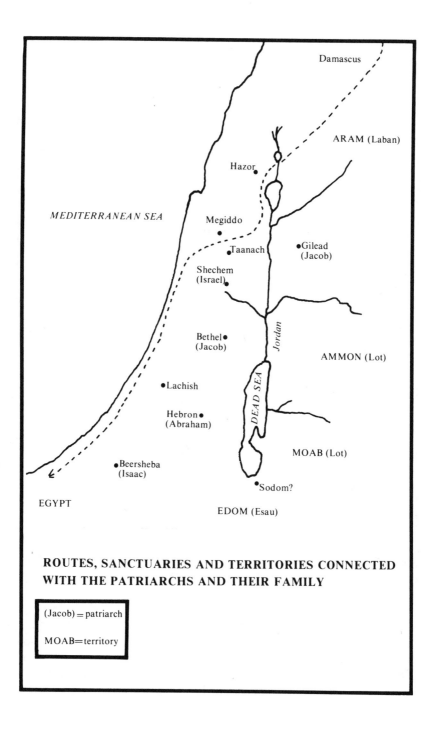

Damascus

ARAM (Laban)

Hazor

MEDITERRANEAN SEA

Megiddo

Taanach

•Gilead
(Jacob)

Shechem
(Israel)•

Bethel•
(Jacob)

Jordan

AMMON (Lot)

•Lachish

Hebron•
(Abraham)

DEAD SEA

MOAB (Lot)

•Beersheba
(Isaac)

•Sodom?

EGYPT

EDOM (Esau)

**ROUTES, SANCTUARIES AND TERRITORIES CONNECTED
WITH THE PATRIARCHS AND THEIR FAMILY**

(Jacob) = patriarch

MOAB=territory

27

Dates	Egypt	Asia Minor	Syria Palestine	Mesopotamia
2600	Old Kingdom			After 3500: primitive cities, Sumerian civilization
2400			Ebla Ugarit	Mari, Lagash
2300			(2250) Destruction of Ebla	Akkadian empire: Sargon the Great
2200				Guti invasion
2100				3rd dynasty of Ur: time of Gudea
2000			Rebuilding of Ebla	Amorite dynasty of Isin
1900	Middle Kingdom	Assyrians in Cappadocia	Hurrites	Dynasty of Larsa
1800			Aleppo, Hazor	Mari (Babylon): Hammurabi
1700	Hyksos invasion	Old Hittite Kingdom		
1600	Expulsion of the Hyksos		Destruction of Ebla and Aleppo	Invasions. Kassite dynasties
1500	New Kingdom	Kingdom of the Mitanni (capital: Nuzi)		
1450	Thut-mose III, El Amarna letters		Thut-mose III at Megiddo. Ugaritic alphabet	Kassite domination. Babylon
1300	El Amarna	New Hittite Kingdom		Assyrian revival
1250	Rameses II	Hattusilis III	Arameans. Battle of Kadesh. Exodus?	Shalmaneser I
1225	Merneptah, Peoples of the sea	Peoples of the sea	Joshua, Philistines	
	Beginning of the Iron Age			

Mari. It is not impossible, therefore, that the oral tradition memorialized clan chieftains who had traveled from Ur to Canaan via Haran (cf. map, p. 20).

Abraham and his clan settled in the southern part of Palestine, at Mamre, near Hebron, in the territory of Judah (Gen 13:17).[7] There he is said to have worshiped God under the name of El Shaddai, that is, "God of the mountain" (unless the name ought to be translated rather as "God of the steppe"). According to the Priestly tradition, this was the first name under which Yahweh was worshiped. This assertion is, however, open to challenge, since the name Ya has been discovered at Ebla, that is, back in the third millennium.

In addition to the tradition regarding the birth of Ishmael, son of the serving-woman Hagar, which may reflect a legal situation comparable to that found in the code of Hammurabi, we should note the fact that Abraham, who was presumably to have no posterity, had adopted a servant, Eliezer of Damascus. This practice, unknown in Israel, is well attested at Mari.

The Bible complacently tells the story of Abraham passing off his wife as his sister; in fact, it tells the story twice about Abraham, and then tells it again of Isaac. The story may preserve the memory of Hurrite law which acknowledged the position of a wife who was also a sister and enjoyed the same rights as her husband over their entire property.

The purchase of the cave of Machpelah has striking parallels in Hittite law. The latter forbids purchasing a cave without also purchasing the field in which it lies, and the trees as well must be included in the agreement (Gen 23).

Isaac: Genesis 17; 21–22; 24; 26–28

The Isaac cycle has to a large extent been drawn into the orbit of the Abraham cycle, with Isaac becoming Abraham's son; this is to be explained by geographical proximity. Isaac moved about in the Negeb around Lahai Roi and Beersheba. The Isaac cycle gives us a good description of the life of semi-nomads at the beginning of the second millennium: shift of flocks from pasture to pasture on the edge of the fertile areas, search for water holes, occasional stay in a frontier town, quarrels with the townsfolk.

At Beersheba the Canaanites worshiped El under the title of El Olam (Gen 21:33). At Lahai Roi, another clan, that of Ishmael, worshiped God under the name of El Roi. The proximity which the sharing of wells made inevitable drew the two clans together.

The great event in the life of Isaac was the sacrifice of the young Isaac by Abraham. In all likelihood this was not a real event but a myth celebrated at Beersheba to explain why El Olam had come to forbid the sacrifice of human children and replaced it by an animal sacrifice. When Isaac was turned into a son of Abraham, he naturally became the hero of the story, a hero until then anonymous.

The Lot cycle, which had its setting on the desolate shore of the Dead Sea, likewise became associated with Abraham and Isaac. When the story of Lot was thus linked to that of Abraham, Moab and Ammon, the clans

Fresco of a procession of Canaanites coming to Egypt during the time of the patriarchs. Beni Hassan, about 1850 B.C.

descended from Lot, likewise became distant relations. This provided justification for these peoples being subject to David.

Jacob: Genesis 25–50

The Jacob cycle is by far the most important and most complex of all. Part of it deals with the antagonism between Jacob and Esau, between settler and hunter both of whom probably claimed the same territory, Gilead. Esau eventually became subject to Jacob, thus prefiguring the difficult relationship of dependence of Edom,[8] descendant of Esau, on Israel, heir of Jacob.

A second part of the cycle explains relations between Jacob and Laban, between Israel and the Arameans of the Damascus region. They eventually concluded a treaty by erecting a pile of stones; this treaty between nomadic groups is attested at Mari. The heap of stones is suggestive of the temples of Canaan, in particular the temple at Hazor.[9]

Finally Jacob took possession of the central part of Canaan, and there God appeared to him at Bethel. Bethel was the site of a Canaanite cult that went back to 2100 B.C. The "Mighty One of Jacob" is therefore to be identified with the Canaanite El.

Israel

Jacob has two names. Is this a sign of a profound change in Jacob's life, as theology would have it? Or have two clans been confused: a clan descended from Jacob, whose Amorite name means "God protects," and a clan tracing its line back to an Israel, which is a name attested at Ugarit

in the fourteenth century but probably also at Ebla, back in the third millennium? If there were two clans we can better understand the story of the two wives: there would be a Jacob/Leah group and an Israel/Rachel group.

The name Israel is linked to another Canaanite sanctuary, Shechem, where El Berit, God of the covenant, was worshiped. Archeologists have found the ruins of an ancient sanctuary, a veritable fortress 60 × 75 feet, oriented toward the rising sun. Shechem is a very old city, in which palaces succeeded one another from the eighteenth century on and which was perhaps conquered by two other clans connected with Jacob: Simeon and Levi (Gen 34).

The Patriarchs and Egypt

In the story that runs from Abraham to Joseph we are told several times of nomads being forced by drought to go down into Egypt.

We know, in addition, that from as early as the third millennium Egypt had an interest in Syria-Palestine. A scribe named Uni has left an account of an expedition to Byblos for the sake of obtaining wood. On this occasion, he tells us, he destroyed many fortresses and cut down fig-trees and vines.

The instruction for King Meri-ka-Re at the end of the third millennium recommends that he distrust the Asiatics who periodically invaded Egypt. Pharaoh Armenemnes I imitated the kings of Babylon and built a wall against Asiatic incursions along the isthmus of Suez.

There was thus ongoing contact between Egyptians and Asiatics, and it was easy to travel from the one area to the other, as is shown by the story of Si-nuhe, an Egyptian official who crossed the wall in flight from Egypt and took refuge in Damascus. His story prefigures that of Moses.

The story of Si-nuhe, overseer of the king's domains in the countries of the Se-tyou, is known to us from five papyri and about 20 ostraca; the story originates in the 20th century B.C. and is 335 lines long.

The part that interests us here speaks of Si-nuhe's flight after the death of Amen-em-hat I.

"When I set out southward, I had no intention of going to court. I expected that there would be a rebellion, and I did not think I could live on after that. I crossed the waters of Ma 'aty near Sycomore; I reached Snefru Island and spent the day there on the edge of the tilled fields. I set out as soon as it was light, and I met a man who stood in my path; he greeted me respectfully, but I was afraid of him. I directed my steps northward and reached the Wall of the Ruler that had been built in order to turn back the Setyou and crush the Sand-Crossers. I crouched down under a bush lest the watchmen on duty that day should spot me. I set out again when it was dark and I reached Peten the following morning. . . . I was unexpectedly attacked by thirst; I was suffocating and my throat was dry. I said to myself: "This is the taste of death." But I took heart and got to my feet again when I heard the lowing of cattle and sighted some Setyou. Their leader, who had been in Egypt, recognized me; then he gave me water and, when I had gone with him to his tribe, he had some milk boiled for me. They treated me well."

The well-known fresco in the tomb at Beni Hasan shows Asiatics coming in peace to trade in Egypt. But there are many representations showing them forced to do the hard labor of slaves.

During the period of the Middle Kingdom in Egypt relations with the Asiatics became increasingly tense, as can be seen from the execration texts. The oldest of these date from the end of the twentieth century B.C.; the names of hostile or rebellious princes were written on potsherds, which were then broken and buried in a sacred place. Scholars have recognized thirty-one names of Asiatic princes, names of Amorite origin; also mentioned are fifteen cities and twenty-one peoples distributed on a line from Syria to Egypt. From the indications collected it seems that the countries along the Sea-road were already well organized and controlled. On the other hand, the system was much more lax and fluid in the interior, where a tribal regime was still followed. Byblos is an already familiar name, but these early execration texts provide the first written mention of Jerusalem, an Amorite city, and of Ashkelon on the coast.

The second group of execration texts dates from the end of the nine-teenth century B.C.; this time the names are written on tiny statuettes representing crouching prisoners with their hands tied behind their backs. Scholars have made out about a hundred names of places which were to have a long and varied history. The northern cities mentioned include, for example, Damascus, where the Sea-road and the King's Highway met; Hazor, the major city and in practice the capital of Upper Galilee, well known too for its trade with Mari; Acco, the great port at the northwestern end of the Jezreel valley; Aphek, where Joshua would defeat the coalition of thirty Canaanite kings; and Beth-shemesh in the territory of Judah. But also to be noted are various cities of the Transjordan and, in particular, Ashtaroth, the capital of Bashan, where the Hebrews will fight one of their first battles against the Amorite king Og, in order to gain entrance into Canaan (Jos 12; Dt 3:1–6).

The Hyksos

Egypt had good reason to be distrustful: at the end of the eighteenth century B.C. it was invaded by the Hyksos, who were princes of foreign countries. Manetho, an Egyptian priest of the third century B.C., calls them "Shepherd Kings." But the data he provides, which are transmitted by the Jewish historian Josephus, are not very reliable.

Two hypotheses are offered: the Hyksos came from the East and were the first Indo-Aryans to enter the region; or the Hyksos were the princes of Canaan whom the Egyptians had cursed. I shall accept this second ex-

---

Text of Manetho of Sebennytus (3rd cent. B.C.) cited in the work
***Against Apion* of Josephus.**

"In the reign of Tutimaios, for some reason which I do not know, the divine wrath was enkindled against us, and suddenly a people of unknown race came from the East and had the boldness to invade our country. By sheer force, without difficulty or combat, they took possession of it; they captured the leaders, burned the towns without mercy, razed the temples of the gods, and treated the inhabitants with the utmost cruelty, cutting the throats of some of the men and taking the children and wives of others as slaves. Finally, they even made one of their own, a man named Salitis, king. This ruler took up residence at Memphis, where he levied tribute on the upper and lower lands and left garrisons in the most suitable locations. Above all, he fortified the eastern region, for he foresaw that some day the Assyrians would grow stronger and attack his kingdom. When he found a city in a very favorable location, situated east of the Bubastis branch and called Avaris in accordance with an ancient theological tradition, he rebuilt it and fortified it with very solid walls. . . .

"This nation as a whole was called the Hyksos, that is, Shepherd Kings. For in the sacred language *Hyk* means 'king' and *sos* means 'shepherd.'"

planation while realizing that the support for it is weak. The problem is that subsequent pharaohs exercised their wits to erase all traces of this inglorious period of Egyptian history.

The Hyksos first settled at Tell el-Yehudiyeh, north of Cairo, where they built a huge entrenched camp for 40,000 men. The camp was surrounded by a glacis of packed sand that was covered with brick and plaster. On one side a 180-foot-long ramp protected by two towers gave access to war chariots. Then the Hyksos built their capital, Avaris, in the eastern part of the delta (map, p. 47).

The same type of fortification was introduced far and wide in Canaan. We can see that modifications were made in the fortifications of the ancient cities of the Early Bronze Age: Megiddo, Gezer, Tell el-Far'ah north of Naplus, Hazor. It was in this last named city that the new works were most extensive: the glacis was 2,250 feet long, 270 feet wide and 45 feet high; the moat in front of it was 45 feet deep and 240 feet wide at its top. Battering rams and chariots could no longer draw near. To these defenses must be added the fortified gateway with its two or three portals, such as is found at Hazor, Shechem and Beth-shemesh. One of the most imposing Hyksos citadels was doubtless Lachish in southern Judah (map, p. 20).

The Hyksos invasion probably began before the eighteenth century B.C. and must have continued as long as this people was in a position of strength. It was therefore not difficult for clans comparable to those of Abraham or Jacob to make their way into Egypt. Nor is it surprising that Asiatics should have attained to the highest positions under the Hyksos. One such Asiatic often mentioned is Hur, chief treasurer, whose scarabs have been found even in Palestine. There is, however, no basis for identifying Hur with Joseph.

Nor was Hur an isolated case, any more than the Hyksos were the only Egyptian rulers to make use of Asiatics. High Asiatic dignitaries are known at the court of Akh-en-Aton in the fourteenth century B.C., and others appear as late as 1250 B.C.; Joseph resembles figures known to us over a period of about five centuries.

Beginning in 1600 the Egyptians rebelled against the Hyksos, under the leadership of Ka-mose, prince of Thebes, who is immortalized at Karnak (map, p. 20). In 1550 his brother Amosis finally drove out the Hyksos for good. Archeologists have discovered that a number of towns were destroyed at this period, especially Lachish, which was burned.

The Hyksos surely did not leave unaccompanied. Their allies, that is, clans similar to those of Abraham and Jacob, were surely expelled along with them. For this reason, some scholars think that 1550 is the date of the exodus or at least of a first exodus, an exodus-expulsion.

Joseph: Genesis 37ff.

Genesis has a very lengthy narrative about Joseph that has all the earmarks of a novel. It is probably a story that was composed in the time of Solomon. Does not Joseph manifest all the characteristics of the wisdom that was so dear to this king?

Scholars have thought they can discern various sources for this novel. Behind Joseph's dream about the stars there is, they claim, an Aramaic story close in character to the story of Ahiqar. The genius of the biblical tradition is to be seen in the fact that it uses this story to interpret the history of Israel and Judah, Israel being represented by Joseph who is in opposition to his brothers of the south: Judah, Simeon and Levi.

The pharaoh's dream about the fat cows who are succeeded by the lean cows would be inspired by an Egyptian tale. The explanation of the tale initially justifies the pharaoh's possession of the entire land and his right to store up part of the harvest in granaries. The story in its biblical form justifies the same policy as practiced by Solomon.

The Joseph narrative fits in very nicely with the legends of the Near East. In addition, however, it fills them with an historical content. To begin with, it makes reference to the Asiatics who exercised important functions in Egypt; then it gives contemporary relevance to the story in order to justify what is done in the time of Solomon. However it does not simply praise; it also issues a warning to Solomon's successors: Like Joseph they must learn forgiveness and the need of reconciliation and unity among the tribes of north and south.

Egypt and the Hurrians

After freeing itself of the Hyksos, Egypt had to face a new Asiatic power: the Hurrians from the kingdom of Mitanni. The Hurrians are mentioned for the first time in a document of Sargon of Akkad (twenty-fourth century B.C.), according to which they had already established a kingdom beyond the Tigris. By slow steps they infiltrated into Mesopotamia (nineteenth century B.C.), then into Syria-Palestine. They occupied Ugarit in the eighteenth century.

The Hurrians were Semites, but they were ruled by an Indo-Aryan aristocracy, the Maryannu. It is thought that these last made the use of horse and chariot a permanent part of the art of war. According to other scholars, however, it is the Hyksos who are to be credited with this innovation. We still do not know the precise relation of the Hurrians to the

---

A stela at Karnak tells of Thut-mose III's advance on Megiddo and of the battle

"The southern wing of His Majesty's army was on a hill south of the river Qina, and the northern wing was north of Megiddo. His Majesty was positioned in the center, where Amon protected his life in the melee and the power of Seth was in his limbs.

"Thereupon His Majesty won the victory over them (the wretched foe from Kadesh, and the rulers of all the foreign lands as far as Naharin who were assembled around him, namely . . . those of Hurru, those of Kode, their horses, their armies and their people). Then they abandoned their horses and their gold and silver chariots and with fear on their faces fled headlong to Megiddo, in order that the residents might hoist them up by their garments into the city. Then, if His Majesty's army had not decided to take possession of the enemy's goods, it would have taken Megiddo immediately."

After describing the capture of Megiddo, the stela gives a "list of the booty which His Majesty's army carried away from the city of Megiddo: 340 living prisoners and 83 slaves, 2041 horses, 191 mares, 6 stallions . . . 1 chariot worked in gold with a body of gold, belonging to that enemy, 892 chariots of his wretched army . . . 1 fine bronze coat of mail belonging to that enemy . . . 502 bows and 7 poles of meru-wood, worked in silver, belonging to that enemy."

Hyksos. We know only that the Hyksos had such a love for their horses that they had these buried with them (Jericho) and sometimes their chariots as well (Tell el-'Ajjul near Gaza).

Toward 1500 B.C. the Hurrians established the mighty kingdom of Mitanni between the Upper Euphrates and the Tigris. They gradually installed their powerful city-states on all the plains of Syria-Palestine. Theirs was the first feudal system. From this point on, they were a dangerous threat to Egyptian trade, for they controlled the Sea-road that ran from Egypt to Mesopotamia.

We have gained a good deal of information about Mitanni from the tablets found at Nuzi, its capital. In addition, the progress of the Hurrians can be followed thanks to the tablets from Ugarit. For the following century we have a number of documents in the form of the tablets from El Amarna and those of Taanach, located in the southern part of the plain of Jezreel.

As early as 1470 B.C. Thut-mose III, one of the greatest of the Egyptian pharaohs, began a series of seventeen expeditions against the Mitanni and their possessions; he left a permanent record of these expeditions on stelas at Karnak. One of the stelas tells of the battle of Megiddo in which Thut-mose III had to face a coalition of three hundred princes. The stela names one hundred and nineteen Canaanite towns that were conquered, beginning with Kadesh on the Orontes, which was the head of the coalition, and various cities of Syria, Palestine and the plain of Jezreel, including Megiddo and Taanach. At Megiddo the booty was immense because the city was rich. In its palace archeologists have found a bathroom paved with shells and directly connected to a well. There was an underground treasury which the invaders did not discover; it has yielded gold jewelry and engraved ivory plaques. Nor were the cities of the coastal plain spared; Thut-mose III says he captured Gezer.

Thut-mose III's list shows that he was not interested in central Palestine or the Transjordan. His aim was control of the Sea-road. He advanced into the kingdom of Mitanni and commemorated his victory on a stela erected on an island in the Euphrates.

While military campaigns are only too often our best sources of information, a discovery can open up new perspectives. In the reign of Thutmose III some Canaanites came to work in the turquoise mines of Serabit, in the southwestern part of the Sinai peninsula. They left there a number of small statuettes bearing so-called "protosinaitic" inscriptions. These are probably written in a Canaanite dialect that was transcribed using only fourteen signs. Other traces of this writing have come to light, especially at Gezer; the potsherd discovered here dates probably from the beginning of the second millennium. The writing may be a link between hieroglyphics and alphabetical writing.

Canaan

We are now in a position to form a fairly good idea of what the Canaanite cities were like. I mentioned their fortifications and the kind of thing found in the palace at Megiddo. At the center of each city or town there was a temple—as at Megiddo, Lachish, and Gezer. Each city was ruled by a king who was mediator between God and his subjects. The king had about him a retinue of land-owning notables, the elders. In the cities the craftsman class was well-to-do, and luxury was evident. Nomads would come to regard the city as the place of all vices and all forms of idolatry. It is the story of Sodom and Gomorrah: the city represents man's proud rebellion against God; it is the work of Cain.

We have a very good knowledge of the religion and pantheon of Ras Shamrah/Ugarit,[10] with its principal god Baal, the thunder-god who rides the clouds, the god of the spring rains who ensures the harvest, and at his side his consort, the goddess Anath. I may also mention Dagon, for these three gods have a place in all the religious controversies between the Jews and their Canaanite neighbors and, subsequently, the Jews and the Philistines.

Ugaritic placque of a fertility goddess.

But Ugarit has also yielded a fundamental discovery; for its trade the city made use of all the languages already familiar to us: Sumerian, Akkadian, Egyptian, Hurrite, but also of a language close to Phoenician and Hebrew, namely, Ugarit. Moreover, this language could henceforth be written with the aid of an alphabet comprising thirty signs. An abecedary, probably from the fifteenth century, has been discovered; it is presently the oldest known to us.

The campaigns of Amen-hotep II, son of Thut-mose III, tell us that alongside the Hyksos-Hurrian mixed population of Canaan, there was another people called the Habiru. Amen-hotep, like his father, fought the Mitanni in the plain of Jezreel, and he brought back with him, among others, 3,600 Habiru. Who were they? Are we to see in them Hebrews who were taken as slaves to Egypt?

El Amarna Letters: Letter of Biridiya of Megiddo to the Pharaoh

"To the King, my Lord and my Sun, say: Thus speaks Biridiya. Seven times and seven times I fall at the feet of the King, my Lord and my Sun. The King, my Lord, is to know that since the departure of the troop of soldiers Lab'ayu has been making war against me. We are unable to go out for the shearing or to go out by the main gate because of Lab'ayu. And now that he has learned you have not given me a troop of soldiers, he intends to capture Megiddo. Therefore let the king save his city lest Lab'ayu take possession of it."

Letter of Abdu-heba of Jerusalem to Amenophis IV

"To the King, my Lord: Thus Abdu-heba, your servant: I fall seven times and seven times at the two feet of my Lord. Behold, Milkilu [your governor] does not break off relations with the sons of Lab'ayu and the sons of Arzayu, who are claiming the king's land for themselves. Why does the king not investigate a governor who does such a thing? Behold, Milkilu and Tagi have captured the town of Rubutu. And now Jerusalem: if this city belongs to the king (it ought to be defended).

"Are we to act like Lab'ayu who gave the land of Shechem to the Habiru? . . . Let the king realize that I have no royal garrison here with me. . . . The entire land of the king is in rebellion. Send Yanhamu to take possession of the king's land.

"To the scribe of the King, my Lord, thus speaks Abdu-heba, your servant: Speak eloquently to the king. I would gladly be wounded and die for you; I am your servant."

The Fourteenth Century

After this campaign Amen-hotep II signed a treaty of peace with the Mitanni. Henceforth the threat both to Mitanni and to Egypt would come from a new empire, that of the Hittites who had been settled in Asia Minor since the sixteenth century.

In 1530 the Hittites had already captured Babylon a first time. Now in the fourteenth century they began a vast expansion under the leader-

Akhenaton worshipping the sun disc Aton with its life-giving rays (seen as hands); together with his wife and daughter.

ship of Suppiluliumas I (1370–1340). They very quickly overcame the Mitanni, occupied Syria, captured Ugarit and Kadesh, and threatened
Egypt. One of the factors contributing to their power was the discovery of
a method for separating iron from its oxides.

At the time when it had to face this mighty empire, Egypt was under
the leadership of Amen-hotep IV, known as Akh-en-aten (1370–1340). He
allowed his Asiatic empire to fall apart; his concern was mainly for a radical
religious renewal. He wanted to unite his kingdom around the exclusive
worship of Aten, the solar disc. In order to escape the influence of the cult
of Amon, Akh-en-aten decided to build an entirely new capital, El Amarna
(cf. map, p. 20).

The city was abandoned after the death of Akh-en-aten and was buried beneath the sand. As a result, it was to preserve for us some very valuable archives on the situation of Egyptian possessions in Palestine. More
than one hundred and fifty letters written in Akkadian were sent to the
pharaoh by the rulers of Palestine.

Egypt never occupied Palestine but was content to safeguard the
trade route. Egyptian administrative headquarters were at Gaza, but there
were troops stationed at Beersheba and especially at Megiddo in the
north. Each Palestinian ruler had an Egyptian governor resident. As long
as this Egyptian sovereignty was not challenged, the local rulers were free.

It is at this period that we find these local rulers writing to the pharaoh
in order to accuse their neighbors of treachery, ask for reinforcements,

---

Inscription on the wall of the temple at Karnak

"Year 1 of the King of Upper and Lower Egypt, Seti I. The desolation which the
mighty arm of the pharaoh—life, prosperity, health be his!—has caused among the
enemies belonging to the Sheshu, from the fortress of Sile to the city of Canaan. Like
a ferocious lion His Majesty vanquished them. They became corpses in all their val-
leys, lying there in their own blood as though they had never been."

On the walls of this same temple there were engraved what seem to be pictures
of the various fortresses that secured the Sea-road. The easternmost of these fortresses
is thought to be Sile; it is situated on both sides on an artificial canal. The pharaohs
probably used this canal for bringing the products of the Mediterranean to the interior
of Egypt. Is this artificial canal the Shihor of the Bible (Josh 13:3)?

The fortifications of the caravan route from Gaza are also attributed to Seti I.
Megiddo and Beth-shean in the north were intended as garrison cities enabling the
Egyptian army to intervene as needed.

At Beth-shean archeologists have uncovered a triumphal stela of Seti I on the
occasion of his victory over the king of Pella and his allies.

and, in particular, to complain of the Habiru. These complaints focus especially on a Habiru soldier-of-fortune who was daring enough to attack even the fortified cities of Shunem in the north and Gezer in the south. He was captured and sent to the ruler of the city of Acre.

This man, whose name was Lab'ayu, and his sons after him seem to have carved out a territory for themselves in the then wooded hill country of Ephraim. He became ruler of Shechem, but seems to have governed it from a distance. He did not live in the city but he and his Habiru promised to keep the city secure. In return for this he received taxes.

Habiru = Hebrews?

The name "habiru" in its various forms is attested throughout the Near East. The Habiru are known to have been present in Sumer in the third millennium, and their name was to disappear only in the twelfth century.

Wherever found, the Habiru were foreigners and remained unassimilated. At Sumer they were plunderers from the desert; at Mari, dangerous armed bands. Among the Hittites they formed a corps of mercenaries. The pharaohs brought them home from Palestine after military campaigns there, and were to employ them for construction work under Rameses II.

Their diffusion in time and place, their names with their varied overtones, their status which differed from place to place: all this seems to warn us not to regard them as a single people. Father de Vaux points out, however, that Hittite documents speak of the "gods of the Habiru." Are we to think of them as an ethnic group?

Abraham and his descendants in their relations with the Egyptians, the twelve tribes in their relations with the Philistines, and David in particular when working as a mercenary for the king of Gath: these are all described as "Hebrews." In the minds of foreign peoples, then, the descendants of Abraham were identified with the Habiru, perhaps because they had the same status, perhaps because they came from the same Semitic ethnic group. According to the Hebrew explanation of the word "Hebrew," this group would have come from beyond the river, i.e., the Euphrates.

Oppression in Egypt: Exodus[11]

It is impossible to date the entrance of the Hebrews into Egypt, since Asiatics were constantly coming and going. We must therefore think of different entrances at different times. Some Hebrews entered freely in order to trade with Egypt. Others made their way in times of famine, in order to escape the drought. Still others entered as conquerors along with the Hyksos or, on the contrary, as prisoners of war of Thut-mose III, Amen-hotep II, Seti I and Rameses II. This last-named had to conduct a campaign in Syria-Palestine and face the Hittites at Kadesh; these struggles, the results of which were dubious for Egypt, ended in the treaty of Kadesh, which was celebrated at Karnak as a great victory (map, p. 20).

Forced labor was also something that went on constantly in Egypt. A tomb from the period of Thut-mose III (1500 B.C.) shows Nubian and Syrian workers making bricks for the storehouses of Pharaoh. Under Rameses II, two hundred and fifty years later, some Habiru were used for works at Memphis. We would like to identify these Habiru with our Hebrews, but the latter, according to the Bible, labored at Pi-Rameses and Pithom. A century later, in the time of Rameses IV, the same Habiru were still in Egypt.

The redactor of the Bible tells of oppression in Egypt, but of course he sees it only from the standpoint of his people. The Egyptians for their part regarded the employment of migrant workers or slaves as something perfectly normal and necessary. In time of war with the Asiatics, whether the latter had sided with the Hittites or were simply in rebellion against the authority of the pharaoh (even Ashkelon rebelled under Rameses II, ca. 1292), it was absolutely necessary that the Egyptian authorities exercise a firm control over populations that might otherwise take up the enemy cause.

Rameses II.

> **Lines 26–27 of the stela for the 5th year of Mer-ne-Ptah; discovered in this pharaoh's funerary temple west of Thebes**
>
> "The rulers are prostrate asking for peace. Of the nine bows not one lifts its head. Tehenu [Libya] is devastated, Hatti is at peace; Canaan is stripped of all its evil-mindedness. Ashkelon is deported, Gezer captured. Yanoam is as if it were no more. Israel is annihilated and has no more posterity. Hurru is now a widow in Egypt's eyes. All the lands have been pacified."

In addition, everything made these semi-nomads alien to the Egyptians who were a sedentary people: their status, their life-style, their culture, their language and their religion. We read in Genesis 46:34 that "every shepherd is an abomination to the Egyptians." Doubtless the converse was also true.

Given our present knowledge of history, we can no longer tell the story of the exodus from Egypt as though it were a single event. In fact, the Bible itself seems to speak of two exoduses: an exodus-expulsion which might coincide with the expulsion of the Hyksos, that is, in 1550, and an exodus-flight on the occasion of a serious catastrophe in Egypt, the tenth plague. This flight, which started from Pi-Rameses and Pithom, must be dated in the reign of Rameses II, perhaps during the difficult period when a peace treaty had just been signed with the Hittites but Egypt was now threatened by the Libyans.

Mer-ne-Ptah, successor of Rameses II, was forced to campaign both against the Libyans and in Canaan. On a stela dated 1220 he writes: "Israel is annihilated and has no more posterity." Therefore a group called Israel existed at that time in central Canaan. But this very brief mention does not yet justify our identifying this Israel with the Hebrews of Moses.

There is, however, a further indicator pointing in that direction. It is that Rameses II and his son Mer-ne-Ptah had to contend with two new kingdoms, Edom and Moab, that is, the same kingdoms which the Hebrews had to get by in order to enter Canaan.

Moses, Exodus, Numbers, Deuteronomy, Leviticus[12]

It is extremely difficult to get behind the story as we have it and to determine precisely what the historical figure of Moses was like. In the course of time the tradition made him liberator, charismatic leader, prophet, legislator, founder of the Jewish religion, and author of the Pentateuch. Abraham is father of the race, Moses is father of the nation.

The account of Moses' birth is modeled on that of Sargon of Akkad; his adoption fits the Sumero-Akkadian legal pattern. All we have, then, is his name which, despite the Jewish explanation of it as meaning "drawn from the waters," is in fact related to such Egyptian names as Thut-mose or Rameses. Like a good many other Asiatics, Moses was certainly brought up at the court of the pharaoh and trained as a scribe, and he doubtless climbed the ladder rapidly. From the outset, therefore, he was heir to two cultures: that of his clan and that of Egypt.

Once he sided with his brethren, Moses was forced to flee Egypt after the manner of Si-nuhe (cf. p. 31). He found refuge in Midian in the house of Jethro, who, we are told, was a priest. Moses would marry Zipporah, daughter of Jethro, and Jethro himself was a descendant of Abraham through Keturah (Gen 25:1–2). Did Jethro acquaint Moses with the old patriarchal traditions? Was it he who revealed the name Yahweh to Moses, as being the name of the God of the fathers? This is simply a hypothesis, but one thing is sure: Jethro, the Midianite priest, had a good deal of influence over Moses. It was he who recommended that Moses appoint a council of elders (Ex 18), while his daughter Zipporah reminded Moses of the requirement of circumcision. This remembrance of the role played by the Midianites must go back to a very ancient tradition, since the Midianites very soon became formidable enemies of Israel (Num 31:1–12).

According to another tradition (Jgs 1:16) Moses' father-in-law was a Kenite. The Kenites, who were the descendants of Cain, seem to have become connected at a very early date with the tribe of Judah. The name "Judah" may mean "Yahweh be praised"; in any case, it was Judah that saw the establishment of the Yahwist tradition according to which God has been worshiped under the name of Yahweh ever since Enosh (Gen 4:26). The Kenites and the Midianites were closely related; to the Egyptians they seemed to belong to a people closely related to the Habiru, namely, the Shasu. Egyptian documents, moreover, speak of "the Shasu of Yhw." We can hardly fail to be impressed by this link-up of names. Was it through contact with the Midianites or with the Kenites or with both that Moses came to give the God of the fathers the name Yahweh?

According to the two other main traditions, the Elohist and the Priestly, the situation was reversed: it was to Moses that the name of Yahweh and its meaning were revealed, whereas previously this God had been worshiped only under the name El or Elohim. These opposed interpretations can be explained by the fusion of two groups: one from the south, in Judah, Midian and the Kenite Negeb, which worshiped God under the name Yahweh, and one from the north which until its union with Judah worshiped God only under the name El. This solution is all the more plausible since the name Yah seems to be already attested not only among the Shasu but at Ugarit.

Moses also acquired the help of Aaron, who certainly belonged to the tribe of Levi, as we are told so often (Ex 4:14). Aaron seems frequently to be introduced into the stories by the Priestly tradition, but he must in any case have been a historical person. He seems closely linked to the idea of festival and is always present when Hebrews eat and drink in honor of God. In particular, it is he who organizes the celebration in Ex 32, in which the God who led the Hebrews out of Egypt is adored in the form of a bull, probably a sculptured bull that was covered with gold. On this occasion Aaron stood opposed to Moses; the two men did not adore God in the same manner. Was Aaron a witness here to an ancient practice?

When Moses returned to Egypt, he became an opponent of the pharaoh; in this respect, he was a precursor of the prophets—Elijah, Elisha, Hosea—who in like manner courageously opposed the kings of Israel. Moses is the central figure in the story of the plagues, an epic literary composition that combines several traditions in a dramatic crescendo. In the various incidents the author sees the hand of Yahweh, who is bringing the Egyptians, and even the pharaoh himself, to acknowledge the lordship of the God of Moses.

Everything in this story serves to glorify God and to give an historical content to three ancient feasts. Passover, a ritual for the departure of shepherds on their annual migration, had involved the smearing of blood on the tent posts to ward off the evil spirit from animals and humans, along with a meal taken in haste; this ancient ritual now became a feast commemorating God's action in bringing his people out of Egypt. The feast of Unleavened Bread, a ritual of sedentary farmers who offered their first sheaves to God and avoided mixing yeast with the new grain so as not to pollute the new harvest, became a commemoration of the Israelites' hasty departure from Egypt, of their flight in that night of terror. The offering of the first-born, an ancient rite resembling the sacrifice of Isaac, commemorated the mercy of the God who, during the night when the first-born of Egypt died, spared the children of his own people.

The Exodus from Egypt

It is impossible to retrace now the route followed by the Hebrews in their departure from Egypt. The Bible has more or less fused the three traditions—Yahwist, Elohist and Priestly—each of which doubtless described a different itinerary. In addition, the precise location of the majority of the places mentioned cannot be determined with certainty.

Here is but one example: the mountain of revelation is called Horeb by the Elohist and Sinai by the Yahwist. According to Exodus 17:6 and Numbers 20:1, 13, the mountain was near Kadesh in the northern part of the Sinai peninsula. According to the old itineraries for pilgrims it was in the south, but even then one had a choice of three peaks: Jebel Mousa, Jebel Katherina and Jebel Serbal. A third explanation, however, seems more satisfactory: the people approached an active volcano (Num 14:14). Then, with Paul (Gal 4:25), we would have to speak of Mount Sinai as being in Arabia. Do not many passages of the Bible have God coming from the south, from the land of Midian (Jgs 5:4; Dt 33:2; Hab 3:3)? This tradition is still preserved among the Arabs who will point out the volcano Hala' el-Bedr, where the cave of the servants of Moses is located.

But against this rational explanation one may appeal to the comparison that seems to be made between God and Baal. Does not the text as we have it seek to depict the God of Moses after the manner of Baal, the torchbearer (Ex 20:18) who thunders and whose shout makes heaven and earth tremble (Ex 19:16)? The God of the fathers here takes to himself the attributes of the Semitic storm-god and perhaps makes Kadesh, ancient locale of worship of a Baal-healer, his own locale. If this interpretation is defensible, then Horeb-Sinai can only be on the northern route between Kadesh and Baal-zephon.

In this tangled mass of possibilities there are two fixed points: the Hebrews departed from the Nile delta and specifically from the area near Pi-Rameses, the capital of Rameses II, and they arrived at Kadesh, where the memory of Miriam was honored (Ex 15). Between these two points four routes are theoretically possible:

The northern route[13] (Ex 13:17) is one which would fit in well with an exodus-expulsion and which the text anachronistically calls the way of the Philistines. The lake crossed by the Hebrews would then be Lake Sirbonis. This route, which was well secured by Egyptian fortresses,[14] does not fit in with an exodus-flight. It is along this route that the bedouin have always collected the quail who land exhausted after their migration.

The second route crosses the Bitter Lakes and heads directly for Kadesh, where Miriam will be buried and where the incident of the spring of Meribah will take place when the people rebel against Moses (Num 20). The hostilities with the Amalekites would best be explained as occurring on this route.

The third route is a variant of the second. It crosses the Bitter Lakes but then goes straight ahead to the Gulf of Aqaba and Arabia. This route, like the preceding, allows the possibility of gathering the manna at the foot of the tamarisk trees. These first three routes allow only for Horeb being near Kadesh.

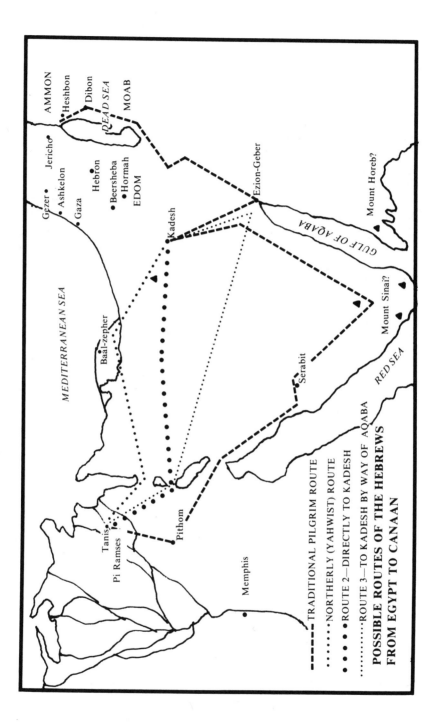

POSSIBLE ROUTES OF THE HEBREWS
FROM EGYPT TO CANAAN

- - - - TRADITIONAL PILGRIM ROUTE
· · · · NORTHERLY (YAHWIST) ROUTE
● ● ● ● ROUTE 2—DIRECTLY TO KADESH
· · · · · · ROUTE 3—TO KADESH BY WAY OF AQABA

The fourth route is that followed by Christian pilgrims from the fourth century on. It passes south of the Bitter Lakes and heads for the southern part of the Sinai Peninsula. According to Agatharchides (second century B.C.) that is where Mara was.

The Pentateuch has combined its sources and regards geography as unimportant, for its purpose is to celebrate the deed by which God saved his people by bringing them across the Sea of Reeds. Even more than an epic, the Pentateuch is a song of adoration; this aspect is highlighted by the canticle of Miriam (Ex 15).

A similar liturgy is celebrated later on at the time of entrance into the promised land, as the people sing of God opening the waters so that the ark may cross (Jos 3–4). Since the same act of worship celebrates the exodus from Egypt and the entrance into Canaan, we may ask: Were there in fact two events or only one? The important thing is the praise and acknowledgment of God as liberator of his people.

Sinai and the Law

The tradition regarding Sinai, which extends from Exodus 19 to Numbers 10, is extremely complex. The various juridical traditions are joined together as though all of Israel's laws through all time had been given to it on that one day and in that one place: the Decalogue and Leviticus, laws

---

Code of Hammurabi 250–252

"If an ox runs wild, strikes a man and kills him, the case allows of no claim. If a man's ox has by repeated gorings made his defect known to the man but he has not clipped the horns nor tied up the animal, then if this ox gores a son of a free man and kills him, the owner shall pay a half mina of silver. If it is a slave of a free man that is gored, the owner shall pay one third of a mina of silver."

Compare Ex 21:28–32

"When an ox gores a man or a woman to death, the ox shall be stoned, and its flesh shall not be eaten; but the owner of the ox shall be clear. But if the ox has been accustomed to gore in the past, and its owner has been warned but has not kept it in, and it kills a man or a woman, the ox shall be stoned, and its owner also shall be put to death. If a ransom is laid on him, then he shall give for the redemption of his life whatever is laid on him. If it gores a man's son or daughter, he shall be dealt with according to this same rule. If the ox gores a slave, male or female, the owner shall give their master thirty shekels of silver, and the ox shall be stoned."

Hammurabi of Babylon receives the law from the sun-god Shamash.

applicable only to nomads and laws applicable only to a sedentary folk (Ex 20:22–33:19). Very ancient laws which, according to the Yahwist and Elohist traditions, go back to the patriarchs are intermingled with the laws of the Priestly Code which were enacted only during the Babylonian exile (Lev).

As it stands, the Sinai episode is presented as the making of a covenant between God and his people. As a result, scholars have thought to shed light on it by comparing the account with treaties between Hittite sovereigns and their vassals (texts from the thirteenth century B.C.).

The treaties in question contain a preamble giving the name and titles of the king, and an historical prologue listing the benefits accorded by the king; these are followed by the commands laid upon the vassals, the clauses regarding the keeping of the document itself, and the requirement that it be read in public; the treaty ends with blessings and curses.

It is a fact that the decalogue begins by presenting God and what he has done for his people; on the other hand, the ten commandments hardly resemble the quite specific obligations imposed on vassals. A public reading occurs only in Joshua 24. There is no list of gods who are called to bear witness, nor can these gods be compared with the seventy men invited to share a communion-meal on the mountain. Curses and blessings do not come at the end of the document but are to be sought throughout the Pentateuch.

Despite certain resemblances with treaties, contemporary exegetes emphasize above all the Deuteronomistic style, which is of the sixth century, and they compare the various manifestations associated with the divine theophany to the religion of Baal as made known to us at Ugarit.

Within this whole body of legislation scholars point to the presence of casuistic laws, that is, those which deal with everyday life in Israel. Such laws as these seem to have parallels among the Hittites, the Babylonians and the Syrians. The ten commandments, on the other hand, form a group apart by reason of their absolute character, even if they may be compared with lists of prohibitions found at Babylon or in Egypt. The ten commandments give the appearance of being a core that has been stripped of all the elements of magic, superstition, and taboo found in other peoples.

As the laws have come down to us, they are no longer in the form of the commandments received by Moses, but have rather undergone a lengthy development. To take but one example: Exodus 20 connects the sabbath obligation with God's rest on the seventh day, whereas Deuteronomy 5 connects the same commandment with the exodus from Egypt.

This gift of the law—augmented over the centuries by all the traditions needed for the life of the people—was the ground of unity among all those who based their lives on worship of the one God. He had liberated them from Egypt and had asked, through Moses, that they accept his laws as so many conditions for their happiness. The law as a whole was thus a blessing rather than a set of prohibitions. Did not the very first commandment show God saying to Israel: "I am the Lord your God, who brought you out of the land of Egypt"? It was through meditation and commentary on the law and by rooting its very life in the law that Israel was to become a people set apart.

Chapter 3
The Age of the Conquest

In the Bible the story of the conquest is told in the Book of Joshua. This book comes from the Deuteronomistic school and doubtless acquired its final form during the exile at Babylon, that is, in the sixth century B.C. Its purpose is to show to a people experiencing the tragedy of deportation the work which God formerly did in its behalf, a work which he can begin anew today.

In composing the book the redactor[1] draws upon various sources that sometimes contradict one another. His purpose, however, is not historical accuracy; rather he is collecting traditions and presenting them in an optimistic light. Thus he tells us that all of Palestine was conquered: "Joshua took all these kings and their land at one time" (Jos 10:42). This is clearly not true! We know, for example, that Jerusalem and many Canaanite cities were conquered only in the time of David. The important thing in the mind of the redactor, however, is to praise God who has given Canaan to his people.

Within this theological perspective the redactor does show respect for his sources when, for example, he shows us Joshua's strategems. But at every point he gives his narrative an epic quality. He does not hesitate to tell us that the sun stood still or to use lyric language in describing the capture of Jericho or Ai.

Instead of telling us how the various tribes made their way into Canaan, he supposes the entire people to be united under a single charismatic leader, Joshua, that is, that the union of the tribes has already been accomplished. Yet if we get behind the materials used we find that the tribes followed different itineraries and that they were far from supporting one another. Even greater complexity arises from the fact that throughout the biblical documents inconsistencies emerge. What, for example, were the real historical relations between Machir, a clan which disappeared, Ephraim, which achieved domination, and Manasseh?

It is as difficult to recover the historical figure of Joshua as it is to get back to the historical Moses, because all the traditions about the conquest have now been linked to Joshua. We do know for sure, however, that he belonged to the house of Joseph and the clan of Ephraim (Jos 19:49; 24:29), that he was one of the first scouts (Num 13:8, 16) and that he was buried in Ephraim.

The Book of Joshua deals with Israel,[2] that is, a people understood as comprising all twelve tribes, but it tells us nothing of the actual history that unfolded at the end of the thirteenth century. We must therefore turn to archeology, which will confirm the Book of Joshua, weaken its authority, or force us to challenge it outright.

The Agents of the Conquest

When the house of Joseph left Egypt, it was doubtless taking advantage of the confused situation in which Egypt found itself, confronted as it was by the Libyans on the one hand and a new invader, "the peoples of the sea,"[3] on the other.

This new threat had been sweeping over the Near East since the sixteenth century B.C. According to the Bible these people of the sea came from Caphtor (Dt 2:23); scholars usually identify Caphtor with Crete and speak of an Egeo-Cretan movement that was set in motion perhaps by the Dorian invasion. Its pottery, decorated with checkered squares, spirals and pictures of birds and swans, is related to Mycenean pottery.

These peoples of the sea—Philistines, Tjeker, Zakkala, Denyen—are attested for the first time in the letters of El Amarna. We can trace their progress in the correspondence from Ugarit. The Hittite rulers pleaded for reinforcements, then for supplies. In 1200 the Hittite empire disappeared from the map. Ugarit was invaded, then utterly destroyed; great Ugarit would henceforth be hardly more than an important village.

In the reign of Mer-ne-Ptah the peoples of the sea joined the Libyans in an attack on Egypt. They were thrown back on this first occasion but set sail again ca. 1175. Rameses III conquered them on both sea and land, thanks to his superior weaponry, especially his bows and chariots. To commemorate his victory, this pharaoh had a picture of the battles in the delta incised on the walls of the temple of Medinet Habu. The invaders are represented as tall men with feathered helmets. The soldiers carry lances,

---

Inscription on the temple of Medinet Habu, 8th year of Rameses III

"The foreign countries formed a conspiracy on their islands. All the nations were immediately thrown into confusion and dispersed in combat. No country could resist their weapons; Hatti, Kode, Carchemish, Arzawa and Alashiya were all destroyed at one blow. They pitched camp in a place in Amurru and desolated its people; the country was as if it had never existed. They then turned toward Egypt, while a fire was prepared before them. Their confederation included the Philistines, the Tjeker [who would occupy Dor], the Shekelesh, the Denyen [connected with Dan?], and the Weshesh, all of them countries united with one another.

"Those who reached the frontier have no posterity; their hearts and souls have disappeared for ever and ever. Those who advanced together by sea were met by a burning fire at the mouths of the rivers, while a palisade of lances hemmed them in on the banks. They were forcibly dragged ashore, enclosed, and prostrated on the sand, then killed and piled one on top of the other. Their boats and their possessions were as it were fallen into the deep."

---

short swords and round shields. The cavalry is equipped with very light chariots, but the soldiers must rely on their lances. The wives, children and possessions of the soldiers follow in ox-drawn carts.

After being repulsed by Rameses III, some of the invaders took possession of the coast between Gaza and Carmel. In the south, the Philistines (who gave their name to Palestine) formed a confederation around five cities: Ashdod, Ashkelon, Gaza, Ekron and Gath. We know nothing of Gath and are not at all sure even of where it was located. We are almost equally ignorant of Ekron, knowing only that its inhabitants worshiped Baalzebub, whose name is doubtless represented by the Beelzebul of the New Testament. Ashdod and Ashkelon are among the cities mentioned in the Egyptian execration texts; like Gaza, they were Egyptian fortified places before being occupied by the Philistines. Each of these five cities had its own ruler; the confederation as such intervened only in political and military difficulties. We know from the extensive pottery that the Philistines built up a fruitful trade with Cyprus. Unfortunately, excavations have not as yet uncovered any Philistine document, so that we know nothing of their language. As for their religious practices, they seem to have adopted the Canaanite gods: Baal at Ekron, his consort Astarte at Bethshean, and Dagon at Ashdod.

The most important remains are still their tombs, which have been found at Lachish in the southern part of Judah, Bethshean in the extreme east of the plain of Jezreel, and Tell el-Far'ah near Gaza. Some terra cotta sarcophaguses have been uncovered, their lids adorned with human masks

that are encircled by two miniscule arms. These tombs have also yielded
ceramic vessels, jewelry, and weapons, some of the latter made of iron. At
this period iron was a precious metal which the Philistines were able to
monopolize for a time.

Though the Egyptians were driven from the coastal plain, they kept
up relations with the Canaanite cities. Moreover, they still occupied the
Arabah rift between the Dead Sea and the Red Sea. They had again begun
to mine copper at Timna under Seti I, but it was Rameses III who rebuilt
a temple there in honor of the goddess Hathor. This Egyptian temple also
shows some Semitic aspects, in particular a whole row of standing stones.
Among the objects given to the temple some are Egyptian, but others undoubtedly came from the inhabitants of the Negeb. It seems, therefore,
that Egyptians, Midianites, Amalekites and Kenites not only worked side
by side but also worshiped the gods together. This discovery forces us to

**Scene of battle between the Egyptian army of Rameses III and the Sea-
peoples, pictured on the wall of the Temple of Medinet Habu.**

rethink many questions about relations between Egyptians, Kenites and Midianites in the time of Moses. We may add to all this the discovery of a very beautiful bronze serpent half covered with gold, which looks like the brother of the one Moses elevated in the wilderness in order to heal snake-bites.

In the interior of the country the chief adversary of the Hebrews at the time of the conquest was the group of Canaanite city-states. But connections between the city-states were often quite loose, so that infiltration was possible. Nonetheless two barriers remained down to the time of David: in the north, the plain of Jezreel, which was controlled by the fortresses of Megiddo, Akko, Taanach and Bethshean; in the south, Gezer, Aijalon and Jerusalem, which formed a second line of fortifications. These two barriers cut Palestine, west of the Jordan, into three regions the occupation of which took different forms once the Hebrews attempted to penetrate into them.

We may note, finally, that Rameses III speaks of victories over the kingdoms of Moab and Edom, which were therefore already in existence. Archeologists have uncovered for this period the towns of Dibon, Madaba, Pella and especially Amman. Near Amman a temple has been found which contains a fine collection of votive objects, Egyptian scarabs and Mycenean pottery, all attesting to extensive trade relations.

The Hebrews did not receive permission to cross through either Edom or Moab; they had to make a lengthy detour in order to enter Canaan.

Ivory decoration from the palace at Megiddo, showing the army returning from battle with prisoners and presenting them before the King on his throne decorated with Cherubim.

The Conquest of the South

The account in Numbers 13–14 speaks of scouts sent by Moses to reconnoiter the land of Canaan. According to the Deuteronomistic tradition, Moses sends a man from each tribe, and these twelve are to explore the whole of Israel. But there is a second and surely older tradition that tells

The name "Israel" as it appears in hieroglyphics on the stele of Memeptah.

of a reconnaissance as far as Hebron, and the central figure in the expedition is evidently Caleb (Num 14:24). A second principal, Joshua, is mentioned along with Caleb, but Deuteronomy (1:22–39) sees Joshua as a kind of "page" to Caleb. This difference in generations is confirmed by Joshua 14:10.

After this reconnaissance, Caleb alone urges the conquest of Canaan; the Hebrews hesitate, however, and are finally defeated by the Canaanites in a battle near Hormah (Num 14:39–45). Oddly enough there is a second battle at Hormah (in Num 21:1–3), but this time the Hebrews are the victors. The victory does not, however, cause them to change their route; they make their way around Edom and Moab.

These two irreconcilable traditions suggest that one group was victorious at Hormah and continued to travel northward. Now it is clear (Jos 15:13–19) that Caleb was the one who conquered Hebron, even if the Deuteronomist adds that he asked Joshua's permission to do so (Jos 14:6–13), and, without fearing to be contradicted, says that the conquest of Hebron was the work of Joshua and all Israel (10:28–40).

As we have seen, such a conquest of Hebron from the north was impossible in the time of Joshua because of the Canaanite barrier formed by Gezer, Aijalon and Jerusalem. Hebron was therefore conquered from the south and by Caleb. This claim is supported by a second narrative dealing with Othniel, brother of Caleb, who conquered Debir (Jos 15:15; Jgs 1:11–15).

Stranger still, the tradition preserves the fact that Caleb and Othniel were not members of the twelve tribes but were Kenizzites, a clan connected with Edom. We can understand, then, that there should still be Kenite towns in southern Judah in the time of David (1 Sam 30:29).

Later on, when the tribe of Judah achieved dominance, the entire territory was assigned to it, the Kenites having been absorbed, and Hebron became the capital of Judah. Further south, Hormah was assigned to Simeon (Jos 19:4); does this imply that it had been conquered by this clan? The majority of the levitical cities were also located south of Hebron (Jos

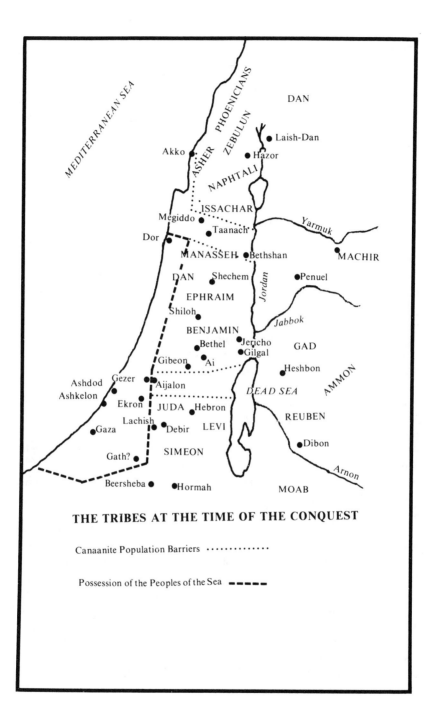

THE TRIBES AT THE TIME OF THE CONQUEST

Canaanite Population Barriers ··············

Possession of the Peoples of the Sea ━ ━ ━ ━ ━

57

21). Moreover, Simeon and Levi are always mentioned together after the patriarchal story of the rape of Dinah at Shechem (Gen 34). Does the story reflect an attempt to capture the city of Shechem?

Simeon, Levi, the Kenites and the Kenizzites all have their history; Judah simply includes all of them. Are we to think that Judah amounted only to the sum of these various groups? Did Judah also absorb the Canaanites through his marriage with Tamar? "Judah" would then be the name not of a person but of an area.

The Transjordan

As I pointed out earlier, it is useless to ask what route the Hebrews followed from Kadesh to their entrance into Canaan. It is especially useless because the journey, as recorded in the Bible, presupposes the union of the twelve tribes and its length is explained primarily on theological grounds: the people sinned and God punished them by keeping them in the wilderness for forty years.

Having bypassed Moab, the Hebrews were confronted with the kingdom of Sihon, king of Heshbon. Sihon was perhaps one of the last Amorite kings to resist the advance of Moab between the Arnon and the Jabbok. The Moabites for their part were to claim that the Hebrews took Heshbon from them; such was the origin of all the later frictions between Israelites, Moabites, Ammonites and Arameans, who all claimed to be the rightful owners of the lands north of the Arnon.

The territory thus won was assigned (according to Num 32:33–39) to the tribes of Gad and Reuben. Heshbon having been given to Reuben, it is logical to think that Reuben was credited with the victory. It is to be noted, however, that as a result Reuben occupied a position in the center, surrounded by Gad on all sides.

The stela of King Mesha of Moab (ninth century B.C.) states that Gad had always dwelt in the land of Ataroth, that is, the area north of the Arnon. However, Joshua (13:15–28) offers a different division: Gad south of the Jabbok, Reuben north of the Arnon.

This contradiction suggests that we try to introduce some order into the account. There is no reason for doubting what is said on the stela of Mesha. Gad was doubtless settled in the Transjordan ever since the patriarchal age, its settlement there being comparable to that of Jacob in Gilead. Like a good many other clans, Gad had not gone down into Egypt. In addition, Gad seems to have been a tribe of only the second rank: Gad was a son of Zilpah, a slave-girl.

When the Hebrews came on the scene, Gad was inspired by ethnic kinship to take the opportunity of fighting at the side of Reuben against Heshbon; the city then was assigned to Reuben. In time Reuben was fused with Gad or was crushed by Gad, if that is how the blessing of Moses (Dt 33:20) is to be interpreted. At the time when the blessing was being composed Reuben was already a dying tribe (Dt 33:6). As with Simeon and Levi, the disappearance of Reuben is explained in the blessing of Jacob as the outcome of a crime: Reuben supposedly dishonored his father's bed (Gen 49:4).

Gad and Reuben were essentially nomadic tribes, with pastures at their disposal; therefore they remained on their side of the Jordan. They did not take part in the conquest of the Cisjordan, a fact of which Deborah complains bitterly (Jgs 5).

The clan of Machir settled in Gilead, north of the Jabbok. But here again the story is not clear.

According to the Song of Deborah, which seems to be very old, Machir settled in the Cisjordan and occupied the central part, from Shechem to the plain of Jezreel. Judged by the etymology of their name, the Machirites would originally have been mercenaries in the service either of the Canaanites or the Egyptians. But a more general interpretation of "Machirites" has been proposed: "They who are sold." Could they have been taken into slavery like Joseph? At the time of the entrance into central Palestine, the Machirites were gradually driven out by Manasseh and would then have settled in Gilead; in the history of the clans Machir thenceforth became a son of Manasseh.

Still further north there was question of another son of Manasseh, Jair, who occupied sixty towns (Jos 13:30); according to the Book of Judges he had only thirty towns, and their location is very uncertain.

The north may have been won as far as the other side of the Yarmuk by a victory over another Amorite king, Og of Bashan; as far as we know now, this victory seems to have existed only in epic legend.

Central Palestine

The Book of Joshua devotes twelve chapters to this section of the country. It tells of numerous events which are all connected with the territory of Benjamin and its sanctuary at Gilgal.

Gilgal, the site of which has thus far not been discovered, was a very important sanctuary. Here, within a circle of twelve standing stones, the people were circumcised with primitive knives of flint in order to purify

The Song of Deborah (Judg 5)

Then sang Deborah and Barak the son of Abinoam on that day:

That the leaders took the lead in Israel,
   that the people offered themselves willingly,
   bless the Lord!

Hear, O kings; give ear, O princes;
   to the Lord I will sing,
   I will make melody to the Lord, the God of Israel.

Lord, when thou didst go forth from Seir,
   when thou didst march from the region of Edom, the earth trembled,
   and the heavens dropped
   yea, the clouds dropped water.
The mountains quaked before the Lord,
   yon Sinai before the Lord, the God of Israel.

In the days of Shamgar, son of Anath,
   in the days of Jael, caravans ceased
   and travelers kept to the byways.
The peasantry ceased in Israel, they ceased
   until you arose, Deborah,
   arose as a mother in Israel.
When new gods were chosen,
   then war was in the gates.
Was shield or spear to be seen
   among forty thousand in Israel?
My heart goes out to the commanders of Israel
   who offered themselves willingly among the people.
   Bless the Lord.

Tell of it, you who ride on tawny asses,
   you who sit on rich carpets
   and you who walk by the way.
To the sound of musicians at the watering places,
   there they repeat the triumphs of the Lord,
   the triumphs of his peasantry in Israel.

Then down to the gates marched
   the people of the Lord.

Awake, awake, Deborah!
   Awake, awake, utter a song!
Arise, Barak, lead away your captives,
   O son of Abinoam.
Then down marched the remnant of the noble
   the people of the Lord marched down for him against the mighty.

From Ephraim they set out thither into the valley,
   following you, Benjamin, with your kinsmen;
from Machir marched down the commanders,
   and from Zebulun those who bear the marshal's staff;
the princes of Issachar came with Deborah,
   and Issachar faithful to Barak;
   into the valley they rushed at his heels.

Among the clans of Reuben
    there were great searchings of heart.
Gilead stayed beyond the Jordan;
    and Dan, why did he abide with the ships?
Asher sat still at the coast of the sea,
    settling down by his landings.
Zebulun is a people that jeoparded their lives to the death;
    Naphtali too, on the heights of the field.

The kings came, they fought;
    then fought the kings of Canaan,
at Taanach, by the waters of Megiddo;
    they got no spoils of silver.
From heaven fought the stars,
    from their courses they fought against Sisera.
The torrent Kishon swept them away,
    the onrushing torrent, the torrent Kishon.
    March on, my soul, with might!

'Then loud beat the horses' hoofs
    with the galloping, galloping of his steeds.

'Curse Meroz, says the angel of the Lord,
    curse bitterly its inhabitants,
because they came not to the help of the Lord,
    to the help of the Lord against the mighty.
Most blessed of women be Jael,
    the wife of Heber the Kenite,
    of tent-dwelling women most blessed.
He asked water and she gave him milk,
    she brought him curds in a lordly bowl.
She put her hand to the tent peg,
    and her right hand to the workmen's mallet;
she struck Sisera a blow,
    she crushed his head,
    she shattered and pierced his temple.
He sank, he fell,
    he lay still at her feet;
at her feet he sank, he fell;
    where he sank, there he fell dead.

'Out of the window she peered,
    the mother of Sisera gazed through the lattice:
"Why is his chariot so long in coming?
    Why tarry the hoofbeats of his chariots?"
Her wisest ladies make answer,
    nay, she gives answer to herself,
"Are they not finding and dividing the spoil?—
    A maiden or two for every man;
spoil of dyed stuffs for Sisera,
    spoil of dyed stuffs embroidered,
    two pieces of dyed work embroidered for my neck as spoil?"
So perish all thine enemies,
    O Lord!
But thy friends be like the sun
    as he rises in his might.'"

them of the uncleanness contracted in Egypt; at Gilgal, too, they celebrated the first Passover. Later on, in the reign of Saul, who was a Benjaminite, Gilgal was to be the national sanctuary, until it was rejected by
the eighth-century prophets and worship was centralized at Jerusalem.

The set of rites celebrated at the sanctuary of Gilgal suggests less a
series of real events than a great national liturgy commemorating the exodus from Egypt and the entrance into Canaan.

Was this liturgy linked to an older cult celebrated at Gilgal, in a sanctuary whose description is so reminiscent of the Phoenician open-air sanctuaries? Whatever the answer to this question, here, as in the case of
Passover, the rites were actualized in terms of an historical event, the entrance of the people into Canaan.

Scholars disagree on whether this liturgy was celebrated as a feast of
all Israel under the monarchy; it may have been so celebrated in the time
of Saul.

Jericho[4]: Jos 2:6; 24:11

The traditions regarding Jericho are very confused. A first tradition
tells of how the city was conquered with the aid of Rahab. Her house, located on the city-wall, was supposedly preserved when the walls fell. A
second tradition (or is it in fact the same tradition?) speaks of a battle (Jos
24:11). But the main tradition is the one about the walls of Jericho col-
lapsing at the sound of the sacred trumpets (Jos 6).

This third tradition became part of the liturgy celebrating the conquest. It took the form not of a battle but of a procession led by the priests
on seven successive days. The story is really a canticle in honor of God who
gives victory; this canticle is comparable to the story in Genesis which
sings of God creating the universe in the course of a week. Jericho is a
symbol of all the forces that will be overcome simply by God's intervention. What are the weapons and fortresses of men as compared with God?
The story served as a psalm of encouragement to the Jews who were exiled
in Babylon, and it retains this power even today when sung by blacks, who
derive from it the courage to believe that all the white fortresses will some-
day collapse.

What historical value does the story have? Excavations have shown
that the walls of Jericho were thrown down in about 1550 B.C., a date
which corresponds to the departure of the Hyksos from Egypt but not to
the exodus under Moses three centuries later. Jericho was inhabited again
from about 1300 B.C. on, but it was no longer a fortified town. Perhaps
this more recent village was captured by Joshua.

Ai[5]: Jos 7–8

The story itself of the capture of Ai raises few if any questions. The Hebrews advanced and were initially thrown back. Achan was then stoned as being to blame for the failure. In a second assault, the Hebrews captured Ai by means of a strategem and then put it under the ban. Ai was destroyed once and for all.

Here again, however, archeology undercuts the story. Ai had been a very important city from the fourth millennium down to about 2500 B.C., at which time it ceased to exist. Only in about the thirteenth century, that is, the period of the entrance of Joshua's Hebrews into Palestine, was a small village built once again.

Is the story of Ai, then, a legend pure and simple? But why should such a legend have been invented? Inasmuch as Ai is close to Bethel, did people subsequently take the story of the capture of Bethel (attested in Jgs 1:22–26) and transfer it to Ai?

There is a great temptation to try at any cost to provide a historical explanation of the biblical story. But was Ai itself that important to the redactor? Was he not simply using a story about Ai, the well-known ruin, in order to raise a monument to the glory of the tribe of Benjamin, which had been able to conquer this area?

Gibeon[6]: Jos 9–10

In this story there is no question of a conquest. The need was rather to explain why the Gibeonites, who were foreigners, were not subjected to the theological rule of the ban, which was applied throughout the entire conquest. If it was God who gave the Hebrews this country, then everything should have been offered to him in sacrifice!

The explanation given is that the Gibeonites managed to secure a treaty with the Hebrews by trickery. They thus saved their lives, but they also became second-class citizens, hewers of wood and drawers of water.

Gibeon has today been identified with certainty on a site northwest of Jerusalem. The town was a rich one and engaged in the wine trade; wine jars as well as thirteen cellars for aging the wine have been discovered. The Hebrews had no desire to destroy this town if it offered a treaty; quite the contrary! Moreover, the town was very well defended and had a cistern of extraordinary size holding 180,000 liters of water; as a result it could withstand a lengthy siege. A treaty was thus profitable not only economically but militarily, for the Hebrews now had a town at their disposal.

The Canaanite kings could allow nomads to make their way into relatively unoccupied territory, but they could not countenance these same nomads settling in as powerful a city as Gibeon. The coalition of kings was a logical response, and the memory of a battle had an objective basis, even if an epic dimension has been added: as in the Iliad, moon and sun are decribed as standing still. Archeologists have shown that in fact around 1230–1220 B.C. the fortress of Lachish was once again sacked and burned (Jos 10:32). Lachish was a fortified city in the south of Judah and was often the prize sought in successive conquests.

All these traditions in the Book of Joshua have to do primarily with the tribe of Benjamin; there is almost nothing about Ephraim and Manasseh. Ephraim and Manasseh were to occupy the center of the land, an area which at that time was almost empty of inhabitants and covered with forests. But we may also ask to what extent these three tribes were already differentiated at this period. Did not Benjamin, Ephraim and Manasseh comprise the house of Joseph? We may hypothesize that Joseph, who was sold by his brothers, was a member of the clan of Machir, "the one sold." On its return from Egypt, this clan occupied the highlands of Ephraim, whence its new name; the clan must have divided into a northern branch and thus given birth to Manasseh, and into a southern branch and thus given birth to Benjamin. After all, in Amorite texts Benjamin means "son of the south."

Dan, an Unusual Tribe[7]

The Book of Joshua tells us little about Dan, but the story of this tribe is told at length in the Book of Judges (1–35), especially in chapters 17 and 18.

Joshua and Judges are in agreement that Dan received territory west of Benjamin, with Eshtaol and Zorah as its key towns. Except for these two towns, this territory does not seem to have been conquered by Dan. According to the Book of Judges the Danites were unable to overcome the Amorites; judging by the map they must have been faced by the Philistines to the west and the hot-headed tribe of Benjamin to the east. Evidently, Dan received no help from the other tribes.

In response to this difficult situation the Danites sent scouts to the north. These men traveled toward the sources of the Jordan and did a report on the city of Laish,[8] which had commercial ties with Sidon; they judged the site to be a favorable one. Then, according to the Bible, the migration of Dan began—not really of Dan as such, but of a part of Dan, for there would always be Danites in central Palestine.

How were these Danites able to pass through the territory of Ephraim and Manasseh with their wives, children and flocks? Above all, how were they able to cross the plain of Jezreel, which was guarded by Canaanite cities, and then the territory of Naphtali, before finally reaching Laish and capturing and destroying it?

Archeology confirms the capture of Laish at the end of the twelfth or beginning of the eleventh century B.C., as well as its change of name: it was henceforth known as Dan. How was this victory related to that of Deborah over Sisera? Must not Deborah have broken through the Jezreel barrier before Dan could travel to the north?

At this point the ambiguities inherent in reading the Bible become clear. Theoretically, we should read Joshua before we read Judges, but in fact these books are theological works which use the available documents in order to give an account of the Israelite faith and not in order to write history. It is clear that some of the documents in Judges are older than those of Joshua; nonetheless in the present state of our knowledge it is extremely difficult to construct a serious chronology. All we can do is offer hypotheses; the most attractive one in this context is that Deborah's victory opened the northern route to the Danites.

But the question returns in a new form, since Deborah complains about the absence of the Danites: "And Dan, why did he abide with the ships?" (or: "Why is Dan in the ships of strangers?"—Jgs 5:17 JB). Did Dan hire itself out like Machir and take service on foreign ships?

The Book of Judges tells us a further surprising story in connection with the migration of Dan. Early in their journey the Danites thought it right to steal an idol of cast metal which the mother of a certain Micah had had made for herself. Not only did they steal the idol, but they took with them the Levite who was minister at the sanctuary of this image, and the Levite was none other than a grandson of Moses! When the Danites reached Dan they built a sanctuary for the idol, but a sanctuary in which Yahweh was also honored.

The story is so incredible, and the mixture of Israelite and foreign customs so striking, that scholars have asked what the real origin of the tribe of Dan was. It does not seem impossible that a Hebrew clan should have incorporated foreign elements; Judah did this. In this case, however, the fusion would have been with a people of the sea, perhaps the Danaeans. This would explain both the clearly Hebrew side of Dan (according to the blessing of Moses in Genesis 49, "Dan shall judge his people as one of the tribes of Israel") and, at the same time, the puzzling side (Dan on ships, Dan and its sanctuary that is at once Yahwist and in the service of an idol).

We should observe that Dan, like Gad, is a secondary tribe, being descended from Bilhah, a slave-girl.

The Northern Tribes

Except for the names of the kings involved, the story of the battle in which the north was conquered (Jos 11) is identical with the story of the battle Joshua fought against the Canaanite kings who formed a coalition after the treaty with Gibeon. The complete parallelism of the texts deprives them of all historical probability.

While it is impossible for us to determine how certain tribes reached the north, the capture of Hazor is well attested archeologically. Hazor is mentioned in eighteenth-century B.C. Egyptian documents and in the Mari letters. This city in northern Palestine was the focal point in the tin trade, tin being the metal that had to be mixed with copper to form bronze. Hazor is also known to us from the El Amarna letters; with the support of the Habiru the king of Hazor behaved as an independent prince, threatening those of his neighbors who complained about him to the pharaoh. In the lower city at Hazor a temple was built, probably in the seventeenth century B.C., which measured 75 feet by 50 feet and had three areas: a principal room which gave access to the holiest part of the temple, a part which in turn contained a niche. This is the same plan that would be adopted by Solomon in Jerusalem about four hundred years later. There is evidence that the city was destroyed about 1250 B.C.; the destruction may very well be attributed if not to "all Israel," then at least to the tribes of Zebulun and Naphtali.

Here again we must ask what connection there was between the capture of Hazor and the battle fought by Deborah. Both texts name Jabin, king of Hazor. Are we to conclude that the battle of Taanach preceded the battle of Merom, which opened the way to Hazor? That would doubtless be the most satisfactory solution. We may think that in their presentation the redactors of Joshua and Judges confused the two events, and we may say, once again, that their aim was not to write an accurate history. Rather we are meant to join Deborah in singing the glory of God who gives victory and a land to his people.

The territory of Hazor becomes the share of Naphtali, and this fact confirms the eminent part this tribe played in the conquest. Zebulun is given a territory south of Naphtali. This territory does not extend to the sea, and yet in the blessings of Moses and Jacob Zebulun is said to dwell on the shore of the sea and to be a sailor. Are we to think that originally Zebulun was in the service of the Philistines or that later on the tribe migrated to the coast?

The tribal name "Issachar" means "hired out for wages." Its name thus links it to Machir, but while Machir came down from the highlands of Ephraim to become a mercenary, Issachar hired itself out in the plain of Jezreel for farmwork. This tribe doubtless never left Palestine after the age of the patriarchal migrations; it doubtless entered the service of the Canaanite cities and won its independence only to the extent that the country was conquered by the Hebrews. Since Issachar and Zebulun are always mentioned together, we may draw the same conclusions for both tribes. We may note too that Mount Tabor, which stood on the common frontier of Issachar, Zebulun and Naphtali, was a place of worship for these three tribes but also, it seems, for the Canaanites (Dt 33:19), blessing of Moses).

Of Asher, finally, we know only that its territory was located on the slopes of Carmel. According to the Song of Deborah Asher dwelt on the coast of the sea and near its harbors. Asher, of whom we know so little, was another son of Zilpah the slave-girl.

The Twelve Tribes

Traditionally the "twelve" in the term "the twelve tribes" refers to the twelve sons of Jacob. By Leah Jacob had Reuben, Simeon, Levi and Judah, and then, later on, Issachar and Zebulun; by Rachel he had Joseph and, later on, Benjamin. By Leah's slave-girl Zilpah he had Gad and Asher; by Rachel's slave-girl Bilhah he had Dan and Naphtali.

But the number twelve remained even when the tribe of Joseph was divided into two groups, Ephraim and Manasseh. All that was needed was to suppress Simeon or Levi; this was not difficult inasmuch as these two tribes were fused with the Judah group at a very early time.

As a matter of fact, two groups became clearly dominant which had no contact with each other at the time of the conquest. In the south there was the group that had come from Edom. In the north the dominant group was the house of Joseph; at an earlier stage, perhaps it was the tribe of Machir which would have split into three: Ephraim, Manasseh and Benjamin. This group was undoubtedly the one that had left Egypt with Moses and had had the experience of Sinai-Horeb.

We still do not know how and where these two dominant groups met and shared their traditions and their faith in Yahweh as the only God. Their contact may have come at the oasis of Kadesh, prior to their divergent attempts to enter Palestine. Reuben, originally the eldest of the Jacob-Leah group, would have traveled to the Jordan with the house of Joseph.

This leaves the tribes descended from the slave-girls, as well as Issachar and Zebulun. All these tribes are relegated to secondary roles, either in the north (Naphtali, Asher, Zebulun, Issachar, Dan) or in the Transjordan (Gad). It seems that none of these clans took part in the descent into Egypt. When the house of Joseph came on the scene, they rallied to it.

The Shechem Assembly: Jos 24

The Book of Joshua tells us nothing of the conquest of Shechem. Is this because the Habiru had long been settled there? Archeology confirms that there was no destruction of this city in either the thirteenth or the twelfth century B.C.; on the contrary, it was inhabited without a break. Were the inhabitants of Shechem used to Habiru control and did they accept the Hebrews as obvious successors to the Habiru?

According to the Book of Joshua it was at Shechem that the covenant of Sinai was renewed, and this in terms that show a surprising similarity to Hittite treaties. Oddly enough, in the course of this ceremony two groups are contrasted. Joshua speaks of himself and his house as having already chosen Yahweh. He then challenges the others: "Choose this day whom you will serve."

It is clear that Joshua and his house—doubtless Ephraim, Manasseh and Benjamin combined—had long since abandoned the gods of the other side of the river, that is, of Mesopotamia. But who are the other people being addressed?

Is Joshua speaking to the Canaanites of Shechem? Possibly, for we have already noted how Judah absorbed Edomites and how Dan mingled with foreigners. It is much more likely, however, that Joshua is addressing tribes which are ethnically close to the house of Joseph.

The tribes in question cannot be Judah and its group, for contacts between Judah and the house of Joseph will begin only in the time of David. We must think, therefore, that Joshua is addressing those northern tribes which doubtless had not left Palestine since the patriarchal age. In this view, Joshua is asking Naphtali, Issachar and Zebulun, Dan and Asher whether they are willing to join his house and enter into a covenant with Yahweh, the God who freed Joshua's house from Egypt and revealed his law to it at Sinai.

The Tribal League

We have seen a tribal league being formed at Shechem. The union was not completed on a single occasion, as the Deuteronomistic redactor

We may compare the results of research on the formation of the Israelite tribes with what Regine Pernoud says about our ancestors the Gauls. Note, however, that there was no contact between these two worlds and that the history of the Gauls began only shortly before the Christian era.

Regine Pernoud writes:

"Thus these tribes, which were so independent and so jealous of their freedoms, had nonetheless accepted the arbitration of a higher and indeed sovereign justice to which peoples and individuals agreed in advance to submit themselves. And this justice was of a religious kind. It was religion that united the Catholic world.

"The druids presided over the solemn assemblies of the Celtic peoples. Once a year there was a vast gathering for purposes at once political, judicial and religious. It was held in the neighborhood of Chartres, which was regarded as the center of Gaul."

We may add the information provided by Strabo:

"At the full moon the Gauls celebrate the feast of a great god whom they do not name."

would have us think with his idealistic presentation; it was undoubtedly a gradual achievement.

The tribes, which numbered a symbolic twelve, had for their common bond a cultic law. There was no political bond, and economic ties could hardly have played a significant role. Each tribe still had its independent history; this was a period in which, as the Book of Judges puts it, "each one did as he pleased." There was no concern for the affairs of the other tribes.

There were sanctuaries, but a variety of them: the tent in the wilderness, Gilgal with its twelve standing stones, Shechem, Bethel, then Shiloh (map, p. 88).⁹ The idea of "all Israel" gathering at a single sanctuary, as is presupposed in Joshua 24, actually became a reality only at a late period. Solomon's temple in Jerusalem would be a step in this direction; the decisive point came, however, with the Josianic reform that suppressed all the high places (seventh century B.C.).

Since there was a variety of sanctuaries, it is not possible to think of an annual feast in which the gift of the law was celebrated and to which each tribe sent representatives. That was not possible in this age of anarchy; it required rather a kingdom with a strong central administration. The division into twelve provinces dates only from the time of Solomon (tenth century B.C.).

Martin Noth thought it possible to compare Israel at this period with the amphictyonies of Greece, especially the Delphic amphictyony. It is clear today, however, that this hypothesis is untenable, since there was no central administraton, no common sanctuary, no annual festival. It is true, nonetheless, that the tribes, called by the religious number twelve, did feel bound together by their common faith and that this faith, this respect for revealed law, would gradually lead them to unity. In any case, such unity was to be a wish shared by all devout men. Each knew of the divisions between north and south; each knew that at one point in history they had acted scandalously toward their brothers and had sold Joseph to the enemy. Yet each would want to believe that unity was possible, that the twelve tribes could join together, and that Joseph would forgive his brothers. Such would be Ezekiel's prophecy to the exiles in Babylon; the Deuteronomistic redactor seeks to achieve the same goal by rewriting the history of the twelve united tribes.

Chapter 4
The Age of the Judges

The Judges[1]

In theory the Book of Judges should pick up where the Book of Joshua leaves off, and tell us about the settlement in Canaan. In fact, however, as we have seen, the Book of Judges supplies many items of information about the conquest, which are perhaps older than those in Joshua.

On the basis of the historical events it reports, Judges elaborates a theology that is well summarized at the beginning of Chapter 2: Instead of obeying the Eternal One, the tribes violated his law and were therefore punished. They were constantly being subjected by the Canaanites, the Aramaeans, the Ammonites, the Edomites, or the Philistines. In their distress they cried to God, who heard them, as he had in the time of Moses, and remembered his covenant. Then he raised up a deliverer.

As in the Book of Joshua, so here the redactor speaks of "all Israel," but the documents he uses show that in each case there was question of a single tribe, or at most two or three neighboring tribes, never of the twelve, and practically never of the southern tribes, the Judah group.

When the book tells us of the settlement,[2] we find that far from reflecting a united Israel, the settlement of a tribe often took place at the expense of the other tribes. I have already discussed the migration of Dan, which was given no help to retain its territory. In this chapter we shall see a regular war being waged between Ephraim and Benjamin, two tribes of the house of Joseph. Once again (as with Simeon, Levi, and Reuben) the war against Benjamin is explained by a sexual crime. This accumulation of references to sexual crimes and a comparison with the same theme in the

A Canaanite vase decorated with antelope grazing. Found near Ziglag.

story of the Trojan War make it clear that behind the sexual pretext there were conflicts among the tribes over spheres of influence. Ephraim and Benjamin both claimed supremacy over the central region.

Despite the many figures given in the Book of Judges we are unable to say anything definite about the period proper to each judge. We do not know in what order they arose or whether they judged during the same period. We do not know when the institution of judges began; is it to be traced back to Moses? We are better informed about when it ended, since Samuel is the last of the judges. At the request of the people he will establish a monarchy in Israel.

Nor is there any unity among the judges. We must distinguish between the lesser judges (Jgs 10:1–5; 12:7–15) and the major judges who waged wars of liberation in the name of an inspiration from God. But some judges, such as Jephthah and Samuel, combined the characteristics of both types.

The Lesser Judges

These men are known from two very laconic lists which, in a stereotyped manner, give the name of each man, his place of birth, the number of years he acted as judge, and the place of his burial.

- Tola of Issachar, a native of Shamir, a judge for six years, buried in Gilead.
- Jair of Gilead, a judge for twenty-two years, buried in Kamon.
- Jephthah of Gilead, from Mizpah, a judge for six years, buried in Gilead.

- Abdon the Pirathonite, a judge for eight years, buried in his own city in Ephraim.
- Ibzan from Bethlehem, a judge for seven years, buried in his own city (in Zebulun).
- Elon of Zebulun, a judge for ten years, buried at Aijalon in Zebulun.

One point is clear: all these lesser judges were from the north. Each acted as judge in his own tribe; Jephthah alone moved beyond Gilead, and even he went only into Ephraim. No lesser judge is named for the south.

What was the function of these judges? As their name indicates, they certainly had to interpret the law of God for their people and render judgments in conformity with the law. But surely their function was broader? They acted as governors of their territory and perhaps even of the territory of several tribes; but this is only a hypothesis.

Jephthah: Jgs 10:6—12:7

The list of lesser judges is interrupted by the story of Jephthah. Jephthah is presented to us as a kind of Ulysses: an illegitimate child, thrown out by his brothers at the death of their father, he became head of a band of raiders and because of his military qualifications was called to become leader of Gilead.

In the time of Jephthah Gilead was a clan that had split off from Ephraim. The clan migrated across the river in order to escape from under the thumb of Ephraim, but the latter had no intention of surrendering its rights. The result was a war between Gilead and Ephraim, which was won by Jephthah thanks to a trick involving pronunciation. Jephthah distinguished Gileadites from Ephraimites by their different ways of pronouncing the letter *s*.

Jephthah's main task, however, was to protect his clan not against Ephraim but against enemies from the east. Here the redactor confuses somewhat the Ammonites and the Moabites, but that is unimportant, for in any event it was the everlasting struggle for the territories east of the Jordan, from Ammon to Gilead.

The message is clear and is akin to that of the prophets: Turn away from the gods of neighboring peoples, serve the Lord, and he will save you. Jephthah is the liberator sent to a people oppressed by its neighbors, just as Moses was sent to the people in Egypt.

There is an odd incident in the story of Jephthah. He promised that if he won the victory he would sacrifice to God the first person he would meet as he returned to his home; the person was his own daughter. The

Gezer Calendar.

The Gezer Calendar

This is the oldest Hebrew inscription known to us. Its interpretation is beset with numerous difficulties. One hypothesis regards it as the work of a young apprentice farmer named Abivahu. This calendar gives us at least an idea of how farming was carried on at that time:

"Two months of harvesting,
two months of sowing,
two months of late hay;
one month for cutting flax,
one month for harvesting barley,
one month of harvesting and measuring;
two months of pruning,
one month of summer crops."

---

incident inevitably reminds us of Agamemnon sacrificing his daughter *before* setting out for the Trojan War. There is a difference, however: Jephthah sacrifices his daughter *after* God has supported him in his undertaking and allowed him to overcome his enemies.

Othniel: Jgs 3:7–11

The mention of Othniel in the Book of Judges seems due entirely to the redactor. He seems to have been added in order that there might be at least one judge from the tribe of Judah. This Othniel of Judah, and therefore of the south, supposedly did battle with Cushan-rishathaim, king of Mesopotamia. That is impossible. On the other hand, if we are meant to think of a king of Cush, i.e., Ethiopia, or of an Edomite king, we learn nothing of historical value.

There is an Othniel known to us from the age of the conquest: he was the brother of Caleb and therefore an Edomite, and supposedly conquered Debir. That Othniel is an historically consistent figure. Othniel the judge is simply a copy of the other Othniel and is intended to support the fiction of "all Israel."

Deborah: Jgs 4–5

We are told of a woman who was a judge in Israel; according to the Book of Judges, she used to render judgments while seated under a palm tree between Ramah and Bethel, in Ephraim. Not only is Deborah thus comparable to the lesser judges, but she also ranks among the great liberators of Israel.

We have two versions of her activity, but despite some differences they are in essential agreement. Judges 4 is a prose text, while Judges 5 is a metrical version, a canticle comparable to that of Miriam after the crossing of the sea (cf. pp. 60-1).

The two texts supply many details about the situation in Israel. The powerful Canaanites in the plain of Jezreel prevented any communication among the tribes; it was a desolate period. Then, inspired by God, Deborah arose and summoned for battle the two tribes of Naphtali and Zebulun (Jgs 4) or else a confederation of tribes that included not only Naphtali and Zebulun but also Machir, Ephraim, Benjamin and Issachar (Jgs 5).

Here for the first time (in the canticle) we find a league of tribes and, at the same time, bitter reproaches uttered against others. Gad, Reuben and Gilead remained in their pasturelands beyond the Jordan; Dan and Asher stayed on their ships or in their harbor. Nothing is said of the southern tribes. In the time of Deborah—but when exactly was that time?— there were therefore links among the ten northern tribes, along with the clan of Gilead. Machir had taken the place of Manasseh. But, despite these bonds, all the clans did not feel equally called; six gave a direct answer to the summons.

In order to determine the date we must clarify an obscurity in the text. In addition to Sisera, who is called a general or a king, mention is made of Jabin, king of Hazor. According to the chronology of the Bible, Jabin was conquered by Naphtali and Zebulun. If we are to trust this chronology, then we must admit either that the redactor has confused two events or that the victory of Naphtali and Zebulun was very limited and temporary. Both hypotheses are plausible.

Otherwise we must reconstruct the sequence of events in a different manner. First, Deborah and a group of six tribes won the battle of Taanach and slew Sisera. Then, the road having now been thrown open, Naphtali and Zebulun carried the campaign as far as Hazor and defied Jabin by destroying his city.

The opposing forces are clearly described. The Canaanites sent up nine hundred iron chariots, a number comparable to that of the coalition which Thut-mose III met at Megiddo around 1550 B.C. The Hebrews, on the other hand, had hardly a shield or a spear for their forty thousand men—a laughable number. The statement brings out the relative fewness of the Hebrews, but it makes clear, even more, that the victory will come from God alone. The Hebrew strategy is simple: the chariots are a formidable enemy on the plain, therefore the Hebrews take up their position on Mount Tabor; then heaven comes to their rescue, probably in the form of a torrential rain that causes the river Kishon to overflow and immobilize the chariots. This is a new version of the victory over the Egyptians when the Hebrews emerged from the Red Sea; in both cases God is the victor.

It is also a woman who brings the day to an end. Jael, wife of Heber the Kenite, treacherously murders Sisera, the fleeing king who has sought rest and protection in her tent. Two women carry the colors of Israel on this extraordinary day that puts an end to Canaanite hegemony over the region.

Here, once again, we come upon the Kenites, but this time far from the south. According to Genesis 4:23 the Kenites were a nation of coppersmiths and blacksmiths. They belonged to a group that claimed descent from Cain and, as such, did not adopt a fixed abode but went about offering their services to neighboring peoples.

From the time of the middle kingdom, which was the time of the patriarchs, the Egyptians used to work the turquoise mines at Serabit el-Khadem in the Sinai. Three of the local people inscribed their names on a little obelisk which pictured them; one of them was named Keni, the Kenite.

We have seen that under Rameses III, a short time after the exodus, some Kenites were working in the copper mines of the Arabah. Heber had doubtless brought his skills to the plain of Jezreel.

Shamgar

Shamgar is mentioned twice (Jgs 3:31; 5:6). He is said to have liberated Israel from the yoke of the Philistines; we are told nothing more. Was he a contemporary of Deborah (Jgs 5)? His name is not Semitic but Hurrian. He is twice called son of Anath, and Anath was the well-known Canaanite goddess against whom the prophets will later rail. It was perfectly natural for a Hurrian to worship Anath, but could a Hurrian have been a savior of Israel? To later minds it would have been impossible, but in these early days did not the Hebrews make a treaty with the Hurrians, both groups being threatened by the Philistines?

Ehud: Jgs 3:12–30

Ehud was a Benjaminite; like Shamgar he is treated not as a judge but as a liberator. The danger this time was from the east: Moab had become threatening, to the point of crossing the Jordan and occupying Jericho and

Gilgal. What became of Gad and Reuben at this time? Was this the time when Reuben disappeared and Gad was pushed northward?

Benjamin was forced to rely solely on itself and some individuals who came down from the highlands of Ephraim to drive back not only Moab but, according to our text, a coalition of Moab, Ammon and the Amalekites.

Gideon/Jerubbaal: Jgs 6–8

Gideon belonged to the tribe of Manasseh and the clan of Abiezer, and he had his seat under the oak of Ophrah. His story is told in great and often complex detail. Gideon is also called Jerubbaal; but was this really a second name of the same man, or are we to see in the story a collection of traditions about Gideon of Manasseh and Jerubbaal a Canaanite, both of them natives of Ophrah, both of them having led their village in a victorious struggle against the Midianite invader, against the raids of these nomads who swept in on their camels like a cloud of locusts and destroyed all the harvests?

The existence of two different individuals would clarify many obscurities in the story. Gideon is a faithful worshiper of Yahweh; like the patriarchs, he has dreams and welcomes angels. Like Moses, he is called by God but is unwilling to set out without having first received signs. Like Elijah, he sees fire from heaven fall on his offering and consume it.

Yet at the same time his father is supposed to have been guardian of the altar of Baal in his village of Ophrah. Then, he himself, after winning his victory, supposedly requires each warrior to contribute a gold ring from his booty so that these may be melted down to form a golden ephod which will be set up in Ophrah and become an object to which Israel prostitutes itself. The story here resembles the one we have seen in connection with Dan.

Either we must think that there were two personages who fought whether side by side or successively and whose traditions have been intermingled, or we must accept that at this period the Hebrews were still far removed from the pure and unyielding Yahwism which the redactor praises and that this was a time of confusion, religious as well as political.

Gideon of Manasseh was able, like Deborah, to gather together four tribes for combat: Manasseh, Asher, Zebulun and Naphtali. The last two had already been the privileged companions of Deborah. Manasseh replaced Machir, and this time Asher came in from its ports. Unfortunately it is once again impossible to date Gideon and Deborah in relation to each other.

Gideon did not take all his forces into battle, but only three hundred men, so that the victory might belong to God alone. After winning the battle, he sought to keep Midian from crossing the river and to this end he called upon Ephraim, which did in fact capture two kings. Ephraim bitterly reproached Gideon for not having summoned them for the whole battle; Gideon got out of the difficulty by using a good deal of diplomacy, but once again we can see Ephraim's ambitions manifesting themselves.

Gideon then decided to pursue the enemy into the Transjordan and he asked for the help of Gad. Gad refused, but Gideon carried on his campaign anyway and returned victorious; he then humiliated the elders of Gad and destroyed their city of Penuel (map, p. 57). The unity of the tribes at this time was definitely nothing but a theological hope.

In consequence of this resounding victory those who had followed Gideon asked him to be their ruler, that is, to become king, and even to found a dynasty. According to the Book of Judges, Gideon refused, giving the prophetic answer: "The Lord will rule over you."

Abimelech: Jgs 9

Abimelech was the son of Gideon, or of Jerubbaal, and a Shechemite woman. Contrary to Gideon's theological answer to the offer of kingship, Abimelech's name means: "My father is king." Jerubbaal, a Canaanite, could very well have accepted the title of king, as all the little Canaanite princes did; on the other hand, such an acceptance was still difficult for a Hebrew like Gideon.

In any case, the death of Gideon-Jerubbaal was followed by a real war of succession. In order to win recognition as king of Shechem, Abimelech slew all of his brothers with the exception of Jotham, who survived to bear witness against him. Jotham prophesied against a monarchy, as Samuel and so many prophets were to do after him; he was a witness who anticipated the later prophetic movement.

The city of Shechem had a long history behind it. It had been founded by the Hyksos as a fortified city and, according to Genesis 12:1–7, was the place of Abraham's first contact with Palestine. With Shechem, too, was associated the name of Israel who is said to have worshiped El Berith, the God of the covenant, there. In the time of Abimelech people would have been worshiping Baal-berith, since they had now turned to the cult of Baal along with the rest of Canaan.

Abimelech did not reign at Shechem, but he did receive taxes derived from the temple; he thus renewed the royal role of Lab'aya the Habiru (fourteenth century B.C.). The mutter of rebellion was soon heard in

Shechem, and Abimelech had to overcome a rival, a man named Gaal. Not content with this success, he killed by asphyxiation the Shechemites who had expected to find refuge in their sacred cave; then he destroyed the city. This act of destruction does not seem to be confirmed by archeology, which, however, has indeed found traces of destruction in the temple of the city, a temple which was doubtless that of Baal-berith. Unfortunately, it is not possible to date this destruction more closely than between 1200 and 1100 B.C.

Abimelech, whose monarchic rule cost the lives of his brothers and the populace of Shechem, was killed by a woman who dropped a millstone on his head. Once again, monarchy was rejected. The conclusion of the story of Dan will demand an end to anarchy. This conflict announces the entrance of Samson on the scene.

Samson: Jgs 13–16

Samson is the hero of the tribe of Dan, but this sprightly popular tale will not provide us with any historical information. We do not even know whether the episodes narrated have to do with Dan before or after the migration of the bulk of the tribe to the north.

The story of Samson opens with an account of a barren woman, thus linking his birth with that of Isaac, but even more with that of Samuel and, later, of John the Baptist. The remainder of the story, however, belongs to the cape-and-sword genre with its ups-and-downs, its improbable battles using the jawbone of an ass, its tricks like tying the foxes and sending them to burn the harvest, and also its love affairs which thrust poor Samson, a somewhat naive fellow, into the arms of beautiful Philistine women. Nor is Samson himself free from taint; but this is not yet the age when mixed marriages will be rejected.

Samson is in fact less a judge (he passes judgment on no one and sweeps no one into battle) than a popular hero whose strength and weaknesses make him resemble Hercules. He overcomes a lion with his bare hands and falls victim to Delilah, as Hercules does to Omphale.

Is this similarity a sign that Dan intermarried with the peoples of the sea?

Chapter 5
Samuel and the Establishment of the Monarchy

Samuel[1] is a very complex figure. To begin with, his story relates him to the judges. Thus we are told that his birth was miraculous in the same way as Samson's. But then we are told that he was raised in the temple of Shiloh, where the ark was kept; he is therefore to be not only a judge but a priest, that is, a man jealous of his authority as being alone authorized to offer sacrifice. It may be however that this assertion is a later addition, intended to bring out the separation of powers between king and priest.

Samuel's life is summed up in the same manner as that of the judges had been: "Samuel judged Israel all the days of his life. And he went on a circuit year by year to Bethel, Gilgal, and Mizpah; and he judged Israel in all these places. Then he would come back to Ramah, for his home was there, and there also he administered justice to Israel. And he built there an altar to the Lord" (1 Sam 7:15–17).

Like his predecessors, Samuel judged only a very limited sector of the total tribal territory, namely, the highlands of Ephraim. Like them again, he was called during a period of distress, after Israel had been defeated by the Philistines in the battle of Aphek around 1050 B.C. Not only did the Philistines seize the ark, but they also occupied the hilltops. Samuel would therefore have to lead his people in war, push back the Philistines, and as a sign of gratitude erect a stone to the Eternal One: "Ebenezer."

Samuel's victory only removed the danger for a time. The Philistines were not vanquished, and Israel's neighbors were organizing against it on all sides. In the north, Phoenicia controlled the coast and protected its hinterland. The Aramaeans became a power strong enough to disquiet the Assyrian ruler, Tiglath-pileser I, even though he had conquered Babylon. In the west and south Ammon and Edom were consolidating their kingdoms.

In the face of these many dangers, the political solution would be to unite the tribes under the authority of a king. Did Samuel think of this solution? Did he envisage establishing his sons as a kind of dynasty of judges? If he did, his plans did not succeed, and the people, Ephraim, called for a king such as the other nations had. They would no longer look for a leader raised up by God, but wanted a recognized military leader. They wanted a leader capable of rescuing them from the control of the Philistines who had a monopoly on iron and thus kept Israel at their mercy not only for arms but for farming tools.

This providential rescuer was to be revealed when Jabesh in Gilead was besieged by the Ammonites: his name was Saul of Benjamin. He was a farm laborer, yet he succeeded in raising an army and freeing Jabesh. He then asked the tribes to gather at Gilgal, and he had himself proclaimed king by "all Israel." In actual fact, "Israel" here consisted of Benjamin, Gilead and doubtless Ephraim. The other tribes were not affected.

Once he became king, Saul organized a standing army (1 Sam 13:2; 14:52) and successively repulsed the Ammonites, the Philistines, and, in the south, the Amalekites. He thus established in the hill country a territory that ran from the edge of the plain of Jezreel in the north to Ramah, Gibeah, and Gilgal in the south, and extended across the Jordan to the area around Jabesh and Mahanaim. Saul thus effected a tribal union from the center and doubtless also established the first links with Judah in the south in order to fight off the Amalekites. This explains the presence at his court of David, a Judean.

This kingdom did not as yet have any administrative organization. Gibeah can hardly be called its capital. Archeologists have uncovered an eleventh century B.C. citadel there: a yard 90 by 150 feet, surrounded by

Typical Philistine pottery decoration of a bird looking backward.

a casemated wall. Four rectangular towers guarded the angles. This was perhaps a Philistine fortress that was subsequently used by Saul.

The edifice erected by Saul was thus very insecure. His army was capable of bold raids and could defend the hill country, but it could not face the Philistine war-chariots in the plain. For attempting to do so, Saul and his son Jonathan would fall in the battle of Gilboa around 1010.

I have just told the story of the hero of Jabesh who was anointed king. But the First Book of Samuel offers another tradition: a popular legend according to which a young keeper of asses is mysteriously anointed king by Samuel, who this time dons the prophet's robes.

Samuel called Saul to be king, not however because of the latter's exploits but because Samuel was notified by God in a dream. From his earliest years Samuel had been listening to the word of God, and his role, like that of the later prophets, was to warn Israel.

As a prophet he delivered a very anti-royalist sermon to the people. If Israel chooses a king, it is because it no longer trusts in its God. And whom does it choose as king in God's place? A young man who hides among the baggage (1 Sam 10:17–27), an action which hardly wins the enthusiasm of the people.

Campaign of Tiglath-pileser I against the Aramaeans

"Tiglath-pileser, mighty king, king of the universe, king of the four countries. At the order of Anu and Adad, the great gods who are my lords, I went to Mount Lebanon, I cut down and carried off the trunks of the cedar trees for the temple of Anu and Adad, the great gods who are my lords. I passed into Amurru, I conquered the land of Amurru in its entirety. I received tribute from the lands of Gubal (Byblos), Sidunu (Sidon) and Armada (Arvad). I boarded the ships of the town of Armada in the land of Amurru and successfully travelled three leagues from the town of Armada, which is by the high seas, to the town of Samuru in the land of Amurru. On the open sea I slew a blower, which they call a sea-horse. I received a crocodile and a large monkey that lives on the seashore. And on my return I subjugated the land of the Hatti (the Hittites occupying Syria). I forced Ili-Teshup, king of the Hatti, to hand over hostages, rents, tribute and cedar wood. I went to Milida in the great land of Hatti and received tribute from Allumaru. I conquered the town of Enzata in the land of Ishua, as well as the land of Suhma. From these I deported prisoners whom I carried off to my own country. During the past year I twice crossed the Euphrates in pursuit of the Ahlamu Armayu (Aramaeans). I defeated them from the foot of Mount Lebanon, from the town of Tadmar (Palmyra) in the land of the Amurrru, from Anat in the land of Suhu (west of the Middle Euphrates), as far as the town of Rapiqu (west of Baghdad) in the land of Kar-Duniash (Babylonia). From them I took prisoners and possessions to my own city of Ashur."

Samuel goes further in his denunciation of the monarchy and launches into a violent indictment of royal power and of the evils that will come with a king: the king will have all the rights, he will take your sons and daughters, he will seize your best lands. God saved you by the hand of his judges and prophets; as followers of your king, you will advance to destruction. Samuel is here repeating the remarks of Jotham (cf. p. 79).

To some, the monarchy represents political salvation; to others, a serious sin: forgetfulness of God. We shall find this twofold tradition continuing throughout the history of Israel. Samuel represents the prophetic

---

Call for a King: I Samuel 8

"When Samuel became old, he made his sons judges over Israel. The name of his first-born son was Joel, and the name of his second, Abijah; they were judges in Beersheba. Yet his sons did not walk in his ways, but turned aside after gain; they took bribes and perverted justice.

"Then all the elders of Israel gathered together and came to Samuel at Ramah, and said to him, 'Behold, you are old and your sons do not walk in your ways; now appoint for us a king to govern us like all the nations.' But the thing displeased Samuel when they said, 'Give us a king to govern us.' And Samuel prayed to the Lord. And the Lord said to Samuel, 'Hearken to the voice of the people in all that they say to you; for they have not rejected you, but they have rejected me from being king over them. According to all the deeds which they have done to me, from the day I brought them up out of Egypt even to this day, forsaking me and serving other gods, so they are also doing to you. Now then, hearken to their voice; only, you shall solemnly warn them, and show them the ways of the king who shall reign over them.'

"So Samuel told all the words of the Lord to the people who were asking a king from him. He said, 'These will be the ways of the king who will reign over you: he will take your sons and appoint them to his chariots and to be his horsemen, and to run after his chariots; and he will appoint for himself commanders of thousands and commanders of fifties, and some to plow his ground and to reap his harvest, and to make his implements of war and the equipment of his chariots. He will take your daughters to be perfumers and cooks and bakers. He will take the best of your fields and vineyards and olive orchards and give them to his servants. He will take the tenth of your grain and of your vineyards and give it to his officers and to his servants. He will take your menservants and your maidservants, and the best of your cattle and your asses, and put them to his work. He will take the tenth of your flocks, and you shall be his slaves. And in that day you will cry out because of your king, whom you have chosen for yourselves; but the Lord will not answer you in that day.'

"But the people refused to listen to the voice of Samuel; and they said, 'No! but we will have a king over us, that we also may be like all the nations, and that our king may govern us and go out before us and fight our battles.' And when Samuel had heard all these words of the people, he repeated them in the ears of the Lord. And the Lord said to Samuel, 'Hearken to their voice, and make them a king.' Samuel then said to the men of Israel, 'Go every man to his city.'"

current which will ceaselessly resist the abuses committed by the kings. He is a prototype of the later prophets, a hero of God, a man who in the face of royal claims recalls the sovereignty of God and demands that God's rights be respected.

According to this tradition, there can be no kingship by popular acclaim; only the prophet or the priest (Samuel embodies both types of authority) can anoint a king. And the king will then be subordinate to him; specifically, he will not be able to invoke God without Samuel's aid. The reason for Saul's rejection by God will be that he himself offered a sacrifice without waiting for Samuel.

The king God really wants is Saul's young page, David, who is anointed by Samuel in accordance with God's will. This theological statement does not succeed in hiding the tension between two tribes, Judah and Benjamin, which wanted to have leadership in Israel. Saul is not mistaken when he warns the Benjaminites that if they follow David of Judah, they will lose many of the advantages which he, Saul, and his house guaranteed to them.

Saul and his house were wiped out in the battle of Gilboa; Saul was supposed to have reigned for twelve years, but the number is very problematic. He laid the foundations for a state, but was unable to remove the danger from abroad or to bring about internal unity, for the Canaanites continued to live in the midst of the Israelites. But perhaps Saul did attempt to reduce the power of the Canaanites; the hatred of the Gibeonites for him would point in this direction (2 Sam 21:2).

Chapter 6
The Reigns of David and Solomon

The sources of information on David are numerous: 1 and 2 Samuel, 1 Kings, 1 Chronicles, a large number of psalms, and some discourses of the prophets. In dealing with these many sources, however, it is difficult to separate what is history from theology, epic poetry and legend. It is all the more difficult because the reign of David occurred during a period when the great neighboring powers were not on the scene. As a matter of fact, it was this absence that made possible the extension of the kingdoms of David and Solomon.

Our surest source is the Books of Samuel, which evidently contain very ancient parts: the elegy for Samuel and Jonathan, the royal annals, the history of the succession. There are remarkable pages among them that bring the figure of David alive to us more than any other in the Bible.

The First Book of Chronicles repeats the Books of Samuel and Kings; when it adds otherwise unknown information, this seems to be of later origin than the traditions in the Books of Samuel and relates primarily to dogmatic questions. Thus according to 1 Chronicles it is David who makes all the preparations for the building of the temple, and Solomon is simply the executor of these plans.

The Book of Psalms reminds us that David was a musician and poet at the court of Saul. We do not know whether this or that psalm may go back to David himself or to the dedication of the temple of Solomon. The psalms emphasize David's position as servant of God, the man who was tested unto death but remained faithful. In every situation and despite everything he placed himself in the hands of God and believed in God's promise and in the divine mercy. If this picture reminds us of the one in the Books of Samuel, it is also very close to the portrait of the suffering Servant of Second Isaiah, the prophet of the return from exile. David reflects the hope of the humble folk of Israel who commit themselves to God; he prefigures the Messiah who is to come.

As for the prophets,[1] they continue to reflect on the person of David, on his faith, and on the promise connected with his name: the hope of a posterity that will never die out. David is the focus of all the hopes of a national restoration, but also of all the spiritual hopes linked to the coming of a Messiah who will restore purity and fidelity to the Lord alone.

David

David, born around 1040 B.C. at Bethlehem of Judah, appeared one day at the court of Saul. We have three traditions regarding his entrance on the scene. The simplest explanation shows David as a splendid fighter whose courage has been noticed by Saul. It is against this background that the story of David and Goliath is told;[2] it is an epic story, for another tradition tells of a single combat between Goliath and a hero named Elhanan (2 Sam 21:19). To augment the greatness of David, his deeds of valor are confused with those of his companions. The story of David and Goliath is also a theological tale which emphasizes that David's victory comes from the Lord.

The second tradition, which is very hostile to Saul, makes the king of Israel a sick man. Only David's handsome face, his psalms, and his harp-playing can solace the king. This side of David as poet and musician is certainly true to life. It is equally true that he became an intimate of the house of Saul, being linked by friendship with Saul's son Jonathan and marrying Saul's daughter Michal. We should think that Saul, rather than being jealous, had a very justified fear of seeing himself and his family ousted from the kingship to the advantage of David, a man of Judah rather than of Benjamin (1 Sam 2).

Finally, the third tradition, historically the least susceptible of proof but theologically the most important, is that Samuel had another dream. The Lord bade him anoint David as king to replace Saul. Thus David, unlike Saul, is not a king forced on God by his people but the king whom God chose for his people.

The jealousy, or anxiety, of Saul forced David to flee far from the court. The narrative turns into an epic as it tells us of David acting like a Robin Hood, a magnanimous bandit who plays with Saul but, out of fidelity to God, is unwilling to make an attempt on his life.

One thing is clear: pursued by Saul, David was forced to take refuge

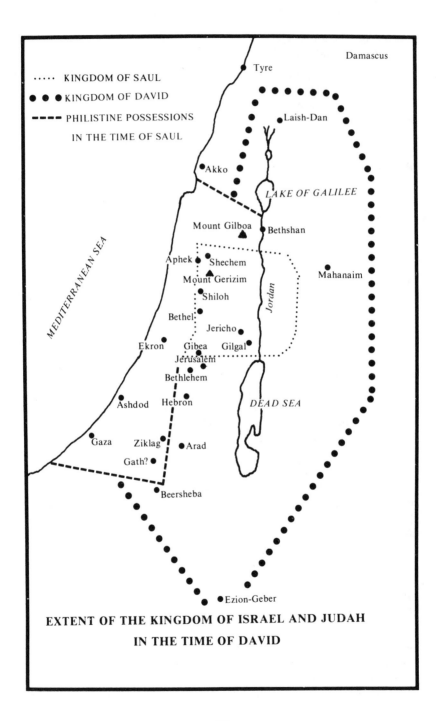

KINGDOM OF SAUL

KINGDOM OF DAVID

PHILISTINE POSSESSIONS
IN THE TIME OF SAUL

Damascus

Tyre

Laish-Dan

Akko

LAKE OF GALILEE

Mount Gilboa

Bethshan

Aphek

Shechem

Mount Gerizim

Mahanaim

MEDITERRANEAN SEA

Shiloh

Jordan

Bethel

Jericho

Ekron

Gibea

Gilgal

Jerusalem

Bethlehem

Ashdod

Hebron

DEAD SEA

Gaza

Ziklag

Arad

Gath?

Beersheba

Ezion-Geber

**EXTENT OF THE KINGDOM OF ISRAEL AND JUDAH
IN THE TIME OF DAVID**

with his old enemy, the Philistine prince of Gath, who gave him the town of Ziklag. Thenceforth he fought for the Philistines but skillfully avoided fighting against his own brothers; he attacked the nomad peoples who were a threat to both the Philistines and Judah. More than that, when he returned from his expeditions he gave a part of the booty to the elders of Judah, thus increasing his merits in their eyes.

When the Philistine princes united against Saul and Jonathan, David was excluded from the battle. He subsequently learned of the death of the heroes, including his friend, of their tragic lot, and how their remains were displayed at Beth-shean.

The defeat of Israel, terrible though it was, did not utterly destroy Israel's power. In the north, Saul's general, Abner, tried to rally the scattered tribes. Fearing the might of the Philistines he crossed the Jordan to Mahanaim. There he had the royal anointing conferred on a son of Saul named Ishbaal or Ishbosheth, the latter ("man of shame") being the sobriquet bestowed on him by the authors of the First Book of Samuel.

In the south, David had himself proclaimed king of Judah at Hebron. The elders enthroned him because of his military feats, even though the theology of the book reminds us of the secret anointing by Saul. David immediately wrote to the inhabitants of Jabesh-gilead to compliment them for having buried the remains of Saul and Jonathan but also to let them know that he could serve them as Saul had (2 Sam 2:6). Was it at this period that a sanctuary was built at Mamre in honor of the patriarchs?

Ishbaal, doubtless with reason, suspected Abner of wanting to seize power. Abner then turned to David, but by doing so he threatened the interests of Joab, David's general. Abner brought David the support of the elders of the northern tribes. A grateful David made a covenant with Abner, but Joab assassinated the latter in an ambush. Ishbaal was likewise assassinated—all this, says the Second Book of Samuel, without the approval of David!

In any event, it was David who emerged triumphant; the elders of Israel came to Hebron and acknowledged him there as their king. For the first time, there was unity between the northern and southern tribes, as David reigned over both Israel and Judah. After having reigned for seven years over Judah alone, he was to reign for thirty-three years more over combined Israel and Judah. The number forty is doubtless symbolic; it signifies the completeness of David's rule and God's blessing on it.

Israel and Judah united became a real threat to the Philistines, and immediately after David's anointing they launched an attack on the new kingdom. Skilled in maneuvering, David traveled the length of his kingdom and drove them back to the plain. It even seems that the Philistines finally acknowledged David as a kind of overlord and supplied him with troops.

David's second step was to choose a capital for the new kingdom. At the heart of the realm stood Jerusalem, an independent Canaanite city. It was well fortified; the hill had been supplied with stone terraces on which the houses were arranged in tiers; the wall around it dates from 1800 B.C. Moreover the city had an advantage rare in the land of Judah: its own spring, named Gihon. Joab captured the city by a bold stroke: he entered the city through the tunnel that brought the water from Gihon.

Jerusalem was not part either of Israel or of Judah and was therefore an ideal capital for purposes of political unity. David added religious unity by having the ark brought there with great pomp. The priests Abiathar and Zadok were to guard the ark in its tent.

David had a palace built for himself, and would have liked to imitate the monarchs of the east by having the temple of God joined to it, but Nathan the prophet was instructed by God to forbid this. There is here an echo of a dispute that was to divide Israel for a long time: to some prophetic circles the temple was an offense against God, representing a desire to make a prisoner of him instead of allowing him to be the leader. In the view of these circles it was not for David to build a temple but for God to build a house for David by ensuring him an unfailing posterity.

After Jerusalem, all the Canaanite cities were subjected to taxation and thus to David. At last the kingdom described in Judges 1:28 became a reality. The kingdoms of Moab, Edom and Ammon, which had so often disturbed the tribes, now became the marches of David's empire. It was on the occasion of the expedition against Ammon that David had Uriah murdered in order that he might marry Uriah's widow Bathsheba, who would later be the mother of Solomon. This is one of the most vivid episodes in the story of David; the description could only have come from someone close to the king.

David extended his conquests in the direction of Syria, signed treaties with the Philistines, and cultivated good relations with Egypt.

He had established a kingdom, but its unity was still only superficial. There were really two kingdoms, Israel in the north and Judah in the south; Jerusalem had replaced Hebron as capital of Judah. Absalom, David's son, would later be able to play on the accumulated grudges against David's centralizing state; he had himself recognized as king at Hebron and came close to overturning his father.

In this last-named situation David showed himself a man full of love for his children despite their faults, but at the same time a very astute man: he did not confront his son, but he managed to surround him with false counselors who caused his downfall.

The unrest did not come only from David's children. During the rebellion of Absalom, David was disturbed by the attitude of Mephibosheth (Meribbaal), son of Jonathan and grandson of Saul. Had he perhaps joined the ranks of the insurgents in order to win back his kingdom of Israel? On the other hand, had not David welcomed him at his table out of friendship for the man's father, Jonathan? But perhaps David also wanted to keep an eye on him in this way! More serious was the revolt of Sheba, a Benjaminite, who trumpeted: "We have no portion in David" (2 Sam 20:1). Responding to the same cry, the kingdom was soon to be divided.

David tried to ward off these threats of division by establishing an administration. Like Saul he had a standing army commanded by Joab; now he added a special bodyguard for the king, one drawn, it seems, from among the Philistines (2 Sam 8:18).

High officials also made their appearance. There was Jehoshaphat, the *maskir:* was he an archivist or a prime minister? There was Seraiah, the *sopher:* a scribe or private secretary of David? It is beyond doubt that during David's reign a number of traditions were put in writing, perhaps those concerning Abraham and Isaac at Mamre; it is certain too that in the story of the succession we see the appearance of a remarkable literary work. Another minister who came on the scene was Adoram, in charge of collecting taxes, but also perhaps in charge of forced labor.

The priesthood was organized around Abiathar, a former priest of Shiloh and one of David's companions from the first hour, and around Zadok whose posterity was to have a fine future. Did David perhaps have a special priest of his own, named Ira (2 Sam 20:25)? In the Second Book of Samuel David's sons are called priests; the First Book of Chronicles, which could not accept the linking of civil and religious functions, corrects this by saying they were ministers of state.

The Succession[3]

Saul had been proclaimed king after the manner of the liberator-judges. David was anointed king by two gatherings of tribal elders. This time, however, there was a succession: it was up to the king to appoint his successor.

This was a new problem, aggravated by the fact that David had many wives. Very soon, his sons were at odds among themselves. Thus because of a sexual matter Absalom had killed his brother Amnon. Then, after being admitted back into the realm, Absalom rebelled against his father and was killed. David had now become an old man who could no longer keep warm, but he had still not named his successor.

Adonijah, the eldest son, seeing his father grow feeble, decided to go ahead. He had himself recognized as king by his father's oldest servants: Joab the general, Abiathar the priest, and the men of Judah. He organized a great festival and a sacrifice at the spring of En-rogel, on the border of the territories of Judah and Benjamin.

But Adonijah did not take into account the combined diplomatic talents of Nathan the prophet, Zadok the priest, Benaiah the captain of David's personal bodyguard, and Bathsheba the mother of Solomon. They leagued together to warn the king of the doings of his eldest son and reminded him of a promise he had supposedly made to Solomon. Whatever be the facts in regard to the promise, David, who had not been consulted by Adonijah, took up the cause of Solomon. He had him ride down to the spring of Gihon on the royal mule and be anointed there by Zadok in the presence of all the people. The anointing was a solemn one; the trumpet was sounded.

Solomon, thus anointed during the lifetime of David, later settled his own accounts. Again for sexual reasons, he had his brother Adonijah put to death, for though Adonijah had recognized Solomon's kingship, he still represented a threat. In like manner, Solomon had Joab slain in order to make room for Benaiah; Abiathar was superseded, and Zadok alone remained.

Of course, this purely political side of Solomon's enthronement was not enough in the eyes of faith. As a result, stress was put on the visions Solomon had. His first vision at Gibeon was the most important; when asked by God, Solomon requested only the gifts of wisdom and of discernment of good and evil. This request, which pleased God, along with Solomon's good judgment became the basis for proclaiming the king's very great wisdom. This wisdom made him known in far-off places, and the queen of Sheba came to visit him. It made him known through time as well, for later the Book of Proverbs and the wisdom books would be attributed to him.

Solomon's great work was the building of the temple. There was no longer any resistance from the prophets, but only praise for this king who was able to build a temple that was in continuity with the sanctuary of the ark, who by means of the temple worship gathered the twelve tribes in Jerusalem, and who was concerned to provide his people with a history in which its various traditions were gathered and wrought into a unity. The first or Yahwist document dates from the time of Solomon.

The temple was not novel but was built after the manner of the pre-Israelite temples at Hazor and Shechem. The workers were not Jews but chiefly Phoenicians loaned, for a price, by Hiram of Tyre. The time pe-

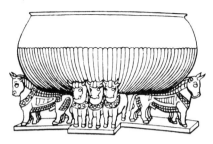

The Bronze Sea from Solomon's Temple.

riods for the construction and dedication match those in the Ugarit documents for the temple of Baal. The ornaments were comparable to those in Egyptian temples. The location on a hilltop recalled the Canaanite temples. But, at the center of the temple, there was no statue of God but only the ark of the covenant.

In keeping with the later theology that centralized everything in Jerusalem, the Bible acknowledges no temple but the one in Jerusalem. Nonetheless the excavations at Arad in the Negeb have revealed a tenth-century B.C. temple which is in every respect like that of Solomon and which fell into disuse only in the eighth century B.C. before being destroyed in the seventh (map, p. 88).

Solomon's wisdom was not wholly concerned with God; it was also the wisdom of a king. He was able to build a temple which not only brought the Israelites together but could also attract the Canaanites and other foreign peoples. Solomon's palace was next to the temple, signifying that he was submissive to God but also that he was God's son (Ps 2:7) after the fashion of the kings of Ugarit. This syncretism understandably disturbed the prophets, all the more so since Solomon also exercised the prerogatives of priests. Thus he offered sacrifices at Gibeon (1 Kgs 3) and blessed the people before the altar (1 Kgs 9). Saul had been sharply criticized for such practices and had even been rejected by God because of them, according to the prophecy of Samuel.

In addition to the temple, Solomon also built a palace for himself, fortified Jerusalem, and rebuilt a number of fortified places, among them Hazor, Megiddo and Gezer. Archeologists have shown that each of these cities was surrounded by a casemated wall and entered by gates with triple outworks. The stables of Solomon, however, have not been found; the stables at Megiddo must be dated from the time of King Ahab, or almost a century later. The oldest agrarian calandar in Hebrew has been found at Gezer, and it dates from this period. Aqueducts dug in the time of Solomon have been found at Jerusalem and Gezer.

One of Solomon's most important works was the building of the port of Ezion-geber on the gulf of Aqaba. This harbor enabled him to trade with the kingdom of Sheba which maintained trade routes to the Indies, eastern Africa and the mysterious land of Ophir whence came gold. Sheba was doubtless the kingdom of southern Yemen, which flourished at that period. With the help of Sheba and the sailors of Phoenicia Solomon built a fleet which undertook voyages of up to three years.

This foreign trade was matched by cultural relations. Solomon was receptive to all forms of wisdom; he welcomed the queen of Sheba; he was interested in botany and zoology. For his undertakings he doubtless reopened the old copper mines of the pharaohs between the Dead Sea and the Red Sea. All of these sources brought him wealth and the ability to control the trade routes to Gaza and Egypt in the south and to Syria in the north; Solomon's wealth became part of his legend.

For his building program and to maintain his luxurious life-style as a woman-loving eastern prince, Solomon had to find money. It was from the people that he exacted it. In order to administer his kingdom more efficiently he divided it into twelve areas, each with its governor. Each governor had to feed the royal household, and doubtless the temple staff as well, for one month each year (1 Kgs 4).

Since this sort of tax did not provide for his major undertakings, Solomon added forced labor. Did this obligation fall particularly on Israel? In any case it was one of the reasons for the schism that occurred at Solomon's death.

In order to pay back Hiram of Tyre, Solomon gave up the towns of Galilee—twenty in all, says the First Book of Kings (9:10–14). The Chronicler seeks to correct the impression by saying that Hiram offered these towns to Solomon, but this attempt to glorify Solomon deceives no one.

In like manner, Solomon's relations with Egypt are not entirely clear. The Bible praises his international relations and his marriage with an Egyptian princess. Yet it seems that Solomon was forced to meet the pharaoh in his own home territory. It was only after the capture and partial

**A drawing of one of Solomon's
ships "of Tarshish," built in the
Phoenician style.**

destruction of Gezer by the pharaoh (1 Kgs 9:16) that Solomon agreed by treaty to marry the pharaoh's daughter. This would not prevent the pharaoh from receiving Hadad of Edom and giving him too one of his daughters or from promoting the independence of Edom at the end of Solomon's reign (1 Kgs 11:14–22).

It was the pharaoh again who welcomed Jeroboam when he rebelled against Solomon in the name of the northern tribes, that is, in the name of Israel. Jeroboam would return from Egypt to effect the schism and become king of Israel as distinct from Judah.

At the end of Solomon's reign, Aram in the north also regained its independence under the leadership of Rezon, who defeated David's ancient enemy, Hadadezer, king of Zobah (1 Kgs 11:23). The new kingdom, with its center at Damascus, would reach its apogee during the ninth and eighth centuries B.C.

By the end of Solomon's life, his reign reminds us of the reign of Louis XIV. From the standpoint of the arts, trade and culture it was a magnificent reign. From the standpoint of the state it marked the beginning of the end; excessive fiscal oppression led to schism. From the religious standpoint, the purity of Solomon's dream as he asked God for wisdom was contradicted by an ever growing syncretism, which was intensified by the presence of foreign princesses.

The Kingdoms of Israel and Judah
at grips with their neighbors and the Assyrian and Neobabylonian empires

Judah	Israel	Mesopotamia	Neighbors
Rehoboam 933–916	Jeroboam 933–911		Sheshonk of Egypt 930: Campaign vs Judah and Israel
Abijah 915–913	Nadab 911–910		
Asa 912–871	Baasha 910–887		Ben-hadad I Alliance of Damascus with Asa
	Elah 887–886		
	Zimri 886		
	Omri 886–875		
Jehoshaphat 870–846	Ahab 875–853	Assurnasirpal 883–859	
	m Jezebel		Ben-hadad II, Damascus
	Prophet Elijah	Shalmaneser III 858–824	853, battle of Kharkar Shalmaneser repulsed
	Ahaziah 853–852		
	Jehoram 852–841		840: Stela of Mesha of Moab
Jehoram 846–841	Prophet Elisha		
Ahaziah 841	Jehu 841–814?		Hazael of Damascus
Athaliah 841–835			
Joash 835–796?	Jehoahaz ?–803	Adadnirari III	Ben-hadad III of Damascus
	Joash 802–787		
	Prophet Amos	Troubles in Assyria	
Uzziah 781–?747	Zechariah		
	Shallum		
Jotham 740–736	Menahem 746–737	Tiglath-pileser III 745–727	Tyre, Damascus, Israel pay tribute. 738
Prophet Isaiah	Prophet Hosea		
	Pekahiah		
	Pekah 735–732		734: Tiglath-pileser in Gaza
Ahaz 735–726 (or 716)			Ahaz allied with Tiglath-pileser
Prophets Isaiah I Micah			

Chapter 7
Schism: 933 B.C.(?)
1 Kings 12

Once Solomon died, the unity of the realm could no longer be maintained. According to the First Book of Kings the reasons for this were theological. The breakup of the kingdom was a punishment for the infidelities of Solomon who joined his wives in worshiping foreign gods, the gods of the neighboring peoples. Let the people return to worship of Yahweh alone and unity will be restored: such is the vision of the Deuteronomist.

But we must also do justice to more political considerations:

1. The union between Judah and the northern tribes had been due solely to the personality of King David. Until he came on the scene, Judah in the south and Israel in the north had lived separate lives. At the time of Solomon's death unity was still a very recent thing.

2. Unity had been threatened on at least two occasions during the reign of David himself: when Absalom had himself chosen king at Hebron, and when Sheba the Benjaminite anticipated the later slogan: "We have no portion in David, and we have no inheritance in the sons of Jesse." Then during the reign of Solomon the northern tribes rebelled under Jeroboam.

3. The rebellion of Jeroboam seems to show that Israel was more heavily taxed than Judah. In any case, the northern tribes had serious complaints about forced labor.

4. It seems that the ideas of Israel and Judah on the monarchy dif-

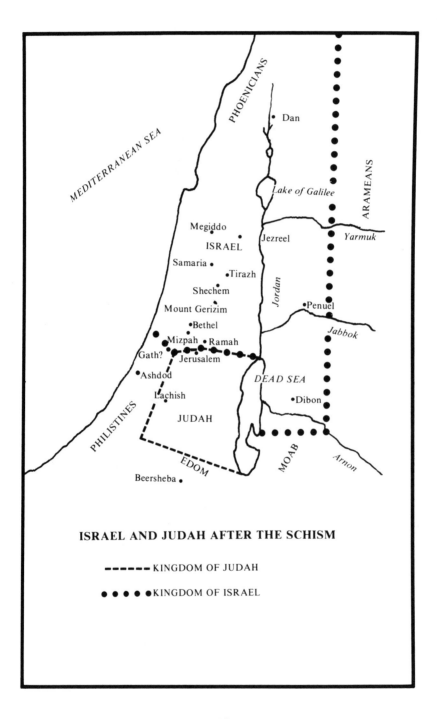

ISRAEL AND JUDAH AFTER THE SCHISM

------ KINGDOM OF JUDAH

● ● ● ● ● KINGDOM OF ISRAEL

98

fered. Judah seems to have adopted without difficulty a dynastic type of kingship. The people relied on Nathan's promise to David that God would make his throne stand firm from generation to generation.

In Israel on the other hand it seems that the king was meant to have the approval of a council of elders, identical with the one that had chosen David as king. This was a more democratic variety of kingship and was in continuity with the election of the liberator-judges who had won recognition for their qualities. These qualities were a sign of God's blessing.

The episode of the succession is recounted in 1 Kings 12. Rehoboam has been designated as successor to his father in Judah, and he goes to the sanctuary at Shechem in order that he may there be acknowledged as king of Israel also.

At Shechem the general assembly first presents him with their grievances. In response to their suit, he must choose between Solomon's advisers who counsel him to listen and put himself at the service of the people, and his own advisers who urge him to assert his royal authority. Rehoboam chooses this second course, promising Israel to be even harder on it than his father had been. At this point the break takes place, as the ancient rallying cry is raised: "To your tents, O Israel!"

Then Rehoboam endeavors to negotiate but, with an incredible lack of diplomacy, sends as his ambassador Adoram, who was in charge of forced labor. Adoram is stoned. Rehoboam must then take flight, and will now reign over Judah alone. The union of Israel and Judah has thus not lasted more than seventy-five years.

Dating

Beginning with the schism we can follow the history of the two kingdoms, and it ought to be easy to establish dates. Unfortunately, we do not know in every instance how account was taken of a year in which there was a change of kings; in Israel, such a year of change was accounted as a year of reign both for the departing king and for the new king. As a result, between the coming of Jehu and the fall of Samaria we count 165 years in Israel but only 144 in Judah. To complicate matters, Judah initially used a calendar in which the year began with the month of Tishri (September–October) but later adopted the calendar already in use in Israel, according to which the year began with the month of Nisan (March–April). The date of this shift is not known for certain.

Some kings reigned conjointly, as, for example, David and Solomon.

Since quarrels arose in Israel at the time of the succession, some kings must have reigned at the same time.

Fortunately, it is possible to date a certain number of events thanks to the very precise lists kept in other countries. Thus we have very exact dates for Assyria between 892 and 648 B.C. and a complete list of its kings down to 757 B.C. This list can be filled out with the aid of the canon of Ptolemy which, though dating only from the second century, is very precise and gives numerical data on the reigns of the Babylonian kings from 747 B.C. on. Finally, many Babylonian tablets and various inscriptions contribute to the work. It is thus possible to achieve increasingly greater accuracy, but the task is one that must be constantly tackled anew in order to take into account all the data, which unfortunately are not always in agreement.

Jeroboam, King of Israel and Rehoboam, King of Judah: 1 Kgs 12–14, 1 Chr 10–12

The history of the period I deal with in this chapter and of the further period down to the destruction of the northern kingdom, Israel, can be followed in the First Book of Kings, which we have in a Deuteronomistic redaction. The theological framework is very specific: the kings are to be judged in terms of their fidelity to Yahweh alone. But within this framework the book uses various sources; these are often mentioned but are unfortunately lost: the Book of the Acts of Solomon, the Book of the Annals of the Kings of Judah, the Book of the Annals of the Kings of Israel.

The principal source of the First Book of Chronicles is the First Book of Kings; when the former refers to other documents, it is very difficult to judge their antiquity.

Jeroboam, who had fled to Egypt in the time of Solomon, returned to Israel; we cannot date this event. The northern tribes called him to Shechem to be their king. He does not seem to have intervened, perhaps being persuaded by the prophet Shemaiah who saw the schism as God's will.

Jeroboam chose ancient Shechem as his first capital, but later moved to Tirzah in the north. He fortified these two cities, as well as Penuel in the Transjordan (see map, p. 98). But the religious problem proved to be more challenging, for he had to provide alternatives to the pilgrimages to Jerusalem where the ark was kept.

As a result, he decided to call attention to Bethel and Dan by new

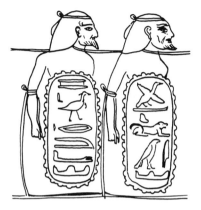

**Representations of Canaanite
cities captured by the Egyptian
pharaoh Sheshonk I in 930 B.C.
The names of the cities are
written in the ovals.**

buildings. At Bethel in the south men remembered the patriarchs and Jacob in particular; all that was lacking was a priesthood, and this Jeroboam could not acquire from among the Levites, who doubtless remained faithful to the house of David. He therefore established a new priesthood.

The situation was easier at Dan. There the tribe of Dan had long ago established its own sanctuary which, despite its idol, was dedicated to Yahweh. Dan also possessed a levitical priesthood which claimed descent from Moses himself (Jgs 18:30).

At both Bethel and Dan Jeroboam set up bulls in honor of Yahweh; these were intended as a kind of support for the divinity. He did this in imitation of the Canaanites and their cult at Baal-hadad. The purpose was not to have the bulls be worshiped but rather to give the presence of God a sensible aspect, since some equivalent of the ark had to be found. In fact, the bull readily attracted the Canaanite population of the north, while the name of Yahweh drew Israel. This practice was a disgrace to the kingdom of Israel in the eyes of all the prophets. Jeroboam and his successors were syncretists—or did they think they were returning to the tradition of Aaron in which God was worshiped under the form of a bull?

Meanwhile Rehoboam reigned over the kingdom of Judah, a territory now considerably diminished. If the list of fortifications in the First Book of Chronicles is ancient, then Judah hardly reached as far as the plain of Beersheba in the south (Edom had regained its autonomy) or the coastal plain (the Philistines were once again in command there). The fortifications needed refurbishing at Lachish and Azekah (where the work done by Rehoboam has been brought to light). In the north the frontier was under challenge; the territory of Benjamin lay between the two kingdoms, but was to be linked to Judah by its proximity to Jerusalem.

Statue of a bull representing an Egyptian god. This could be a model for the golden calves made by Jeroboam.

In about 930 B.C. Pharaoh Sheshonk I came up from Egypt and, profiting by the weakness of the two kingdoms, laid waste to them. Perhaps Rehoboam was able to preserve part of his kingdom by offering the treasures of the temple. On the other hand at Karnak this pharaoh tells of his campaign against the plain of Megiddo and of the capture of Penuel; of this the Bible says nothing, just as it says nothing of the capture of Gezer and with it Egypt's renewed control of the entire Way of the Sea. At this period too Taanach was completely destroyed.

War between Judah and Israel: 1Kgs 15–16:3, 2 Chr 13–16

The great worry of the kings of Judah was the location of Jerusalem, situated as it was on the frontier of the area belonging to Israel. The policy of the kings of Judah, therefore, was to push back the border to the northern side of Benjamin. Neither Rehoboam nor his son Abijah (or Abijam) succeeded in doing this against Jeroboam.

Israel in the north was much richer than Judah, for through it passed the routes from Egypt to Damascus. But the wealth tempted others and Israel was exposed to the hostility not only of Judah but of the Philistines, the Phoenicians and the Aramaeans, these last soon to be replaced by the Assyrians. In the east there was still the ancient rivalry with Moab. Surrounded by these many dangers Israel sorely needed a stable government. Yet because it had no dynastic tradition the north was to have twenty-nine kings in two hundred years.

Jeroboam of Israel died in 911. His son Nadab succeeded him for two years, then was assassinated by Baasha of Issachar (910–887). Baasha thought himself strong enough to attack the kingdom of Judah. In order to counter this threat Asa of Judah used skillful diplomacy to turn Israel's northern neighbor, Ben-hadad I of Damascus, against it. This judicious alliance enabled Asa to be victorious, conquer Ramah, and push his northern border out as far as Mizpah. Ben-hadad, for his part, seized the northern part of Israel, from the Transjordan to the land of Naphtali.

Asa of Judah is praised by the First Book of Kings not only for his victory over Israel but also because he supposedly pushed the Cushites further south and thus extended his realm in that direction. But the favorable judgment on Asa is due primarily to the fact that he is said to have undertaken a religious reform by destroying the idols on the high places of Judah and Benjamin.

Israel: The Omrid Dynasty: 1 Kgs 16:8–22:54

The death of Baasha (between 883 and 889) ushered in a new succession crisis. His son Elah reigned for two years before being assassinated by Zimri, a commander of Elah's chariotry. But Zimri could not defend his position, for the people appealed against him to Omri. After overcoming the two pretenders, Zimri and Tibni, Omri inaugurated a major dynasty that would rule in Israel for almost fifty years.

According to the Bible Omri was even worse than his predecessors. This religious judgment should not be allowed to obscure the fact that he

Ivory decoration in the form of a sphinx, from the time of King Omri in Samaria.

was a very great king. His major undertaking was the choice and construction of a new capital, Samaria. The site was an excellent one, since the spot was located at the meeting of the roads leading south to Shechem and Jerusalem, north to Megiddo, Damascus and Phoenicia, and west to the coast. Samaria[1] stands even today like a marvelous watch-tower set amid fertile hills. Omri also began to build there a remarkable palace on which he spent the riches obtained from trade in old wines and fine oil.

This king so impressed mighty Assyria that henceforth all the rulers of Israel would be called sons of Omri, even after his dynasty had disappeared.

We know from the stela of Mesha of Moab that Omri conquered his neighbor.

Ahab: (875–853 B.C.)

At the death of Omri his son Ahab succeeded him and continued the work of his father. It was he who built the fortifications of Samaria; within these were depots and warehouses where ostraka would later be found. Ostraka ("potsherds") are fragments of pottery on which bills were written with pen or stylus in the Phoenician alphabet; the bills inform us regarding the extensive trade carried on at Samaria and the luxury that reigned there.

A palace identical with the one at Samaria has been uncovered at Dan; its warehouses have yielded over three hundred jugs.

Ahab's architectural work did not stop there. From his reign date important hydraulic systems by which water was brought up through stepped tunnels into the cities of Hazor and Megiddo. This technique was henceforth so reliable that King Mesha of Moab, conqueror of Ahab, would use Israelite prisoners to build comparable systems in his kingdom (stela of Mesha).

These admirable policies were supported through a judicious alliance with the Phoenicians, one of whose princesses, Jezebel, became Ahab's wife. This political alliance in the north enabled him to defeat the Aramaeans of Damascus and to regain control of the northern Transjordan.

The alliance with the Phoenicians also made possible a considerable extension of trade. In addition, doubtless on the advice of Jezebel, the king did not hesitate to take for himself properties he wanted, as in the case of Naboth. In the view of the Phoenician princess who was Ahab's wife, it was legitimate for a ruler to reapportion lands, extend the royal domain and develop the economy. But in doing this Ahab forgot the ancient Jewish

The Stela of Mesha

of black basalt stone, 1,10 m high, 60 cm wide, containing 34 lines

"I am Mesha, son of Chemosh, king of Moab, the Dibonite. My father reigned over Moab for thirty years and I reigned after my father. I made this high place for Chemosh . . . because he saved me from all attacks and gave me victory over all my foes.

"Omri was king of Israel and he crushed Moab for many days, because Chemosh was angry at his own country. And his son succeeded him and said: 'I will crush Moab.' In my time he spoke thus, but I triumphed over him and his house. And Israel was laid low for ever. Now Omri had taken possession of Madaba and had lived there during his own days and half the days of his sons, forty years in all. But Chemosh restored it to me in my time. And I built Baal-meon and constructed the reservoir there, and I built Qaryaten.

"The people of Gad had always lived in the land of Ataroth, and the king of Israel had built Ataroth for himself. I attacked the city and captured it. And I slaughtered the entire populace; the city was a sacrifice for Chemosh and for Moab.

"Chemosh said to me: 'Go and take Nebo from Israel.' I went by night and attacked it from break of dawn to midday. I captured it and slew everyone: 7000 people along with foreigners, foreign women and concubines, for I had devoted them to destruction in honor of Ashtar-Chemosh. From that place I took the vessels of Yahweh and dragged them before Chemosh.

"The king of Israel had built Jahaz, and he resided there while waging war against me, but Chemosh put him to flight before me. From Moab I brought 200 men, all its elite fighters, I launched them against Jahaz, and I captured it to annex it to Dibon.

"I built Qarhoh: the wall around the park and the wall around the citadel. I built its gates, I built its towers, I built the royal house, I built the double reservoir for water within the city. There had been no cistern within the city of Qarhoh and I said to the people: 'Each of you is to build a cistern in your house.' I had the Israelite prisoners dig ditches for Qarhoh.

"I built Aroer and I constructed the Arnon road. I built Beth-bamoth, for it had been destroyed. . . . . I built Madaba."

law which ensured each family a portion of the land which God had given and which had been distributed in accordance with his laws.

The reign of Ahab saw a considerable enrichment of the well-to-do classes, but at the same time the small farmers were at the mercy of the rich. They were forced to borrow, then mortgage their property, and finally sell themselves into slavery. This is the situation denounced by the northern prophets beginning with Elijah.

Finally, in order to secure his power, Ahab had to enter into an alliance with the kingdom of Judah by marrying his daughter Athaliah to Jehoram, son of King Jehoshaphat. Nonetheless Ahab was to die in battle, being slain at the siege of Ramoth-gilead where he was facing the Aramaeans once again.

Jehoshaphat, King of Judah (870–848 B.C.): 1 Kgs 22:41–51, 2 Chr 17–21

Despite his alliance with Israel, Jehoshaphat found favor in the Books of 1 Kings and 2 Chronicles. He was a devout king, even if he did not believe the warnings of the prophet Micaiah about the disaster at Ramoth-gilead.

His reign was one of economic prosperity and reorganization of the country. In order to develop his trade he has to subjugate Edom and re-open the port of Ezion-geber. He then tried to restore Solomon's fleet in order to renew commercial ties with Tarshish, but for reasons unknown to us the fleet was destroyed.

Of his son Jehoram (2 Kgs 8:16–24; 2 Chr 21) we know nothing except the hatred which the redactor of the Second Book of Kings has for him because he married Athaliah, a northern princess who brought with her all the vices and especially the worship of the Canaanite gods. In the reign of Jehoram Edom once again recovered its independence and Solomon's port of Ezion-geber was destroyed.

The Battle of Kharkar (853 B.C.): (downstream from Hamath on the Orontes)

The Bible says nothing of this important event; at most it mentions that there was an alliance betweeen Ben-hadad II of Damascus and Ahab. The reason is that this was not the time to be concerned about such rivalries between minor kingdoms, for in the north Assyria was on the move.

Until the tenth century B.C. Assyria had remained confined to the upper Tigris valley, but with the accession of Assurnasirpal II, 883–859 B.C. (a contemporary of Omri and Ahab), a vast Assyrian empire developed in the direction of the Mediterranean. Even in the time of Omri the Phoenician cities had to pay a heavy tribute and saw their populaces deported and massacred.

Shalmaneser III (858–824 B.C.) continued this expansion in the direction of central and southern Syria. There he faced a coalition including Ben-hadad of Damascus, king of Hamath (map, p. 122) and Ahab, at Kharkar in 853 B.C. According to Shalmaneser it was a great victory for him.

Shalmaneser III's account of the battle of Kharkar

"I set out from the Euphrates and reached Halman (Aleppo). They were afraid of my attack and they grasped my feet. I received silver and gold from them in tribute. I offered sacrifices before the god Adad of Halman.

"I set out from Halman and reached the two towns of Irhuleni in the land of Hamath. I conquered the towns of Adennu, Barga and Argana, which were his royal cities. I took prisoners and the possessions of his palaces from him, and I set fire to his palaces.

"I set out from Argana and reached Kharkar. I destroyed Kharkar, his royal city, demolished it and fired it. There were 1200 chariots, 1200 saddle horses, and 20,000 foot soldiers of Adad-'idri of the land of Aram; 700 saddle horses, 700 chariots and 10,000 foot soldiers of Irhuleni from the land of Hamath; 2000 chariots and 10,000 foot soldiers of Ahabbu (Achab) from the land of Sir'ila (Israel); 500 foot soldiers from the land of Gubal (?); 1000 foot soldiers from the land of Musri; 10 chariots and 10,000 foot soldiers from the land of Irqanata; 200 foot soldiers of Matinu-ba'lu from the town of Armada; 200 foot soldiers from the land of Usanata; 300 chariots and 10,000 foot soldiers of Adunu-ba'lu from the land of Shian; 1000 camels of Gindibu' from the land of Arba (Arabia); 12000 foot soldiers of Basa, son of Ruhubu, from the land of Amana.

"He received the help of these twelve kings. They lined up against me to do battle and combat. With the superior forces given to me by Ashur my lord and with the mighty arms given me by Nergal, who goes before me, I fought against them and inflicted a defeat on them between Kharkar and Gilzau. I struck down with my weapons 14,000 of their fighters; like the god Adad, I caused a flood to descend upon them; I scattered their corpses, I covered the surface of the plain with their vast armies, and with my weapons I made their blood flow . . . the broad countryside did not have space enough to bury them. With their bodies as with a dike I dammed the river Arantu (Orontes). During this battle I took from them their chariots, their saddle horses and their cart-horses."

Yet all the information we have suggests that on the contrary he was repulsed. There is a stela that gives us an idea of the size of Ahab's army: it tells us that for the battle of Kharkar he supplied ten thousand foot-soldiers and two thousand chariots. And in fact archeologists have uncovered Ahab's stables at Megiddo.

The agreement between Damascus and Samaria cannot have lasted very long, for Ahab was killed a short time later in a war against the Aramaeans.

Elijah[2]: 1 Kgs 17–19, 21, 2 Kgs 1–2

Israel was threatened not only from without but from within as well. For while in the eyes of history the Omrids were great kings, they

**The god Baal shown as a
Stormgod with his thunder club
and lightning spear.**

achieved their prosperity by trying to amalgamate two cultures, the Israelite and the Canaanite.

The Israelites, who were faithful to God alone, rebelled against the
syncretism of the king. It is impossible to worship both Baal and Yahweh.
Yahweh is the only God, there is no other, and it is illicit to make room
for the Canaanite god Baal in order to satisfy cultural or commercial needs.
The conflict reached the critical stage with the appearance of Elijah who
went so far as to challenge the prophets of Baal in the name of his own
God, Yahweh. He overcame them at the religious level and then finished
them off with the sword at Carmel. But he then had to flee the wrath of
the Phoenician queen, Jezebel.

Elijah's anger was not inspired solely by a determination to see Yahweh alone worshiped; he also provided a voice for all the people who saw
the Mosaic laws trampled on, especially the laws concerning property. Elijah certainly represented the poor of Israel against an all-powerful aristocracy and commercial class. There was a striking example of this social
division: Tirzah, the former capital, was divided in two by a wall on one
side of which stood large stone houses fronted by imposing courtyards,
while on the other stood little houses piled one on top of the other in the
unsanitary and wretched quarter of the poor.

From the Death of Ahab to Jehu

On the death of Ahab his son Ahaziah succeeded him for two years. Elijah criticized the new king harshly for consulting Baal instead of Yahweh (2 Kgs 1). Jehoram then succeeded his brother and reigned for twelve years (2 Kgs 3). He conducted a campaign against the Moabites with the aid of Jehoshaphat of Judah; he followed this up with an alliance with Jehoram of Judah and then with the latter's son Ahaziah. Together the two kings fought Hazael of Damascus; during the battle Jehoram of Israel was wounded and returned to Jezreel. Ahaziah went to visit him there, and the two men died in the rebellion of Jehu.

Elisha: 2 Kgs 2–9:13

Elisha belonged to a community of the "sons of the prophets"; this type of community had existed even back in the time of Saul, and its members lived in great poverty (2 Kgs 4:1–7). They were the unyielding followers of Yahweh and the humble folk consulted them regularly. Like his predecessor Elijah, Elisha worked miracles and was spokesman for Yahweh, the only God, but his message was much more political than Elijah's had been. In the name of God he intervened directly in affairs of state, not only in Israel but even at Damascus. He was the prophet who foretold the end of the house of Omri and the anointing of Jehu. But his vision became universalist, for in the name of Yahweh he welcomed and healed Naaman, a high Aramaean official.

In Elijah and Elisha we see the appearance of those prophetic circles upon which the Elohist tradition drew for its interpretation of the traditions that had been handed on orally.

Jehu (841–814 B.C.): 2 Kgs 9–10

Jehu rebelled against Jehoram and the whole house of Omri. He assassinated not only Jehoram but his relative, Ahaziah of Judah, Jezebel the wife of Ahab, the whole house of Omri at Samaria and some princes of Judah. Nor did he stop there, but exterminated all the servants of Baal, the supporters of Jezebel.

Like Saul of old, Jehu was enthroned by an envoy of the prophet Elisha and recognized by the Israelite army. He founded a dynasty but,

---

Annals of Shalmaneser III

The annals contain the story of his campaign against Hazael of Damascus:
"In the 18th year of my reign I crossed the Euphrates for the 16th time. Hazael
of Damascus trusted in the size of his army which he called up in large numbers. He
took as his fortified place Mount Senir, a peak opposite Mount Lebanon. I fought
against him, I defeated him, I overthrew with my weapons 16,000 soldiers of his army.
I took from him 1121 chariots, 470 riding horses and his camp. He fled to save his life.
I pursued him. I shut him up in Damascus, his royal city. I cut down his gardens. I
advanced as far as the mountains of Hauran. Towns without number I destroyed: I
laid them waste, I burned them. I took from them booty beyond counting. I proceeded as far as the mountains of Ba'li-ra'si which are above the sea. There I set up
my royal statue. Then I received tribute from the Tyrians, the Sidonians, and Jehu,
a descendent of Omri."

---

despite having assassinated the king of Judah, he was unable, because of
his many enemies, to reunite Judah and Israel.

The Bible tells us that he had to face Hazael of Damascus who wished
to reoccupy the Transjordan. The victorious Hazael was to be a particularly
harsh conqueror, as the prophecy of Elisha emphasizes: "You will set on
fire their fortresses, and you will slay their young men with the sword, and
dash in pieces their little ones, and rip up their women with child" (2 Kgs
8:12). A short while later, Amos would be condemning the man who had
threshed Gilead with sledges of iron (Am 1:3; cf. Is 9:16).

The Bible once again ignores Assyria. But the black obelisk of Shalmaneser III (858–824 B.C.) depicts Jehu, who is called a son of Omri, as
paying tribute, doubtless in order to escape being invaded.

According to 2 Kings 10:15 Jehu met Jehonadab (or Jonadab), ancestor
of the Rechabites of whom Jeremiah will speak later on (35:5–11). The Rechabites represented a small part of the Jewish population that had refused
the sedentary life as contrary to the will of God. They rejected everything
that was the glory of the Omrids: buildings, a flourishing economy, the
wine trade. Neher says: "They carried with them, and presented as a challenge to the world, a bit of the past, namely, the Nazirate, which had the
power to shatter the pride of the present age. They were convinced that
the religious conscience could adapt itself to everything else: to a mini-
mum of room in society, to existence as a diaspora of pariahs, but not to
compromise with reasons of state."

There thus survived in Israel a family which preserved the ideal of a
people which followed its God without knowing where they were going.
Like the prophets, they believed that life in the wilderness made fidelity

The "Black Obelisk" of Shalmaneser III showing King Jehu submitting himself as a vassel after the battle of Qarqar in 841 B.C. and bringing tribute.

111

to God easier. Every settling down and every institution imposes compromises and choices contrary to those of God. Because they were concerned for their salvation, the Rechabites refused to become part of the world. Not much later, others would leave the world behind in the same search for fidelity: I am referring to the Essenes of Qumran, shortly before Christ.

Judah: Athaliah and Joash: 2 Kgs 11–12, 2 Chr 23–24

After the rebellion of Jehu and the death of Ahaziah it was the queen mother Athaliah, daughter of Jezebel, who took power in Judah. She had all the possible successors of David put to death. Joash (or Jehoash) alone was spared, because the priests were able to hide him in the temple where he remained for six years.

Athaliah was hostile, then, not only to the house of David but also to the priestly circles, which remained faithful to it. At the end of six years, and after having come to an agreement with the king's personal bodyguard, the priests had Joash publicly acknowledged. Athaliah was slain.

Jehoiada the priest solemnly renewed the covenant between God and the king and between the king and his people. The monarchy was once again characterized by fidelity to Yahweh and service to the people. Jehoiada doubtless acted as regent and took advantage of his position to get rid of the altar of Baal from Jerusalem.

Joash, who had been educated by the priests, wanted to restore the temple of Solomon. He entrusted the task to the priests but discovered that they were keeping the money for themselves. From that time on he himself took charge of the temple finances. The treasury grew but, like Rehoboam and Asa before him, Joash used it in order to avoid an invasion of Judah by Damascus, this time by Hazael.

Hazael had become a formidable power, for he had conquered the Transjordan to the east and had taken control in the west of the route from Egypt to Gath (2 Kgs 12:18).

Joash's life ended in assassination. Like his ancestor David, he reigned for forty years. The figure is doubtful, for it reflects the theology of Deuteronomy: Since Joash was a good king, i.e., was faithful to Yahweh, his reign was complete and therefore forty years in length. But according to the Second Book of Chronicles he had turned away from God and had gone so far as to have the sons of Jehoiada murdered. This is why the very ones who had put him on the throne also assassinated him.

Kings Jehoahaz and Joash of Israel, King Amaziah of Judah: 2 Kgs 13–14

The successors of Jehu once again found themselves having to face Damascus. Ben-hadad III imposed a heavy tribute on Israel, but the Bible says rather mysteriously that the Lord gave Israel a savior (2 Kgs 13:5).

Are we to understand this savior as being the new ruler of Assyria, Adadnirari III (811–791 B.C.)? The latter undertook a campaign in 803–802 B.C. during which he levied tribute on Tyre, Sidon and Aram but also on Joash of Samaria.

According to the Second Book of Kings, Amaziah, king of Judah, successor of Jehoash of Judah, was bent on waging war against Joash of Israel. Having conquered Edom, Amaziah believed he could take on a very weakened kingdom of Israel. It was unfortunate for him that he did, for he was conquered and Joash penetrated the country as far as Jerusalem, breached its wall and took possession of the temple treasures. Amaziah continued to reign until he was assassinated at Lachish in about 781; in all likelihood Joash of Israel could not have consolidated his victory over Judah unless he had annexed the country (2 Chr 25).

Jeroboam II of Israel and the Prophet Amos (781–743 B.C.): 2 Kgs 14:23–29

Jeroboam II reigned from 783 to 747 and benefited from a lengthy breathing space in relation to Assyria, which now had to face Urartu, a new kingdom located in Armenia. Jeroboam was able to restore the ancient frontiers of Israel "from the entrance of Hamath as far as the Sea of the Arabah" (2 Kgs 14:25). This means he reconquered the whole Transjordan from south of Damascus to the Dead Sea. By so doing he fulfilled the prophecy of a certain Jonah.

But Jeroboam II was also a great builder; it was he who gave Samaria its final fortifications and who above all made it a place of luxury. Most of the ebony and ivory adornment comes from his time. Alongside scenes depicting foliage and animals, scenes resembling those in Assyrian art have also been discovered, as well as representations of the Egyptian gods Horus, Isis and Ra. Especially notable is a sphinx with a human head; this figure might have closely resembled the cherubim in the temple at Jerusalem.

There are also more intricately carved ivories with inlays of lapis lazuli or of glass paste, and occasional ivories covered with thin gold plate. These

Seal of Shema, an official of Jeroboam II of Israel, found in the ruins of Megiddo.

ivories doubtless adorned some luxurious piece of furniture, perhaps the ivory beds of which Amos 6:4 speaks.

All this luxury was supported by a flourishing trade. The majority of the ostraka—lists of prices on potsherds—date from the reign of Jeroboam III.[3] They suggest that the court had monopolized the trade in famous wines and precious oils. In addition, the ostraka supply lists of names which clearly show the intermingling of worshipers of Baal and worshipers of Yahweh.

Amos, who was a prophet from Tekoa, a little village in Judah, and who owned flocks, stepped forward right in the sanctuary at Bethel and uttered this condemnation:

> Woe to those who lie upon beds of ivory,
>   and stretch themselves upon their couches,
> And eat lambs from the flock,
>   and calves from the midst of the stall;
> Who sing idle songs to the sound of the harp,
>   and like David invent for themselves instruments of music;
> Who drink wine in bowls,
>   and anoint themselves with the finest oils,
>   but are not grieved over the ruin of Joseph!
> Therefore they shall now be the first of those to go into exile,
>   and the revelry of those who stretch themselves shall pass away
>   (Am 6:4–7).

Amos[4] was scandalized by this luxury but even more by the injustice that was practiced everywhere (5:10–12). What justice did they show to the poor? "We . . . buy . . . the needy for a pair of sandals" (8:4–7). With all his energy he attacked the veneer of polish on Israelite life and denounced the false security it gave. There was no salvation except in Yahweh and in the observance of his law. Could not Israel see that the breathing space had now passed and that Assyria was coming to slaughter and deport?

With the death of Jeroboam II a new period of troubles began. His son Zechariah was overthrown by Shallum after only a year on the throne. Shallum was overthrown in turn after a month by Menahem of Tirzah, the last strongman of Israel.

Judah	Israel	Mesopotamia	Neighbors
Hezekiah ?–687	Hoshea 732–724	Shalmaneser V 727–722 Sargon II 722–705	732: Damascus falls; Israel pillaged
Prophet Isaiah I	Fall of Samaria 721		722–721: fall of Samaria 720: first con-frontation of
		Troubles in Assy-ria Sennacherib 705–681	Egypt & Assyria at Gaza Hezekiah allies himself with Egypt & Babylon Capture of Baby-lon, Tyre and Si-don 701: Siege of Jerusalem
Manasseh 687–642		Esarhaddon 681–669	Campaign vs Syria & Phoeni-cia
Prophet Nahum Amon 642–640 Josiah 640–609		Ashurbanipal 669–630 Weakness of Assyria	Babylon rebuilt 660: Assyria loses control of Egypt 626: Nebupolas-sar, king of Bab-ylon
		614: Assyria con-quered by the Medes	
Jehoahaz, a pris-oner in Egypt		612: Nineveh taken and de-stroyed	Intervention of Egypt on the side of Assyria
Jehoiakim 609–598	Josiah slain at Megiddo, 609		
Prophet Jere-miah		605: battle of Carchemish Nebuchadnezzar of Chaldea, 605–562	601: Babylonian troops stopped short of Egypt
Jehoiachin de-ported to Baby-lon			598: Siege of Jerusalem
Zedekiah 597–587			587: Destruction of Jerusalem

Chapter 8
Assyrian Domination
and the End of Israel

Tiglath-pileser III[1] (745–727 B.C.)

It was just at the time when Menahem came to the throne that Assyria became powerful once again under the leadership of Tiglath-pileser III, who won a decisive victory over Urartu. He annexed the southern part of Armenia and deported its populace.

Tiglath-pileser was bent on leaving no political autonomy to the countries he conquered. He meant to occupy them and fully incorporate them into his realm. Initially, a conquered state was allowed self-government, but Tiglath-pileser had to be given annual expressions of submission. The least attempt at rebellion was met with military intervention; all trained personnel were deported, the king was replaced, and a part of the territory was attached to the crown or assigned to faithful vassals.

If these measures still proved inadequate, the state in question simply disappeared and became an Assyrian province under the government of palace officials. All leaders were exiled, while new peoples were brought in from elsewhere; it was hoped in this way to keep all conquered states under control.

Judah under Uzziah and Jotham: 2 Kgs 15, 2 Chr 26–27

I must point out right at the beginning that the entire chronology of the reigns of Uzziah, Jotham, Ahaz, and Hezekiah is still very difficult to establish.

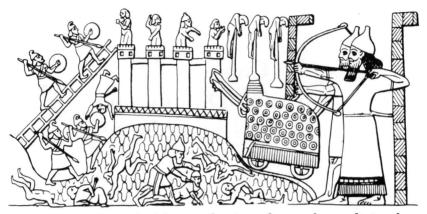

An Assyrian palace relief showing the siege of a vassal town during the
time of Tiglath-pileser III. Note the use of the battering ram, siege
ladders, impaling of prisoners, and removal of the heads from dead
enemy soldiers.

Uzziah succeeded his father Amaziah of Judah in 781 B.C. He was a
contemporary of Jeroboam of Israel and like him enjoyed a time of peace.
He was able to rebuild the walls of Jerusalem and once again extend the
frontiers of his kingdom by regaining from the Edomites control of Elath
(the name of which prior to this reign had been Ezion-geber). He also
gained the upper hand over the Philistines and destroyed Ashdod and
Gath (map, p. 98).

Uzziah was interested in agriculture and stockbreeding. Cisterns
were dug, thus making new lands available for cultivation. He supposedly
introduced improvements into oil presses, thus making possible a more
extensive trade in this commodity with Egypt and Phoenicia. As a skilled
technician he is also made responsible for innovations in the art of war (1
Chr 26).

Archaeologists have uncovered Ramath-rachel,[2] a small fortified village south of Jerusalem that owed much to Uzziah. The high standard of
workmanship on the interior of the walls recalls the palace of Ahab at Samaria. We may still admire the superb gateway adorned with capitals that
are doubtless of Phoenician origin. Noteworthy among the finds made
there is a sizable number of seals stamped for the king, whose name is
followed by that of a town. Trade flourished. This little fortress near Jerusalem was perhaps the residence of this leprous king.

Because of his father's illness Jotham became co-ruler at a very early stage. According to 2 Chronicles he followed the policies of his father and conquered the Ammonites. Most notable among his building efforts is the upper gate of the house of the Lord and perhaps the gate of Benjamin on the north side of Jerusalem. The summary given of this reign is extraordinary: "Their land is filled with silver and gold, and there is no end to their treasures; their land is filled with horses, and there is no end to their chariots" (Is 2:7). At the same time, however, it was perhaps under Jotham that the Syro-Ephraimite War began.

Isaiah[3]

The prophet Isaiah of chapters 1–39 was a man of Judah. He lived in Jerusalem and was doubtless an aristocrat. He shared in all the decisions regarding the realm and spoke with authority to high officials and kings. He lived through four reigns, those of Uzziah, Jotham, Ahaz and Hezekiah. He proclaimed the word of God during a forty-year period that saw the rise of Assyria, the destruction of Samaria and the siege of Jerusalem.

His preaching resembles that of Amos. He attacks hypocrisy, immorality, love of finery, luxury on the part of women, idolatrous cults, the anarchy that reigns in the city, and a people who have turned away from God.

On the positive side, he proclaims the wisdom and plan of God. If Judah is unwilling to follow its God, if Judah prefers the wisdom of its king, its scribes or foreigners, then like Samaria Judah is on the road to destruction and punishment. It is urgent that Judah listen to what its God is saying through the mouth of his prophet. Not only Judah but all the nations are obliged to listen to God because he is the universal sovereign. He has a plan for Judah but also for Assyria and Egypt. If the nations refuse to listen to him, they too will fall under his condemnation. Isaiah accuses and warns, but he still thinks that peace and reconciliation are possible. He foresees a day when all nations will come together to pray to God, the God who exercises justice on Zion.

Isaiah thus makes his own the prophecy of Nathan. He states that God cannot turn away from the house of David. Is not the birth of the child "Emmanuel" a sign of this gracious fidelity of God? Whatever happens, says Isaiah, there will always be a remnant, a stump that can bud again. This preaching of Isaiah, which historically was meant to support a tottering monarchy and a despairing people, was to have a decisive influence on the Jewish hope of a Messiah from the stock of David.

The Last Years of Israel (743–722 B.C.):
2 Kings 15:17–17:41

When Menahem took power in Israel, he had to deal immediately with a campaign by Tiglath-pileser who was invading the kingdoms of Tyre, Damascus and Israel. After this campaign of 738 B.C. the three kings had to pay a heavy tribute and give proof of their allegiance. Because Tiglath-pileser had problems in the north, he did not advance as far south as the kingdom of Judah.

At the death of Menahem (Uzziah was still king of Judah) his son Pekahiah succeeded him for two years. He was overthrown by his equerry Pekah, who had the support of the Gileadites.

Pekah in his turn had to deal with a new campaign of Tiglath-pileser III. Having brought the Hittite kingdom of Zinjirli in the Taurus Mountains to its senses, Tiglath-pileser this time advanced as far as Gaza, whose king took refuge in Egypt (734 B.C.).

It was during these years that a new prophet, Hosea,[4] arose in the northern kingdom. He saw the invasion of Israel and Judah as a divine judgment on their infidelity. He denounced the forcible usurpation of power in Israel, but he also doubtless denounced Judah for taking advantage of the Assyrian invasions to push its frontier further north (5:10).

The entire burden of Hosea's message is a criticism of the authorities of Israel primarily but of Judah as well, for attempting all sorts of political and religious alliances while deserting the one true God. Better than anyone else, Hosea gives expression to God's suffering; but he also brings home the love, the ever renewed love, of God. Despite the catastrophe now looming, a time will come when God will say to Israel: "You are my people," and when Israel will answer: "You are my God." Then God will "abolish the bow, the sword, and war from the land," and will betroth his people to himself in faithfulness (Hos 2).

Ahaz reigned in Judah as the contemporary of King Pekah of Israel. He was doubtless urged by Pekah and the king of Damascus to form a new coalition against Tiglath-pileser. But Ahaz had seen Assyrian might advancing on Gaza, and he therefore refused such an alliance. Aram and Israel in the north and Edom in the south joined forces; they would conquer Judah, set up a friendly dynasty there (Is 7:6), and present a united front to the north. Ahaz quickly found himself in a very bad position and began looking around for help. At this point Isaiah intervened, advising against any alliance and reminding the king of God's word: Yahweh would be faithful to the house of David. The evidence for this fidelity? The invaders would see their own kingdoms laid waste before such time as the child

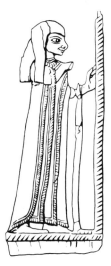

A noble woman from the town of Megiddo.

born of the young woman (most likely the queen) would reach the age when he could reject evil and choose good. The child whom Isaiah calls "Emmanuel" was perhaps young Hezekiah.

The prophet's words did not persuade Ahaz, who countered with arguments from diplomacy: he would make an alliance with Tiglath-pileser against Damascus and Israel. It was a good alliance, but also one dangerous for the future, an alliance that entailed the erection at Jerusalem of an altar to the gods of Damascus (2 Chr 28:23). Was it for the same reason, namely acknowledgment of the gods of Assyria, that the king burned his own sons as an offering?

Tiglath-pileser intervened immediately (723 B.C.). According to Assyrian tablets he received the submission of Ahaz and quickly took control of the Phoenician and Philistine coasts, thus preventing any intervention by Egypt. He then laid siege to Damascus, which held out for three years, and captured Samaria.

Following the usual pattern, Tiglath-pileser took Galilee and Gilead from the kingdom of Israel, turning them into Assyrian provinces. Samaria was now but a tiny state comprising only the highlands of Ephraim and bounded on the east by the province of Dor, on the north by the province of Megiddo, on the east by the province of Gilead and on the south by the kingdom of Judah.

After this terrible defeat, Pekah was assassinated by Hoshea who mounted the throne of Samaria. He immediately paid tribute to Assyria in

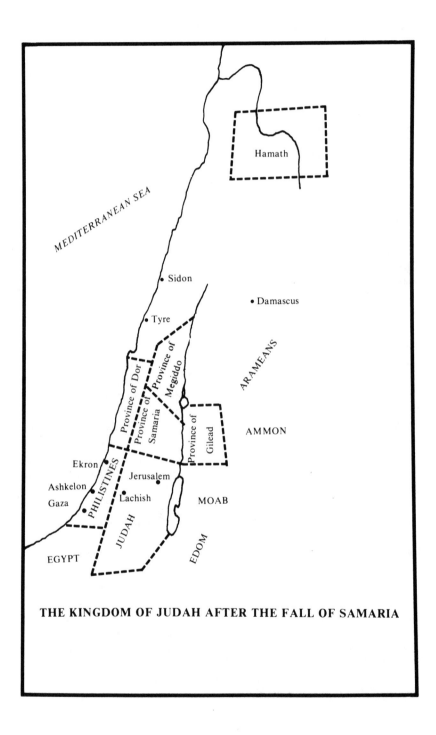

THE KINGDOM OF JUDAH AFTER THE FALL OF SAMARIA

order to win confirmation as king of Israel, a kingdom reduced by both loss of territory and the massive deportation of its elites.

At the death of Tiglath-pileser Assyria experienced its usual succession crisis. Hoshea sought an alliance with Egypt and failed to pay the tribute.

Once Shalmaneser V had consolidated his power in Mesopotamia, he launched a campaign during which he captured Hoshea in unknown circumstances. Then his brother Sargon II took Samaria and razed it (722 B.C.). The fall of Samaria left behind it the memory of scenes of atrocious slaughter, rape, and impaled soldiers; the cruelty of the Assyrians was engraved on the memories of all. The state of Israel was no more, and the region of Samaria became another Assyrian province. The aristocracy and governing classes were deported to Media in upper Mesopotamia (2 Kgs 17:6). Sargon II claimed to have deported 27,290 inhabitants, whose subsequent history we cannot follow here. In return the inhabitants of other conquered cities, such as Hamath on the Orontes, were deported to become the population of Samaria. These new inhabitants would mingle their customs and gods with those of Samaria.

Though Israel disappeared from the map, a Jewish population remained in Samaria and kept close contacts with the temple in Jerusalem; undoubtedly, too, there were also Jews who fled to Judah, bringing with them their traditions and, in particular, the thought of the northern prophets.

Micah[5]

For a short period before the fall of Samaria and then during the years that followed it a new prophet arose in Judah; his name was Micah. He was not, like Isaiah, a man of the city but a countryman. He suffered deeply at the horrors of war and the social injustices his people had to endure. Because (he said) the same wrongs were done in Jerusalem as in Samaria, because there too the lowly were dispossessed (2:1–5), Jerusalem would suffer the same fate as the northern kingdom (1:7–9).

His preaching thus resembled that of Hosea, Amos and Isaiah in its harshness. But like Isaiah he hoped for a scion of David who would be born in Bethlehem. His prophecy would be rediscovered one day by Herod's priests as they searched to find where the Messiah would be born (5:1–5).

Finally, Micah hoped for an age of peace in which all the nations would come and pray to God in Jerusalem where they would all acknowledge his justice.

Annals of Sennacherib

"As for Hezekiah of Judah, he did not bow beneath my yoke. I besieged 46 of his fortified towns, fortresses and countless small towns roundabout; I captured them by erecting embankments and bringing up towers, and by means of shock troops, breaches made in the walls, mines under the ramparts, and battering-rams. I carried out of these towns 200,150 people—young and old, men and women—, horses, mules, asses, camels, large and small livestock beyond numbering. Hezekiah himself I shut up in Jerusalem, his residence, like a bird in a cage. I surrounded him with embankments in order to wreak vengeance on anyone bold enough to venture from the city gate. The towns which I pillaged I took from his country and gave to Mitinti, king of Ashdod, Padi, king of Ekron, and Sillibel, king of Gaza, and in this way I made his country smaller. To the long-standing tribute which he had to give each year I added a further tribute and the alliance gifts due to my empire.

"Hezekiah himself was so terrified by the splendor of my power that he sent to me at Nineveh, the city of my empire, the Urbi (?) and their first-rate troops, which he had brought in to support Jerusalem, his capital, and which he had received as reinforcements. He sent these along with 30 talents of gold, 800 talents of silver, precious stones, rouge, great blocks of red stone, couches inlaid with ivory, pelts, elephants' teeth, wood from maple and yew, all kinds of valuable treasures, and in addition his daughters, his court ladies, and male and female singers. To pay the tribute and protest his submission he sent his ambassador."

Judah in the Reign of Hezekiah[6]: 2 Kgs 18ff., 2 Chr 29–32

Thanks to the alliance of Ahaz with Assyria, Jerusalem had been spared. But at home this policy was far from meeting with unanimous agreement; was this why Hezekiah became co-ruler in 729 B.C.?

Initially the kings of Judah paid tribute first to Shalmaneser V, then to Sargon II, who succeeded him in 722 B.C. and finally devastated Samaria. In 720 B.C. a new coalition was formed against Assyria under the leadership of the kingdom of Hamath and with Aramaeans, Philistines, Egyptians and even Samaritans as members. Once again Judah refused to participate. Fortunately so, for Sargon destroyed Hamath once and for all and made it an Assyrian province; he also descended as far as Gaza and repulsed the Egyptians.

Hezekiah had no trouble understanding what Isaiah was saying: Judah was a remnant miraculously saved by the hand of God. He believed, with Micah, that the time had come to rid Jerusalem of injustice and its venal priests and prophets. Therefore he undertook to unite all the people around the royal house and the Jerusalem temple.

He doubtless looked even further ahead and hoped that with the help of fidelity to Yahweh and an intransigent nationalism he could effect a rapprochement with the Israelites of the north. He knew that they had nowhere to look but to Jerusalem; it was therefore necessary to prepare for unification and look for the right opportunity.

It is very difficult for us to determine what the substance of Hezekiah's reform was. The Second Book of Kings only mentions the fact of the reform, while the Second Book of Chronicles seems simply to embellish the silence. The reform seems to have developed its own theology along the lines of the unity of Israel and Judah and of respect for the feasts in the Priestly code.

Scholars agree, however, that it was in the reign of Hezekiah that the Yahwist tradition of Judah and the Elohist tradition of the north were brought together. Doubtless too it was on the occasion of his reform that the Deuteronomist document first took shape.

Hezekiah was a fine administrator. In particular, he managed to centralize the payment of tithes, which were in kind. As a result he was able to build royal storehouses, develop a profitable trade, and also prepare for time of war.

Initially indeed Hezekiah resisted being drawn into coalitions against Assyria, and instead profited from his position as an ally of Assyria to attack the Philistine principalities. He is said even to have turned one of their royal cities into a fortified city of his own realm. Since Assyrian annals show that the king of Ekron was handed over to Hezekiah, the city in question may be Ekron.

The fortified city of Lachish in the time of Sennacherib's invasion of 701 B.C.

In 713 B.C., however, the situation must have changed, and a new coalition was formed against Assyria. The central figure in the coalition was the ruler of Ashdod who managed to bring together Edom, Moab and Judah. The ruler of Ashdod went to the help of the Egyptian pharaoh, Shabaka.

Isaiah urged Hezekiah to renounce this alliance; he even walked around naked as a sign of what was to happen to Egypt and Nubia (Is 20). Hezekiah doubtless listened to him, for Sargon captured Ashdod and repulsed the Egyptians who tried to help, but did not intervene in Judah.

When Sargon II died in 705, Assyria experienced its usual period of upset at times of succession. There was a general uprising of the empire and it would take Sennacherib four years to settle it.

In this new situation Hezekiah himself now took the lead in an anti-Assyrian coalition. Circumstances seemed particularly favorable. Merodach-baladan, king of Babylon, had rebelled against Assyria and sent ambassadors to Hezekiah. Egypt was always ready to support any revolt against Assyria, and the king of Tyre and Sidon joined the others. The people of Ekron deposed their king who was loyal to Assyria and handed him over to Hezekiah who imprisoned him.

Hezekiah decided to fortify Jerusalem; he also succeeded in having a

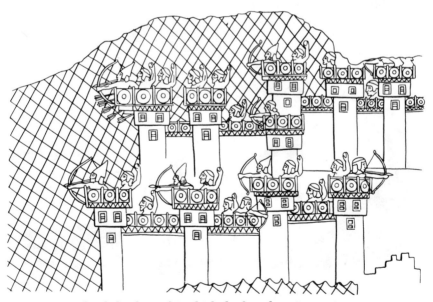

The defenders of Lachish deployed against a siege.

The conquest of Lachish. Israelite prisoners are led before King Sennacherib in his war camp.

tunnel dug which brought water from the spring of Gihon to the pool of Shiloah (2 Kgs 20:20). (An inscription of Hezekiah with details of this work was discovered in 1890.) Judah put out bunting but Isaiah thundered, for he saw only tears and lamentation in Judah's future.

Sennacherib met the members of the coalition one after another. Merodach-baladan and Babylonia were the first to submit. Then Lulli, king of Tyre and Sidon, was forced to flee to Cyprus. At this point, Ashdod and the rulers of the Transjordan immediately paid tribute in order to avoid destruction. Ashkelon and Ekron were captured and the troops of Pharaoh Shabaka were beaten back. Sennacherib was then free to begin the siege of Jerusalem (701 B.C.).

Sennacherib began by destroying a number of Judean cities, Lachish among them.[7] This episode is reported on thirteen stone slabs at Nineveh. Hezekiah then tried to turn Sennacherib away from Jerusalem by paying tribute, but it was too late. Jerusalem had to be punished. At this point Isaiah prophesied: Jerusalem must resist; it will not be captured; on the contrary, the hand of God will fall heavily on Assyria. And in fact, says the Bible, a scourge did strike the Assyrian army, which had to withdraw (2 Kgs 19:35; Is 17:14).

Herodotus explains this rout by an invasion of rats, that is, the plague,

---

Inscription in the tunnel of Siloam

This is the story of how the tunnel was cut through. The miners were wielding their pickaxes and moving toward each other, and when there were now only three cubits to cut through, the voice of one man calling could be heard by the other, for the rock running north-south carried the sound. On the day of the breakthrough, the miners hewed toward each other, and pickaxe struck against pickaxe. Then the water flowed from the spring to the reservoir over a 1200 cubit distance, and the rock over the heads of the miners was 100 cubits high.

---

which was the terror of the age. In addition, Sennacherib's return home became urgent, because there had been a new palace revolution.

According to the Assyrian annals, Hezekiah was imprisoned in his city and forced to pay tribute before seeing his kingdom then divided among the rulers of Ashdod, Ekron and Gaza. But this statement is contradicted by another passage in the annals which shows the kingdom of Judah paying tribute to Sennacherib. Judah was not completely despoiled, for the sudden departure of Sennacherib saved it. But henceforth Jerusalem was only a hut in the midst of a ruin. Hezekiah continued to reign until 687 B.C.; the reign begun so brilliantly had ended in disaster.

The Reign of Manasseh (687–642 B.C.):
2 Kgs 21:1–18, 2 Chr 33

According to the redactor of the Bible, the very long reign of Manasseh was marked by a return to idolatry. Whether from conviction or because he felt compelled, he reintroduced all the cults, including those of Assyria, and, like Ahaz before him, he burned his sons as an offering.

According to the Second Book of Chronicles Assyria once again invaded Judah, and Manasseh was deported to Babylon, whence however he was able to return and resume his reign. According to the author of 2 Chronicles Manasseh also returned to faith in Yahweh.

This deportation cannot have taken place during the reign of Sennacherib, who was fully occupied by rebellions of the Chaldeans, the Elamites and, once again, Babylon. In 689 B.C. Babylon was razed to the ground. But troubles did not cease, and Sennacherib was assassinated in 681 B.C.

His son Esarhaddon succeeded him (681–669 B.C.) and had to attempt a restoration of the empire. In order to placate the Babylonian party he decided to rebuild Babylon. Then he launched a campaign against a coalition headed by the Sidonians. The major campaign of his reign was against Egypt (673 B.C.); he reached Memphis but was repulsed by Pharaoh Tirhakah. Was it on his return from this campaign that he passed by Jerusalem and took Judean captives back home with him? Ezra speaks of the arrival of Jewish emigres under both Esarhaddon and his successor Ashurbanipal.

Ashurbanipal (669–630 B.C.) would be the last great king of Assyria. A learned and brilliant man, he established a library of at least five thousand volumes, some of which were recovered during the excavation of Nineveh. Like his predecessors he had to deal with numerous coalitions, in particular one led by his brother, the king of Babylon. Babylon was captured in 648 B.C., but then the Elamites rebelled in their turn. Susa was destroyed in 639 B.C.

Despite these constant rebellions, Ashurbanipal carried on the policy of conquering Egypt. He had various successes, recapturing Memphis and, in particular, capturing and destroying Thebes (the No-amon of the Bible) in 663 B.C. This was however the last feat of Assyrian military power. Psammetichus I definitively repulsed Assyria in 666–665 B.C.

From the reign of Esarhaddon comes this document of a high official who calls upon Assyrian vassals to take part in the bringing of building materials to Nineveh.

"Then I issued demands to the kings of the land of Hatti and the region beyond the river: Ba'lu, king of the city of Tyre; Manasseh, king of the city of Judah; Qaushgabri, king of the city of Edom; Musuri, king of the city of Moab; Sil-Bel, king of the city of Gaza; Metinti, king of the city of Ashkelon; Ikausu, king of the city of Byblos; Matanba'al, king of the city of Arvad; . . . Paduil, king of the city of Ammon; Ahimilki, king of the city of Ashdod; 12 kings from the shore of the sea . . . in all, 22 kings from the land of Hatti beside the sea and on the high sea.

"I gave them orders and had them transport with great difficulty—from the midst of the mountains whence they came, to Nineveh, my royal city—great logs, excellent pillars, and long beams of cedar and cypress, the products of Mount Sirara and Mount Lebanon, which in time had grown very thick and very tall. Also granite colossi, statues of guardian spirits and sphinxes, blocks of alabaster and granite . . . for the needs of my palace."

We have no information, therefore, about a deportation, but we do learn the details of a corvee involving Judah and all its neighbors, including the kings of Cyprus.

Despite undeniable successes the Assyrian empire was threatened on all sides. Babylon, the Scythians and the Medes revolted. When Ashurbanipal died around 630 B.C., the days of the empire were numbered.

Nahum

It is very difficult to date with precision a series of oracles known as the Book of Nahum; there are, however, some points of reference. To begin with, Nahum knows of the fate of Thebes in 663 B.C., for it is on the basis of the destruction of Thebes that he prophesies the destruction of Nineveh, which will occur in 612 B.C. His preaching is therefore located between these two dates.

Early in his prophecy Nahum says: "Though they be strong and many, they will be cut off and pass away" (1:12), and "Never again shall the wicked come against you" (1:15). The forces of Assyria seem to be still strong. Ashurbanipal has doubtless demanded that Judean troops accompany him to Egypt, and on his way home he may have taken new Judean prisoners with him to Nineveh. But Nahum assures Judah that Ashurbanipal will not come back to them again. Is this a prophetic analysis of the situation? Or is it the prophet's vision in 630 B.C. when he learns of the death of Ashurbanipal and the troubles of the empire? At the very time when Manasseh submits to Assyria, Nahum believes in a triumphant coming of Yahweh (1:1–8); the time is at hand for the authorities in Israel to reestablish justice, for Yahweh punishes injustice. The proof? He will destroy Nineveh.

Then Nahum composes a lengthy prophetic poem in which he sees that Nineveh, despite its wealth and despite its armies, will be destroyed. Nineveh will pay for its crimes and be beaten down by foreign armies. Once again: Is Nahum foretelling what will come, that is, does he have a vision of what the Babylonians, Medes and Scythians will do? Or is he singing of the destruction of Nineveh after news of its fall has come?

In any event it is time for Israel to turn back to Yahweh; it is time for a reform. Josiah is about to succeed the wicked Manasseh.

The Reign of Josiah (640–609 B.C.):[8] 2 Kgs 22–23, 2 Chr 34–35

On the death of Manasseh his son Amon succeeded him, but was quickly assassinated. Was this an act instigated by religious and nationalist circles that wanted a return to faith in Yahweh alone and the shrugging off of the Assyrian yoke?

The text is too terse to allow any conclusions to be drawn. One constant, however, is clear: No one in Judah challenged the dynastic principle. Josiah, son of Amon, took the throne for thirty-one years. According to the Second Book of Kings he was a good ruler, that is, he too effected a religious reform that was rendered possible by the weakness of Assyria.

When Josiah became king he was only a child, and power was in the hands of members of the royal family and of ministers. This was doubtless the period when the prophet Zephaniah exercised his ministry (1:8–9). Zephaniah, like his predecessors, attacked the cult of Baal and the cult of the stars.

In a hostile response to the pride and greed of the governing classes, their skepticism and preference for foreign customs (1:8–13), Zephaniah proclaims the day of Yahweh. On that day Yahweh will impose his law; he will make of the lowly his people and purify them; then he will rejoice and Jerusalem with him; all oppressors will be removed, the lowly will be exalted, and the glory of God will be proclaimed (3:16–20).

Josiah undertook the reform so desired by the prophets. He got rid of the high places, the idols, the Baals, the sacred poles, all the cults of the stars and the fertility deities, all that came from abroad and especially from Assyria. But Josiah went further: he decreed that there should be but a single place of cult, and this was to be in Jerusalem; all the other Israelite sanctuaries, no matter how old, were given over to secular uses, as can be seen from the floor plan of the temple at Arad. All the priests at the Israelite sanctuaries had to come to Jerusalem, where they served as a lower clergy.

Profiting by the weakness of Assyria, Josiah extended the reform to the Assyrian province of Samaria. In particular, he destroyed the place of

---

Deuteronomy 17:16–20

"Only he must not multiply horses for himself, or cause the people to return to Egypt in order to multiply horses, since the Lord has said to you, 'You shall never return that way again.' And he himself shall not multiply wives for himself, lest his heart turn away; nor shall he greatly multiply for himself silver and gold.

"And when he sits on the throne of his kingdom, he shall write for himself in a book a copy of this law, from that which is in charge of the Levitical priests, and it shall be with him, and he shall read in it all the days of his life, that he may learn to fear the Lord his God, by keeping all the words of this law and these statutes, and doing them; that his heart may not be lifted up above his brethren, and that he may not turn aside from the commandment, either to the right hand or the left; so that he may continue long in his kingdom, he and his children, in Israel."

worship at Bethel, which went back to Abraham but to which Jeroboam had given new status as the center of cult for Israel in opposition to Jerusalem.

In 622, Josiah urged the entire populace to celebrate a solemn Passover at Jerusalem. This feast was thus changed from a familial or local feast to a national one. Reenacting the role of Joshua at Shechem, Josiah bade the assembled people enter into a covenant with the Lord.

This entire reform was based on a book discovered in the temple of Jerusalem on the occasion of some renovations. There is agreement among scholars that this book is, if not our present Deuteronomy, at least an earlier version of it which contained the Deuteronomic code and a much shorter introduction and conclusion. Deuteronomy claims, of course, to go back to Moses himself, who is depicted as proclaiming the law of God to all the people and celebrating the covenant. But how could all these laws, including laws concerning the king (Dt 17), go back to Moses?

Scholars are still trying to determine the place where this book took shape. It is clear that in the time of Josiah the book was propagated by the priestly circles of Jerusalem who found in it the order to centralize the cult at Jerusalem. But before being made known under Josiah, the book was doubtless the book that embodied the resistance of the devout during the shameful reigns of Manasseh and Amon.

At the same time, however, the book cannot have originated solely in Jerusalem. Deuteronomy 17, in particular, could not have originated in Judah, for it mentions none of the royal traditions connected with the house of David, and there is no messianic expectation. According to Deuteronomy the king is to be chosen by Yahweh and not appointed by an invader; this rule is in keeping with the tradition of Israel. Above all, the king must, just like Josiah, "write for himself in a book a copy of this law, from that which is in charge of the levitical priests" (Dt 17:18).

This link with the northern kingdom is underscored by the place that Mounts Gerizim and Ebal, that is, Shechem, have in the book (11:24–32; 27:1–11). If the book had been written in Judah it would have focused all attention on Jerusalem.

The idea of centralizing public worship is to be sought in the prophets of the north (Am 4:4–5; Hos 4:13–15), and it was doubtless the Levites in flight from the north who brought their ideas to Judah where they survived until they were applied under Josiah.

The role of the Levites is emphasized in Deuteronomy 18. There is confusion there between the word "priest" and the word "levite"; all the members of the tribe of Levi are regarded as equal and are to share equally in the revenues of the sanctuary. This vision was utterly utopian. There was no room at the Jerusalem temple for all the levites from the provincial sanctuaries, and the priesthood descended from Zadok could not allow them the position they desired. As a result of the Josian reform the levites were no longer priests but servants of the temple; as such, they replaced foreign slaves.

605–562 Nebuchadnezzar	600–559 Cambyses I	587 Destruction of Jerusalem
556–539 Nabonidus	559–530 Cyrus II	
549 Victory of Cyrus over the Medes		Second Isaiah
546 Victory over Croesus of Lydia		
545–540 Capture of Turkestan, Afghanistan		Cyrus' edict of tolerance
539 Fall of Babylon		538 Return from Babylon
	530–522 Cambyses II	Sheshbazzar governor
		Zerubbabel governor
525 Capture of Memphis		Haggai, Zechariah prophets
		Jeshua high priest
	522 Gaumata	Rebuilding of temple
Uprisings of Babylon, Susa, Medes, Parthians, Armenians	522–486 Darius I Building of Persepolis	515 Consecration of temple
Egyptian campaign		
Annexation of Thrace		
Ionian revolt		
490 Defeat at Marathon		
Rebellion of Babylon	486–465 Xerxes	
480 Defeat at Salamis		Malachi?
Liberation of the Greek isles		
Egyptian uprisings	465–424 Artaxerxes	Nehemiah restores Jerusalem
		Governor of Judea
		Conflict with Samaria; Kedar, Ashdod
412 Destruction of temple at Elephantine	422–404 Darius II	
	404–358 Artaxerxes II	Ezra
405 Loss of Egypt		Return to Jerusalem
Egyptian attempt to conquer Palestine 370–360		Establishment of text of Pentateuch
		Ruth, Jonah, Job, Song, Ecclesiastes, Psalms, Proverbs
	359–338 Artaxerxes III	
344 Destruction of Sidon		

Chapter 9
Babylonian Domination
and the End of Judah

In applying the law discovered by the priests of Jerusalem Josiah's intention was not only to unify Judah internally but also, if possible, to unite Israel with Judah once again. This explains why the customs of the north were taken into consideration as well as those of Judah. The same intention also found expression geographically, as Josiah little by little regained control of the ancient kingdom of David. To the south he extended his rule as far as Beersheba; to the west he took control of the land of the Philistines, witness the rediscovered fortress of Yahvne Yam between Jaffa and Ashdod; and to the north he was able to extend his territory to the plain of Jezreel. Among the works of Josiah mention must be made of the oasis of En-gedi,[1] which was to become, in his reign and until 582 B.C., the city of perfumes. En-gedi would subsequently be sung in the Song of Songs and by Flavius Josephus.

Josiah took advantage of the fall of the Assyrian kingdom. In 626 B.C. Nebupolassar, the new king of Babylon, inaugurated a new dynasty; he shook off the Assyrian yoke and expanded his kingdom to the north and the west. In the east the Medes had likewise risen and joined Babylon in fighting against the terrible domination of the Assyrians. In 614 B.C. they captured the holy city of Asshur.

The Assyrians did not think themselves vanquished as yet and they signed an alliance with the Egyptians. The latter did not want the whole of Mesopotamia to pass into the control of a new empire; in addition they coveted Syria-Palestine. Despite this alliance, Nineveh was destroyed in 612 B.C.

All the subject peoples were exultant: "O Judah, never again shall the wicked come against you. . . . O king of Assyria, there is no assuaging your hurt, your wound is grievous. All who hear the news of you clap their hands over you. For upon whom has not come your unceasing evil?" (Na 1:15; 3:19). For to destruction and deportation Assyria had added all kinds of cruelties: prisoners scalped and mutilated, eyes plucked out, men impaled by the thousands. Assyrian sculpture gloated over massacres and the humiliation of conquered rulers who had to pull the imperial chariot by rings through their noses, before then losing their feet, hands, ears, eyes and tongue, all of these being the tortures that preceded death.

After Asshur had fallen and Nineveh had been destroyed, the Assyrians regrouped at Haran. Pharaoh Neco went up to help them and on his way met Josiah, who died at Megiddo. We do not know what policy Josiah was trying to follow at the time. According to the usual rule, his son Jehoahaz succeeded him (609 B.C.).

Neco and the Assyrian army were defeated at Haran. Neco therefore retreated toward Egypt, but on the way asserted his sovereignty by deposing Jehoahaz whom he led into captivity. He appointed instead Jehoiakim who for a very short time would be a vassal of Egypt.

Jeremiah

We do not know when precisely Jeremiah began his ministry: was he already active under Josiah? In any case, his oracles cover the period from the Josian reform to the complete destruction of Jerusalem; his oracles were even sent to Babylon and Egypt where Jews were in exile.

Jeremiah belonged to the priestly family of Anathoth near Jerusalem; this did not, however, keep him from taking up the cudgels for the Josian reform (Jer 1). Is this why he was to experience opposition from the people of Anathoth, a levitical town that had lost its priesthood? The whole life of Jeremiah was permeated with opposition; he is doubtless the prophet who experienced the greatest loneliness; a man possessed by God, he felt forced into a mission that cut him off from his fellow citizens and brought him suffering (17:18–23).

Jeremiah witnessed the return of Israel to foreign cults; this was no longer the age of Josiah but the age of his successors who had to prove their allegiance to Egypt. The suffering of Jeremiah was matched by the suffering of God. God, Jeremiah says, weeps over a people who have turned away from him, his very own people who are on their way to destruction.

For an army will descend from the north and destroy Judah. For reasons unknown to us, Herodotus saw in this people (see Jer 4–6) the Scythians, but it seems much more likely that the people in question were already the Neobabylonians.

Jeremiah took the threat a step further: Just as Shiloh was destroyed of old, so the temple in Jerusalem will be destroyed (Jer 7). The same episode is also known to us from Jeremiah 26, where the priests and the other prophets call for Jeremiah's death. But some elders of Judah save his life by reminding them that a century earlier the prophet Micah had used the same language: "Therefore because of you Zion shall be plowed as a field; Jerusalem shall become a heap of ruins, and the mountain of the house a wooded height" (Mi 3:12). Jeremiah is therefore able to continue preaching; he uses the image of a potter's vessel, and this time he is punished with the bastinado. Jeremiah does not stand out as "the prophet" in an unchallengeable way; he is only one of the prophets in Judah (Jer 28; 29:21), and others also speak in the name of the Lord, but their message is radically opposed to his.

Though Jeremiah cannot prove that he ought to be regarded as sole prophet of the Lord, there is no denying that he is the first prophet to use writing (Jer 36). He has Baruch write down all his prophecies and asks him to take them to the temple and read them to the assembled people. Jeremiah thus makes his own book a foundation, just as Josiah had urged a covenant with God on the basis of Deuteronomy. The people are moved, but the king cuts the scroll in pieces and has it burned. Jeremiah and Baruch must flee to their hiding place; they write down all the prophecies once again and add others (in particular, concerning the end of Jehoiakim and the Babylonian invasion).

Jehoiakim: (609–598 B.C.)

Initially, Jehoiakim seemed justified in trusting in Egypt, for Egypt was victorious over Babylon at Carchemish (607 B.C.). But Nabupolassar died in 605 B.C. and was succeeded by Nebuchadnezzar; in that same year the latter defeated the last Assyrian and Egyptian troops at Carchemish. He then pursued the Egyptians and as he went he took control of Syria and Palestine. Jehoiakim paid tribute to Babylon, to those henceforth known as the Chaldeans.

This is doubtless the period being described by the prophet Habakkuk: "Look among the nations, and see; wonder and be astounded. For I am doing a work in your days that you would not believe if told. For lo, I am rousing the Chaldeans, that bitter and hasty nation. . . . Their justice

and dignity proceed from themselves. Their horses are swifter than leop-
ards . . . their horsemen press proudly on. Yea, their horsemen come from
afar; they fly like an eagle swift to devour. They all come for violence; terror of them goes before them. They gather captives like sand. At kings they
scoff, and of rulers they make sport. They laugh at every fortress, for they
heap up earth and take it. Then they sweep by like the wind and go on,
guilty men, whose own might is their god'" (Hab 1:5–10).

Habakkuk seems to have been mistaken. Nebuchadnezzar was unable
to conquer Egypt, being brought to a halt in 601 B.C. Despite the warnings of the prophet Jehoiakim thought the time had come to rebel. Nebuchadnezzar first sent against him troops from Moab, Edom and Ammon
(2 Kgs 24:2); then he came himself and laid siege (598 B.C.).[2] Jehoiakim
died during the siege, or (according to 2 Chronicles 36) he was deported
to Babylon.

Jehoiachin succeeded to the throne, but only for three months. He
was obliged to leave Jerusalem and surrender. Together with part of the
royal family, the wealthy class, the craftsmen and the soldiers, he was deported to Babylon. According to 2 Kings 25:27–30 he won the favor of the
king of Babylon and lived a comfortable exile in which he ate at the king's
table. He was not the only one to enjoy this privilege, as we see from the
story of the young nobles who became pages at the royal court (Dan 1).

Back in Jerusalem Nebuchadnezzar placed Zedekiah, an uncle of the
former king, on the throne. Like his predecessors, Zedekiah was unable
to heed the prophecies of Jeremiah (Jer 37:2). After having submitted to
Babylon he thought that he in his turn could trust an alliance with Egypt
(Ez 17:14). Again like his predecessors, he tried to win support at home

A fine example of Israelite ivory work: A stag drinking.

by a social reform. Jeremiah tells us how the king ordered the liberation of all slaves and how this new law was quickly circumvented (Jer 34).

Nebuchadnezzar immediately sent an army to besiege Jerusalem. King Zedekiah seemed, however, to have been justified in his actions when the Babylonians had to lift the siege in order to face the Egyptians. But Jeremiah predicted that the Egyptians would go back to their bases and the Babylonians would return. He bade the people surrender (Jer 37). Accused of deserting to the Chaldean side, he was imprisoned in a cistern and owed his rescue to a Cushite servant. In fact the Egyptian army was repulsed. Soon the only fortified places left were Lachish and Azekah (Jer 34:7).

Archeologists excavating at Lachish have found an ostrakon (a potsherd) on which an officer wrote that he could no longer see even the signals from Azekah. On another potsherd we read of those people who weaken the hands of the country and the city: this was the accusation against Jeremiah (38:4).

Once Azekah had fallen it was Lachish's turn; Jerusalem was starved and had to surrender. Zedekiah tried to flee in the night to Ammon (Jer 39:4; 52) but he was captured near Jericho and led to Nebuchadnezzar's headquarters near Hamath. There his own sons and the entire aristocracy of Judah were slaughtered before his eyes; then his eyes were put out and he was made a prisoner in Babylon for the rest of his days.

The walls of Jerusalem were razed, as were the palaces, the homes of the middle class, and even the temple (after it had been looted). It is these ruins that are commemorated in the Book of Lamentations, which tells of Jerusalem's mourning and confesses the sins of the people. The news reached even the exiles in Babylon, who composed Psalm 137, which is at once a lament, a cry of hatred against Edom which profited by the disaster, and an expression of the longing that Babylon in its turn should be destroyed. A direct echo of the response of the Jews in exile comes from the prophet Ezekiel (33:21) who on hearing the news condemned the people and shepherds of Israel for the crimes that had thus drawn down the punishment of God.

After the Destruction of Jerusalem (587 B.C.)

The Babylonians undertook a mass deportation but did not replace the deported with a new population. They put the new Babylonian province in charge of Gedaliah, a friend of Jeremiah (39:14). A seal found at Lachish suggests that Gedaliah played an important role under Zedekiah;

perhaps he was leader of the party that favored the Chaldeans? Since Jerusalem had been razed, Gedaliah moved his capital to Mizpah.

His favorable attitude to the Babylonians led to a revolt among the nobility and he was assassinated along with the Jews and Chaldeans in his company (2 Kgs 25). The Ammonites, who were allied to Zedekiah, were undoubtedly in the plot (Jer 40:14).

Fearing the wrath of the Babylonians, a part of the populace fled to Egypt, taking the prophet Jeremiah with them against his will (Jer 42–43).

What happened next? Our sources of information are extremely limited, since all the elites had been deported. Jeremiah (41:4) speaks of religious activity continuing in Jerusalem despite the destruction of the temple. Pilgrims would have come from the north, but what cult would they have celebrated? What kind of rebuilding could have been undertaken by those left behind, the poorest in the land? The Book of Lamentations tells us of a people prostrated, overwhelmed, incapable of reacting at any level whatever. Such at least will be the condition of Judah later on when the first exiles return.

It is also the situation described by Obadiah (vv. 12–14): foreigners coming to conquer Jerusalem, and brothers, the Edomites, doing abominable things to Jerusalem and its inhabitants (cf. Ps 137; Lam 4:21–22). In his turn he announces a day of Yahweh, for, despite appearances, Yahweh is still Lord of the nations (v. 16) and the guardian of justice. Some escapees take refuge on Mount Zion, which again becomes holy (v. 17).

Obadiah sees the people of Judah robbed of their territory, and Jews returning from exile to expel the robbers. These exiles will return from Sepharad (v. 20), which will give its name to the Sephardic Jews of the Spanish and Moroccan diaspora; Sepharad is doubtless Sardis in Lydia.

The Jews in Egypt

When Jeremiah and his friends reached Egypt, they found other Jews who had been settled there for periods that cannot be determined, since contacts with Egypt had always been continual. These local Jews seem to have taken up residence in the military posts set up on the frontiers, whether in the north to protect Egypt from Mesopotamian raids or in the south to protect it against invasions by the peoples of the Sudan and Ethiopia. Jeremiah 44 speaks of Jews in the land of Pathros, whose practices were strongly tinged with paganism, but also of Jews in Memphis and Jews living in the coastal fortresses of Migdol and Daphne (see, earlier, the inscription at Karnak regarding the expedition of Seti I). We know nothing

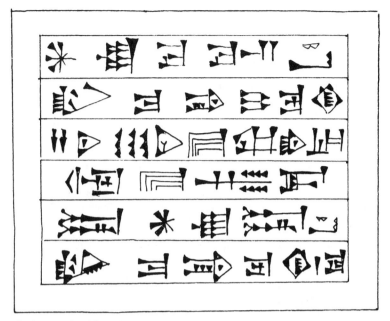

A Babylonian building brick with an inscription of King Nebuchadnezzar: "Nebuchadnezzar, King of Babylon, son of Nabopolassar, King of Babylon, for the temple of Bagila and the temple of Zida."

of the Jews in the land of Pathros; archeologists have, however, discovered a southern Jewish colony at Elephantine,[3] on an island in the Nile below the first cataract. The settlement dates perhaps from the seventh century B.C. and its temple from the end of the fifth. These Jews therefore knew nothing about the reform of Josiah. Their cult was Jewish: they celebrated Passover and the feast of Unleavened Bread and observed the sabbath. However, they did not worship the one God but, it seems, a triad reminiscent of Syro-Phoenician cults: Yahweh, a female goddess, and a god who was their son.

The Jews in Mesopotamia

There was not one but several deportations. There were three deportations to Assyria: in 732 B.C. under Tiglath-pileser III, in 722 B.C. under Sargon II, when Samaria was captured, and, finally, in 701 B.C.

Jeremiah 29:1–14

"These are the words of the letter which Jeremiah the prophet sent from Jerusalem to the elders of the exiles, and to the priests, the prophets, and all the people, whom Nebuchadnezzar had taken into exile from Jerusalem to Babylon. This was after King Jeconiah, and the queen mother, the eunuchs, the princes of Judah and Jerusalem, the craftsmen, and the smiths had departed from Jerusalem. The letter was sent by the hand of Elasah the son of Shaphan and Gemariah the son of Hilkiah, whom Zedekiah king of Judah sent to Babylon to Nebuchadnezzar king of Babylon. It said:

" 'Thus says the Lord of hosts, the God of Israel, to all the exiles whom I have sent into exile from Jerusalem to Babylon: Build houses and live in them; plant gardens and eat their produce. Take wives, and have sons and daughters; take wives for your sons, and give your daughters in marriage, that they may bear sons and daughters; multiply there, and do not decrease. But seek the welfare of the city where I have sent you into exile, and pray to the Lord on its behalf, for in its welfare you will find your welfare. For thus says the Lord of hosts, the God of Israel: Do not let your prophets and your diviners who are among you deceive you, and do not listen to the dreams which they dream, for it is a lie which they are prophesying to you in my name; I did not send them, says the Lord.

" 'For thus says the Lord: When seventy years are completed for Babylon, I will visit you, and I will fulfill to you my promise and bring you back to this place. For I know the plans I have for you, says the Lord, plans for welfare and not for evil, to give you a future and a hope. Then you will call upon me and come and pray to me, and I will hear you. You will seek me and find me; when you seek me with all your heart, I will be found by you, says the Lord, and I will restore your fortunes and gather you from all the nations and all the places where I have driven you, says the Lord, and I will bring you back to the place from which I sent you into exile.' "

---

under Sennacherib, who deported some Judeans. There were also three deportations to Babylon: the first in 597 B.C., the second in 587 B.C. after the destruction of Jerusalem, and a third in 582 B.C., according to Jeremiah 52:28.

How many persons were deported? Perhaps twenty thousand were settled along canals that branched off from the Euphrates in the neighborhood of Babylon (Ps 137); along the Habor, a tributary of the Euphrates (2 Kgs 17:6; 18:11); and near a town called Tel Abib (Ez 1:3; 3:15). But there were Jews elsewhere in Mesopotamia as well—for example, at Nippur where excavations have brought to light the archives of a rich Jewish family, the Murashu.

During the Babylonian regime the purpose of their settlement was that they might develop farmlands (Jer 29), while enjoying a good deal of freedom. We know from Ezekiel (33:30–33) that the Jews could assemble with their priests, and we have seen that the exiled Jewish royal house enjoyed an honored place at the table of the king of Babylon.

On the other hand, these people were all exiles; they had lost their country, the promised land. The temple of God, which was the focus of their worship, had been razed and no sacrifice was henceforth possible. Had the pagans and their gods triumphed?

Ezekiel

Ezekiel belonged to a priestly family and exercised the most important part of his ministry at Babylon. We are poorly informed, however, regarding his early history; did he preach initially at Jerusalem? Or was he included in the first consignment of deportees in 597 B.C., and did he preach only in Babylon? The second hypothesis is the one generally accepted today.

Ezekiel is a very learned man; he is not only a prophet but a theologian, and does not hesitate to draw upon his lore in order to render an account of his prophecies. He is familiar with the great universal sages: Noah, Daniel, and Job (14:12–23), and with the myth of the cosmic tree (Ez 31), while he also knows how to build a boat (Ez 27).

From exile and more specifically from Tel Abib he follows very closely all the events going on in Judah. He condemns in detail all the crimes that will bring Judah to its destruction (Ez 8). Like Jeremiah, he condemns attempts to strike alliances with Egypt. He sees the coming of Nebuchadnezzar and describes it in detail, with special attention to the fate of Tyre (Ez 26–28). He sees the glory of God deserting Zion (11:22–23) because the two sisters, Jerusalem and Samaria, have turned away from God and prostituted themselves with foreigners (Ez 23). Can it not even be said that Jerusalem's corruption is due to its birth from an Amorite father and a Hittite mother (Ez 16:3)?

In addition to uttering these global condemnations, Ezekiel addresses the individual; individuals will not pay for the sins of their fathers, nor will they die if they are converted. The judgment Ezekiel proclaims is one of purification and not of annihilation.

Despite his prophecies, to which no more heed was paid than had been paid to those of Jeremiah, Ezekiel saw the catastrophe come. A messenger brought him news of the destruction of Jerusalem, and Ezekiel was stricken dumb; he bore in his own body the sufferings of his people (Ez 33).

From that point on the prophet set himself to console his people. To a humiliated and despairing people he proclaims, in his famous vision of the bones (Ez 37), that a dead people can return to life. Better still—and this is a constant theme of his message—this resurrected people will be a people reunified, dwelling in its own country, fortifying its own towns (Ez 36) and living under the leadership of a new David who will make his people obey all the priestly laws (Ez 34:24).

This new Israel, gathered from abroad, victorious over its foes, and purified, will have ideal frontiers (Ez 48). The temple will be rebuilt, and from its center will flow a spring of pure water, while the glory of the Lord will take possession of its sanctuary once again.

Ezekiel's vision of a purified Israel will be at the heart of the Judaism now being born.

Babylonian Judaism

Jewish priestly circles were very active at Babylon, although, lacking as we do any clear documentation, we can only suggest hypotheses about this activity.

When the Jews went into exile they took with them all their oral and written traditions, as well as their archives. With this material as a basis, they would be able to rethink their whole past history and reread their traditions with a view to consoling, educating and strengthening the faith of a people in exile. Rereading their history they could believe that, like the captivity in Egypt, the exile was foretold by God and did not disprove his existence and sovereignty. If the people would repent, if they would turn back to God, they would once again experience the miracle of the exodus. Their country was still the promised land, but it could be occupied only by a people who were holy and converted and who followed no law but that of Yahweh. Let Israel be converted, then, and Yahweh would raise up a deliverer. It was this meditation that gave birth to the Deuteronomistic history, the collection of books from Joshua to Kings inclusive.

Meanwhile the priests were also rereading the entire history of Israel from its beginnings, indeed from creation itself. This entire history had existed in function of Israel and it provided the basis for all of Israel's rites, all of its feasts. As a result, the priests completed the documents from Yahwist and Elohist sources by introducing observations on cult and priesthood, as well as the laws on cleanness and uncleanness and on sacrifices. In this way the Pentateuch acquired its final form.

There was, however, one central event that could not be forgotten: the destruction of the temple. Ezekiel and Judaism looked forward to its rebuilding; meanwhile they reorganized the religious life of the people.

Far distant from the temple, each Jew could observe the sabbath and med-
itate daily on God's law as given in the writings that were now taking their
definitive shape. It was certainly Babylon that saw the institution of the
synagogal form of worship, which had its focus no longer in sacrifice but
in prayer and meditation on the word of God.

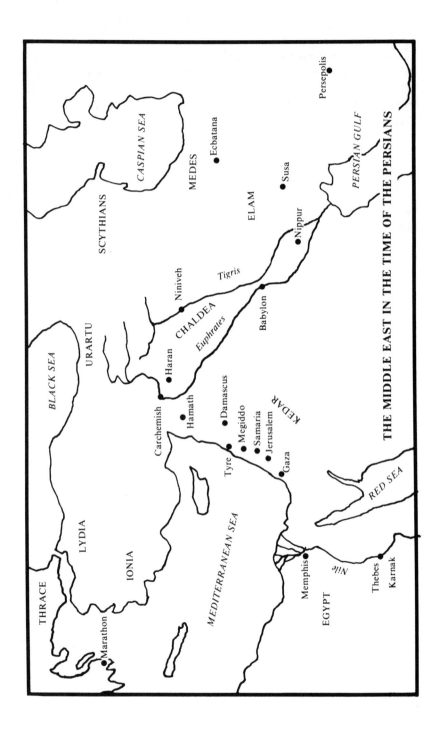

THE MIDDLE EAST IN THE TIME OF THE PERSIANS

146

Chapter 10
Persian Domination
and Return from Exile

End of the Neobabylonian Empire and Birth
of the Persian Empire

The death of Nebuchadnezzar the Great in 562 B.C. ushered in a difficult time for Babylon. Religious clans were in conflict. It was finally a son of a priestess of Sin at Haran who was enthroned under the name of Nabonidus. This choice provoked the anger of the priesthood of Marduk at Babylon.

At the time of Nabonidus' enthronement the great danger came from the empire of the Medes (capital: Ecbatana) who held the entire northern stretch of the Tigris and even Haran as well as the land of the Elamites. In Elam Cyrus came on the scene, determined to shake off the Median yoke with the help of Nabonidus.

In 549 B.C. Cyrus won a decisive victory and had himself proclaimed king of the Persians and the Medes. In 546 B.C. he took possession of the kingdom of Lydia, where Croesus was king, and then of Ionia. He then turned to the plains and plateaus of eastern Iran, occupied Afghanistan and Turkestan, and pushed on as far as India. Having thus consolidated his power and his human and monetary resources, he advanced against Babylon.

Second Isaiah (Is 40–55)

We know nothing about this great prophet whose person is entirely hidden behind his work; it is only the content of his oracles that enables us to date his ministry during the years 550–539 B.C., that is, during the period that saw the rise of Cyrus and announced the fall of Babylon.

To this anonymous writer the fall of Croesus is the sign that Yahweh is about to transform the world, since Cyrus is simply Yahweh's heroic agent. The prophet tells Jerusalem that its sins have been expiated; it is time now to prepare a way for the Lord through the wilderness. He is coming in order once again to feed his flock (Is 40).

Israel in exile had come to doubt its God, yet is not Yahweh the one who brought the Israelites out of Egypt? Now Cyrus is his Messiah (Is 45); he will conquer the nations in order to restore Israel.

Because Babylon was so mighty and its empire so vast, Israel had come to accept the greatness of the Mesopotamian gods, but is not God the one who created the ends of the earth (Is 40:27)?

Cyrus will liberate Israel, and "not for price or reward" (Is 45:13). The return to Israel will not be another journey through a wilderness: "They shall not hunger or thirst, neither scorching wind nor sun shall smite them, for he who has pity on them will lead them" (Is 49:10). Jerusalem's watchmen already see the procession coming, and they cry out their joy: "Break forth together into singing, you waste places of Jerusalem; for the Lord has comforted his people, he has redeemed Jerusalem" (52:9). This return to the holy city and to God is not for the Jews alone; they are accompanied by all the nations: "They shall bring your sons in their bosom and your daughters shall be carried on their shoulders. Kings shall be your foster fathers, and their queens your nursing mothers. . . . Then you will know that I am the Lord" (49:22–23).

At the heart of the preaching of this great poet stands the enigmatic figure of the suffering Servant, who has been appointed by God to save his people. But who is this Servant? Is he the Israelite people as a whole, which through the exodus first and then through this return from slavery has entered the service of God? Is it the elite of Israel, those who have remained faithful and must proclaim God's salvation to the nations (49:5–6)? Or is the suffering Servant an individual person, perhaps Isaiah himself, God's persecuted witness (50:4–11 or even 53)? Or is he a type of the coming Messiah? This last will be the interpretation given by the Targums and, of course, by Christians.

The Persian Period

At the moment when Cyrus turned against Babylon, Nabonidus had just put a strange period behind him: for eight years he had withdrawn to a distant oasis and entrusted the government of the kingdom to his son

---

Clay barrel found at Babylon

It celebrates the entrance of Cyrus into Babylon and the fact that he restored Marduk as supreme god after Nabonidus had preferred Sin.

"Marduk, the great Lord, the guardian of his people, looked with pleasure on the good deeds of Cyrus and on his upright heart, and ordered him to go to his city, Babylon. He made him take the road to Babylon and advanced constantly at his side as a friend and companion; beside Cyrus, girded with their weapons, marched his vast army, their numbers as much beyond counting as the waters of a river. Marduk made him enter Babylon without battle or struggle. He rescued his city of Babylon from oppression and delivered into Cyrus' hands Nabonidus, a king who did not fear Marduk. All the peoples of Babylon and the whole of the land of Sumer and Akkad, its princes and rulers, all bent the knee before him and kissed his feet. They rejoiced to have him as their king, and their faces shone. They did not cease to utter fervent blessings to Lord Marduk who, by his support, had brought the dead gods back to life and had saved all the gods from need and tribulation, and they celebrated his name. . . ."

Belshazzar. This time of withdrawal, perhaps for mystical purposes, perhaps for reasons of health, was later to be exploited by Judaism. Daniel would give an interpretation of it, though one that confuses Nabonidus with Nebuchadnezzar; then the theme would be picked up by the Essenes of Qumran.

When Nabonidus returned to take up the reins of government in 539 B.C. he was crushed by Cyrus at Sippar. The Neobabylonian empire had lasted less than a century.

Cyrus founded the first empire that could claim to be universal. Though possessing absolute power he showed himself much more liberal than the Assyrians and Babylonians. He alone was king, but he divided the empire into satrapies governed by Persian officials. As soon as the royal power was no longer challenged, each state was allowed to live in accordance with its own customs. In correspondence the Persians allowed the use of a variety of language, while official documents were written in three languages: Elamite, Persian and Aramaic. It is this third language that we find used in Syria-Palestine and in such Jewish documents as the Books of Chronicles and the archives at Elephantine.

Cyrus was very careful to restore the local gods. He wanted each people to be at peace, to have its own religions, and, in keeping with its faith, to pray for the king. At Babylon archeologists have recovered the Rassam clay barrel, the text of which is concerned with the piety of Cyrus. Cyrus ordered that all the cultic objects stored up by the Babylonian sovereigns be sent back to the peoples from which they had been taken, and that the temples of these peoples be rebuilt with royal monies. Perhaps Cyrus' faith in Ahura Mazda as sovereign god and wise creator and conserver of the world gave him a feeling for the Jewish faith.

Documentation

We have a good many documents to aid us in dealing with this period. To begin with, there is the work of the Chronicler, who also composed the Books of Ezra and Nehemiah. Here, unfortunately, just as elsewhere in his work, the Chronicler has a quite unsatisfactory idea of history. Thus we do not know the exact temporal relations between Ezra and Nehemiah. But as it stands, the Chronicler's work nonetheless contains many documents concerning the return of the Jews to Palestine.

To these books of the Bible must be added certain prophetic books: Third Isaiah (Is 56–66), Haggai, Malachi and Zechariah, all of which bear witness to Jewish hopes, difficulties and compromises.

We also have archives of various Jewish groups. There are, for example, the documents of the wealthy Marashu family of Nippur, who may stand as symbolic of the Jews who did not envisage a return to Palestine, and the archives of the Jews settled at Elephantine in Egypt, which give

Babylonians and Syrians bring tribute to the Persian king, Xerxes.

evidence of difficulties with the Egyptians. Finally there are some Samaritan documents.

All these must, of course, be compared with the abundant documentation relative to the Persian empire. Josephus' book, *The Antiquities of the Jews,* will be of little help, since it depends almost exclusively on what is said in the Bible.

Return from Exile and Rebuilding

Profiting by Cyrus' desire to see all the ancient cults restored throughout his empire, some Jews at Babylon requested authorization to return to their native land, that is, to the province of Judah which was a dependency of the governor of Samaria. They asked autonomy for a very small area measuring 24 miles on the north-south axis (from Bethel to south of Tekoa) and about 30 miles on the east-west axis (from the Dead Sea to west of Azekah)—in all, about 720 square miles, of which a third was wilderness.

Henceforth Judea would have its own governor; he would be aided by one hundred and fifty heads of families, the "elders" who would one day become the Sanhedrin.

Cyrus authorized the Jews to depart and issued an edict in their behalf which is translated in the Book of Ezra (6:1–5). Not only might the Jews return home and administer their own territory, but they also had restored to them the vessels of the old temple which had been carried off by the Babylonians; an official list of these vessels is given (Ezr 1:7).

How many Jews took advantage of the permission and returned home? Ezra speaks sometimes of 29,818 men, sometimes of 42,630 persons in all; we may doubtless accept this second figure. It is easy to understand the many problems caused by such an influx of people into a country that had been devastated and lacked all structures (Zec 4:10).

It seems obvious that many Jews in Babylon, now well established and enjoying all civic rights, did not plan to return. For this period we have the archives of the wealthy Marashu family which would continue for a century and a half to engage in profitable banking activities and enjoy the trust of all circles. Among their clientele were companies in charge of canals and owners of extensive farmlands, but also slaves. The Murashu family dealt in insurance, rentals, and security for imprisoned debtors. All sums of money were loaned at twenty percent interest.

The Murashu family was but one remarkable example of the way in which the Jews took Jeremiah's advice (Jer 29), settled down, and made both the country and their own interests prosper. The Jewish community

---

Ezra 6:1–12

"Then Darius the king made a decree, and search was made in Babylonia, in the house of the archives where the documents were stored. And in Ecbatana, the capital which is in the province of Media, a scroll was found on which this was written: 'A record. In the first year of Cyrus the king, Cyrus the king issued a decree: Concerning the house of God at Jerusalem, let the house be rebuilt, the place where sacrifices are offered and burnt offerings are brought; its height shall be sixty cubits and its breadth sixty cubits, with three courses of great stones and one course of timber; let the cost be paid from the royal treasury. And also let the gold and silver vessels of the house of God, which Nebuchadnezzar took out of the temple that is in Jerusalem and brought to Babylon, be restored and brought back to the temple which is in Jerusalem, each to its place; you shall put them in the house of God.'

"'Now therefore, Tattenai, governor of the province Beyond the River, Shethar-bozenai, and your associates the governors who are in the province Beyond the River, keep away; let the work on this house of God alone; let the governor of the Jews and the elders of the Jews rebuild this house of God on its site. Moreover I make a decree regarding what you shall do for these elders of the Jews for the rebuilding of this house of God; the cost is to be paid to these men in full and without delay from the royal revenue, the tribute of the province Beyond the River. And whatever is needed—young bulls, rams, or sheep for burnt offerings to the God of heaven, wheat, salt, wine, or oil, as the priests at Jerusalem require—let that be given to them day by day without fail, that they may offer pleasing sacrifices to the God of heaven, and pray for the life of the king and his sons. Also I make a decree that if anyone alters this edict, a beam shall be pulled out of his house, and he shall be impaled upon it, and his house shall be made a dunghill. May the God who has caused his name to dwell there overthrow any king or people that shall put forth a hand to alter this, or to destroy this house of God which is in Jerusalem. I Darius make a decree; let it be done with all diligence.'"

---

at Babylon was also well organized as far as its religious life went, and at this period it was beginning to exert an important intellectual influence.

Those who returned to Judea were, therefore, not poor people but on the contrary often rich both financially and intellectually. It was they who would exercise power; they would also be distrustful of the natives, whose Jewish practices seemed to them highly syncretistic. Evidently, the Jews of Judea and the Jews from Babylon did not fall into one another's arms.

The Persian authorities sent a prince of Judah named Sheshbazzar to be governor of Judea. On the orders of Cyrus he began the construction of the temple but was quickly forced to stop the work because the country was too poor and too lacking in unity. All that was done was to lay the foundations.

It was at this time of despair that a new prophet arose whose message was very dependent on that of Second Isaiah and who for lack of a more specific name is therefore called Third Isaiah (Is 56–66). His purpose is to console his people who, despite the promises associated with the return, do not see salvation on the way. The delay is due to the non-observance of God's laws: those in authority are corrupt; justice is not done to the poor. But God's judgment is coming; he himself will bring justice to the poor and the oppressed; he will separate those who obey his laws from idolaters. The separation will not affect only Jews, for God will also bring justice to foreigners who observe his laws, and they will have entry into the temple (Is 56:3–7).

Cambyses (530–522 B.C.)

In 530 B.C. Cambyses had his brother assassinated and succeeded him. He would be known to history as a terrible conqueror; he further extended the empire by conquering Egypt, where he captured Memphis in 525 B.C. He died on his way home in 522 B.C.

We know very little about his reign that relates to the Jews; perhaps their resettlement continued under his rule. The only sure information we have comes from Elephantine in Egypt. The archives of this Jewish colony express satisfaction that Cambyses spared their temple during his conquest. His action may have been inspired by concern for religion, as in the case of Cyrus; there may have been political considerations as well, since the Jews, unlike the Egyptians, were faithful allies.

At the death of Cambyses a certain Gautama tried to pass himself off as the dead king's supposedly assassinated brother. The result was a palace revolt pitting two claimants, Gautama and Darius, against each other. This internal crisis raised hopes throughout the empire. Had the time come for independence?

In Jerusalem the prophet Haggai urged the people to start again the rebuilding of the temple (Hag 1:2). Poverty and poor harvests were no excuse; the first need was to rebuild the temple and reopen the Lord's house so that he might enter in. Then wealth would be restored; all the nations would bring their treasures to Jerusalem. The temple was to be rebuilt under the direction of Jeshua the high priest and Zerubbabel the governor, the latter being none other than the grandson of Jehoiachin and therefore a descendant of David. Haggai proclaimed Zerubbabel to be the coming Messiah: "On that day, says the Lord of hosts, I will take you, O Zerubbabel my servant, the son of Shealtiel, says the Lord, and make you like a signet ring; for I have chosen you, says the Lord of hosts" (Hag 2:25).

The prophet Zechariah uttered the same message, but he was equally interested in two persons: Jeshua the high priest and Zerubbabel the prince. They were the two olive trees, the two anointed who stand before the Lord of all the earth (Zec 4:11–14). The messianic function is therefore linked also to the priesthood and to a man who for the first time has the title "high priest."

In circumstances unknown to us Zerubbabel disappeared from the scene without having fulfilled the messianic prophecy; only one anointed was left: Jeshua, and it was he who would receive the crown (Zec 6:11–13). Henceforth eschatological expectations would be linked with the person of the high priest.

Darius (522–486 B.C.)

While these messianic hopes were emerging in Judea, Darius got rid of Gautama. Within the space of two years he carried out no less than nineteen campaigns and subjugated nine rebellious kings, a victory celebrated on a bas-relief at Behistun.

From that time forward Darius did all he could to further the organization of the kingdom that Cyrus had begun. He divided the empire into twenty satrapies and exercised a very strict control over their royal governors. To keep watch on the satraps he created a network of spies; at the same time he demanded that the satraps collect heavy taxes so that he might build his new capital, Persepolis.

It was probably on one of these missions of surveillance that a Persian official was disturbed by the rebuilding of the temple in Jerusalem. Would not such an enterprise bring with it a serious threat of nationalism? The Jews were obliged to prove that they had actually been authorized by Cyrus to rebuild their temple. Darius then authorized them to continue the work, and the second temple was completed in 516 (Ezr 6:15–18). The high priest dedicated the new sanctuary in the spring of 515 B.C.

Darius' other activities hardly concerned the Jews of Judea; this was true even of the restoration of the old Babylon-to-Egypt route. Darius turned eastward and made the Indus his eastern frontier.

Back in the west he attacked the Greek colonies and conquered Thrace and Macedonia in succession. He failed, however, against the Greeks at Marathon. The year 490 B.C. marks the coming of a new great power that could rival Persia, provided it could choose its terrain and maneuver while immobilizing the formidable Persian cavalry. Darius died in 486 B.C.

Xerxes (486–465 B.C.)

Xerxes had no sooner taken power than he was faced with a new uprising at Babylon. Unlike his predecessors, he razed the city and its temples. The question of Xerxes' belief has been raised in this context: Was he a sovereign who was influenced by the Zoroastrian reform and who believed only in Ahura Mazda and looked upon the other gods as demons that must be destroyed?

A second event was to leave its mark on his reign: In keeping with the policy of his father he sought to reduce the Greeks to subjection. This second war of the Medes ended in catastrophe for him, however (479 B.C.), and the Greeks were able to regain their foothold in Asia Minor.

Egypt now thought itself in a position to revolt, and Xerxes was obliged to put down rebellions there. Was it on this occasion that the cities of Shechem and Bethel were destroyed? Archeologists confirm the fact but can offer no explanation. The Book of Ezra (4:6) mentions a complaint laid against the Jews, but we have no way of knowing what its substance was, nor do we know what judgment was issued.

As a result of these failures Xerxes was forced to withdraw to his palaces; the end had come for the generous policies of Cyrus. Concerns for justice, order and economic prosperity would be forgotten as the subject peoples were crushed by taxation and every revolt was put down without mercy. In his palace Xerxes indulged in numerous harem intrigues, so that Herodotus regarded him as "more a ladies' man than an energetic man of affairs" (IX, 108–13). He was finally assassinated in 465 B.C.

Esther[1]

It is in this historical context that the Book of Esther is supposedly located. True enough, the author was familiar with the court of Susa, its religious and political customs, and the temperamental and sensuous character of the ruler. But the book makes use of this archeological setting only to tell a story which can hardly be dated prior to the second century. In any case, the book does make clear how difficult it was to be faithful to Jewish particularism in the midst of pagans; the latter planned to extirpate the Jewish community. Did these difficulties begin in Persia or only later under the Seleucids?

Esther saves her people with the aid of harem intrigues; God plays a part only in the Greek version of Esther, which is appreciably different from the Hebrew Esther. Esther is hardly attractive when she causes the slaughter to be directed against the accusers of the Jews and asks that the killing be continued and the goods of the victims be looted.

What we have here is a Jewish nationalist outlook that gives expression to grudges and desires for revenge on the pagans. It is understandable that such a book should have had trouble gaining entry into the Jewish canon; the Qumran community seems to have paid it no heed. Nonetheless it was immensely successful and became the occasion for the autumn feast of Purim, a kind of carnival during which all forms of excess were allowed. Perhaps the feast originated in the Mesopotamian New Year's festival which had won new favor at the Persian court. Was not Persepolis the sacred capital where alone the New Year's festival could be celebrated?

Just as the Iranian king was responsible for this festival celebrating the regeneration of the world and the triumph of good over all the forces of evil, so Purim became the feast celebrating Israel's triumph over all its enemies.

Malachi

In all likelihood it was during the reign of Xerxes that Malachi prophesied. The time of exalted hopes that is reflected in Haggai and Zechariah is now long past; the eschatological perspective has disappeared. Malachi finds fault with a priesthood that lacks zeal, a people who have become skeptics and show contempt for faith in Yahweh. He attacks social dissoluteness; the taxes due to the temple are not paid; men divorce their wives with a word, and even in the priesthood they take foreign wives. Even the sabbath is not observed.

Like his predecessors, Malachi foretells the coming of the Lord. The Lord will, however, be preceded by a messenger. Is this enigmatic figure heavenly or historical? Is the prophet referring to himself? Is he referring to Elijah who had been taken up to heaven and might now be returning?

Artaxerxes I (465–424 B.C.)

Xerxes' successor was a weak king who was much under the influence of his womenfolk and courtesans. Throughout his reign he had to send his generals out to put down rebellions in Egypt and in the province Beyond the River, that is, in Syria-Palestine. The subject peoples in those areas knew that they could count on active aid from the Greeks.

It was in this situation of insecurity that the Persian king became interested in the destiny of Jerusalem, the walls of which had still not been rebuilt. Jerusalem could serve as a fine point of observation in relation both to Egypt and to Syria. At Susa, meanwhile, Nehemiah, a Jew, had won the favor of the king; he pleaded the cause of Jerusalem and obtained from the king an official mandate to rebuild the walls enclosing the city. In the mind of Artaxerxes his own action was political; Nehemiah interpreted it as an act of faith (Neh 2).

Nehemiah came to Jerusalem with his retinue as a man under orders from the great king. He was no longer dependent on the governor of Samaria but himself enjoyed the status of a governor (Neh 5:14).

The rebuilding of Jerusalem and its renaissance as a political center could only be disturbing to its neighbors. Governors Sanballat of Samaria and Tobias of Ammanitis, together with the coastal city of Ashdod and the Arabian kingdom of Kedar,[2] complained to the Persian king and tried to halt the work.

Despite his neighbors Nehemiah carried on his mission from 445 to 433, but had to proceed with caution. The project had to be undertaken secretly and carried out as quickly as possible. The work, done with rapidity and only by Jews clean of any taint, was initially an object of mockery on the part of foreigners and of Jews not allowed to share in it because of their syncretism. But as the work advanced, the uneasy neighbors joined forces and attacked Jerusalem. Henceforth the workers had to build with a trowel in one hand and a weapon in the other. It was necessary to stand guard at the weak points while Nehemiah exhorted the people to cleanse themselves and obey the laws of Yahweh.

Other steps were also taken against Nehemiah; an attempt was made to arrest him for showing a spirit of rebellion against the Persians; an attempt was even made to kidnap him. Despite everything the work was finished in fifty-two days (Neh 6:15). The historian Josephus did not accept this figure; according to him the work lasted for two years and four months, and was still not complete in 437 B.C. Jerusalem had now become a city once again, but it still needed a populace. Nehemiah ordered each village and town in Judah to send a tenth of its inhabitants as a way of repeopling Jerusalem (Neh 7 and 11). It was finally possible to celebrate the dedication of the walls (Neh 12:27–43).

It was not enough to have given Judea a capital again. It was also necessary to deal with social disorder, put an end to usury, and give the debt-ridden peasants the opportunity for the right kind of life. Nehemiah attacked the large landowners and forced them by an oath in the temple to write off the debts owed to them (Neh 5–6); he also undertook a reform to ensure equitable taxation, and in order to set a good example he went so far as to renounce his revenues as governor.[3] In 433 B.C. he was recalled to Susa. He quickly obtained permission to return to Judea a second time;

when he arrived he found that all of his religious and social prescriptions had been disobeyed (Neh 13).

Instead of being the bulwark of orthodoxy, the high priest Eliashib had thrown in his lot with foreigners. One of his grandsons had become the son-in-law of Sanballat, the governor of Samaria. Tobias, the governor of Ammonitis, had a chamber and storeroom in the outbuildings of the temple.

Nehemiah uncompromisingly restored order. He had foreigners ejected from the sacred precincts, forbade all mixed marriages, and reestablished strict observance of the sabbath by closing the gates of Jerusalem to foreign traders. This inflexibility reflects the experience of a Babylonian Jew who was scandalized by the syncretism of the Judeans. With the authority that was his from the king of Persia he rejected all those he regarded as unclean. This interdict affected first and foremost the Samaritans, even though they looked upon themselves as worshipers of Yahweh. Nehemiah thus prepared the way for a break between the two communities, since Samaria remained open to foreigners and especially to trade with Tyre and Byblos.

Our information regarding Nehemiah's mission stops here. We do not know what role Jerusalem played in the strategy of the Persians. Archeologists can confirm numerous destructions on the coastal plain which bear witness to the number of rebellions instigated by Egypt. Similarly, the remains of Persian storehouses and tombs[4] have been found near the frontier; they attest the existence of garrisons. At Lachish the majestic remains of a Persian enclosure have been discovered and, within it, a courtyard surrounded by a portico. Excavations have brought to light magnificent remains of Greek vases.

Darius II (424–404 B.C.)

We know nothing about the Jews in Judea during this period. The only relevant information comes from the Jewish colony at Elephantine. The abundant archives of this community contain a full correspondence with the Persian rulers in regard to civil and religious affairs. For example, in 419 B.C. the community received a document bidding it conform to ancient traditions in celebrating the Passover. We do not know what precisely occasioned this letter, but it shows the unwearying concern of the Persians to see to the observance of religious customs.

The most important event occurred in 412 B.C. During the absence of Ashram the satrap, the temple at Elephantine was pillaged by the Egyptians. The reasons for this act are not known to us, but two may be sug-

Letter of Yedoniah on the destruction of the temple at Elephantine

"In the month of Tammuz, in the 14th year of King Darius, when Arsames left and went to the king, the priests of Khnub, the god at fortress Elephantine, gave money to Vidaranag, the governor there, and said to him: 'Let the sanctuary of Yaho the god at fortress Elephantine disappear.'

"Nefayan, son of Vidaranag and commander at fortress Syene, led the Egyptians and other soldiers to the place. They entered fortress Elephantine with their weapons. They entered the sanctuary there and razed it to the ground, smashing its stone columns. There were also five large porticos of cut stone . . . these they destroyed. They burned the bronze doors and the hinges of the doors, as well as the roof of the sanctuary which was made entirely of cedar planking. They seized for themselves all the gold and silver bowls that were in the sanctuary. It was in the days of the kings of Egypt that our fathers built this sanctuary at fortress Elephantine.

"After this destruction we and our wives and children donned sackcloth and fasted and prayed to Yaho, the Lord of heaven, who made that dog Vidaranag a spectacle for us: they took the bracelets from his feet, and all the possessions he had gained were lost."

The letter goes on to recall that after that event letters were sent to the high priest at Jerusalem over a period of three years without eliciting any response. Then it continues:

"If it seems good to you, our Lord, see to the rebuilding of this sanctuary, since they will not allow us to rebuild it. Consider the grateful friends you have in us here in Egypt, and send them a letter instructing them to rebuild the sanctuary of Yaho the God here at fortress Elephantine, so that it will be as before. Then we will offer oblation and holocaust in your name on the altar of Yaho the God, and we will pray for you at all times, we, our wives and children, and all Jews here.

"If you do see to it that this sanctuary is rebuilt, you will have more merit in the eyes of Yaho, the God of heaven, than one who offers him a holocaust and sacrifices worth a thousand talents of silver. We have sent our instructions concerning the gold.

"With regard to this entire business we have also sent a letter to the sons of Sanballat, governor of Samaria. Furthermore, Ashram himself did not know of all that was done. The 20th of Marheswan, in the 17th year of King Darius."

Observe that the name of the Lord is here vocalized as Yaho and not as Yahweh.

gested. First, as in the days of Moses, Jewish worship was repugnant to the Egyptians; this was especially true of the sacrifice of the Passover lamb when on the same island Egyptians were worshiping Khnum, the god with the ram's head. Second, we know that the Jews of Elephantine were in the service of the Persians and that unlike the Egyptians they did not rebel against the sovereign. The Egyptians therefore had every reason to detest the Jews; the Jews for their part urged their suit with the Persians to have their temple restored.

We have a full correspondence on this subject with the governors of Memphis, Jerusalem and Samaria, and with the high priest of Jerusalem.

After several years of letters the Jews finally received a response from the governors of Judea and Samaria who ordered the Satrap Ashram to rebuild the temple for the purpose of offering sacrifices and incense. Nothing is said, however, of a sacrilege having been committed: was this out of respect for the feelings of the Egyptians?

Despite the authorization to rebuild the temple the days of this community were numbered; the final documents date from 399 B.C. The Egyptian uprising of 405 B.C., which repulsed the Persians for good, undoubtedly also signaled an end to the existence of this Jewish military community.

Artaxerxes II (404–358 B.C.)

At the death of Darius II his successor Artaxerxes inherited the Egyptian rebellion and quickly lost control of Egypt. He also had to deal with his brother Cyrus, whom their mother wanted to see on the throne. Despite the support of Greek mercenaries Cyrus was defeated in Babylonia in 401 B.C. In order to maintain peace and his control of Ionia Artaxerxes had to distribute a good deal of money and sign the peace of Antalcidas in 387 B.C. Despite all these efforts, however, at the end of his reign he could not prevent a rebellion of all the satraps in the western part of the empire, where Hellenism was becoming an increasingly strong attraction.

There is general agreement today that Ezra carried out his mission under Artaxerxes II. It is likely that during this troubled period Artaxerxes put him in charge of settling problems involving the Jews of Judea, Syria and Phoenicia. Ezra was a priest and scribe, with the official title of "Scribe of the law of the God of heaven"; this meant that his function was to see to it that the law of Yahweh, known to the Persians as "God of heaven," was observed. For the purposes of his mission he was empowered to appoint judges and magistrates; the law as interpreted by the Jews of Babylon thus became binding on anyone who wanted to be recognized as a Jew.

To help him in his task Ezra was given permission (Ezr 7:13) to have a contingent of Jews from Babylonia accompany him; five thousand are said to have gone with him. In addition, he acquired funds both from the Persian government and from exiled Jews, who were urged to make an offering for the work of reconstruction in Judea.

On reaching Jerusalem, Ezra organized an assembly at which the law was solemnly proclaimed to all the people (Neh 7). The reading of the law lasted for seven days and was crowned by the feast of Booths. Ezra not only read the law; he also commented on it. The focus of his message was no

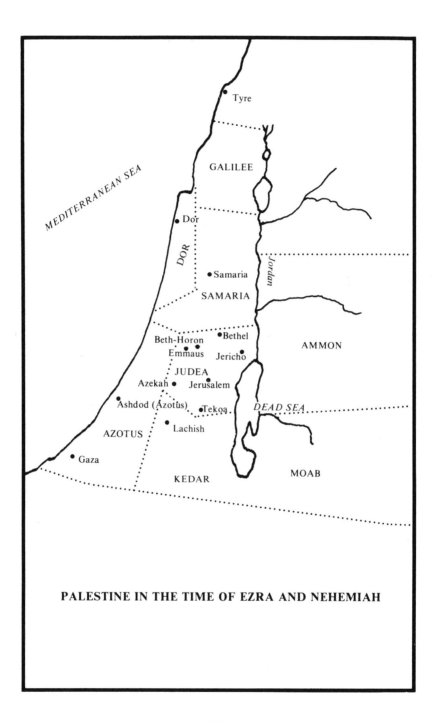

PALESTINE IN THE TIME OF EZRA AND NEHEMIAH

longer sacrifice but the interpretation of the law. The influence of the rabbis and of instruction in the synagogues is evident.

But what law was it that Ezra read to all the people? Was it a collection of laws that he had brought with him from Babylon? Was it the Deuteronomic code of Josiah? Since the reading lasted for seven days, it is thought that Ezra read the entire Pentateuch, doubtless in its definitive form.

The hypothesis that the Pentateuch was read in its definitive form is supported by the fact that the Samaritans have the same Pentateuch as the Jews, apart from a few details.[5] Yet at this time the two communities were already far apart and would soon be separated completely when the Samaritans built their own temple on Mount Gerizim.[6] The definitive redaction of the Pentateuch cannot, therefore, be later than the fourth century B.C.

According to Jewish legend Ezra was a second Moses, the man who rediscovered the Pentateuch and gave it a place of honor. The Samaritans, on the other hand, speak of "accursed Ezra," because he made his own all the laws passed by Nehemiah, dissolved mixed marriages, dismissed foreign wives, and purified Judaism by shutting out any and every foreign influence.

At this point post-exilic Judaism was established: a Judaism lacking in any precise national hope, but on the other hand a Judaism with a very clear idea of its specific nature and in particular of its relation to the law, which had now become something absolute and a criterion distinguishing the Jews from all other peoples. Judaism would henceforth be defined by observance of the law and a scrupulously detailed application of its principles. The center of this Judaism was and would remain Babylon with its rabbinical schools which would send their letters to Judea, as Hillel the Great was still doing in the time of Jesus.

On the other hand, the temple had now been rebuilt, and Jerusalem became the spiritual center for all the Jewish communities of the diaspora. From now on, sovereignty was in the hands of the priests with the high priest at their head. This period also saw the establishment of the canon of Scripture, which included in addition to the Pentateuch the historical books and, gradually, the prophets; these various books became authoritative and were read and commented on in the synagogues throughout the diaspora.

The documents available to us from the Persian period do not allow us to go any further. We know a little about Judea but almost nothing about the two main centers of the diaspora: Egypt in the area of Alexandria, and Mesopotamia. The only detail mentioned is a deportation of Jews in the direction of the Caspian Sea during the reign of Artaxerxes III.

We are better informed about Jewish literary life during this period. In the light of ancient wisdoms Israel was asking itself the meaning of life and death, of evil and suffering. Its reflections gave birth to such works as the Book of Job and the Song of Songs. The Books of Psalms and Proverbs, which had been begun long ago, were completed at this time. On the other hand, the canon was not yet fixed.

Alongside the hyperorthodoxy of Ezra and Nehemiah, and alongside the wisdom literature, other currents of thought existed which represented a challenge to many Jewish ideas. The books of Ruth and Jonah may be taken as expressions of these other currents. Must we not see in these books a polemic against the prohibition of mixed marriages and against the closing in of Judaism on itself? Ruth and Jonah represent a universalist outlook: salvation can come from the pagans and be proclaimed to the pagans.

The opposition is even clearer in the anonymous prophet whom, for lack of a better name, we call Second Zechariah (Zec 9–14).[7] This prophet seems to be launching a vigorous attack on the Jews who had returned from exile and now believed themselves to be the only true Israelites. He asserts that on the contrary the restoration must embrace Israel in its entirety; he defends the despised inhabitants of Judah; he is unwilling to let the believing Samaritans of the north or Jews living in other foreign lands be forgotten and rejected. He does not accept the view that all these people are syncretists. He has a greater sense of history and knows perhaps that only a very small percentage of the population had been deported. According to Sargon, the north had lost only 27,290 inhabitants, which modern scholars estimate to have been three or four percent of the entire population of Israel.

Zechariah proclaims that the poor of Judah as well as the inhabitants of Samaria and of Damascus and even as far as Hamath must have a share in the restoration effected by God. It is not enough merely to rebuild the temple in its pure state. Like Ezekiel, Second Zechariah looks for the reunification of Israel (9:11–10:12). Like Isaiah, he hopes that all the nations will be converted and will come to Zion to honor the Lord. He awaits a good shepherd, but he also knows that this shepherd is and will be rejected by the circles now in power, the leaders of the people. The king whom Zechariah awaits can no longer be identified with an historical figure. He will be appointed by God and not by men. He will be a humble and humiliated Moses, one resembling those whose side Zechariah is taking: the poor, the outcast, the scorned.

It is to be noted that during this period Hebrew ceased to be the language of the people and was replaced by Aramaic, which had long been the language of commerce and diplomacy. Hebrew would henceforth be a liturgical language as well as the language of the sacred texts; these texts would, however, have to be explained in Aramaic, thus giving birth to the Targums.

Beginning in this period, Israel had to come to grips with other cultures, especially that of Babylon. The visions of Ezekiel and his successors bear the profound mark of this culture. Angelology and its correlative, demonology, also make their appearance at this time. Note, for example, how a greater emphasis is placed on the figure of Satan in the Books of Job and Zechariah.

These new elements do not mean a change in the faith of Israel, but they do introduce a new language that will be developed in the apocalypses and the Talmud. The Jerusalem Talmud recognizes what had happened: "The names of the angels came with the people who returned from Babylon."

The Samaritans

In the beginning the Samaritans were part of the tribes of Judah.

According to their chronicles, the ultimate reason for the schism is to be found back in the eleventh century B.C. when Elijah moved the ark from Shechem-Gerizim to Shiloh; this marked the beginning of a period of misfortune.

167 B.C.	Antiochus IV dedicates Mount Gerizim to Zeus Xenios (Zeus the Friend of Strangers) (2 Mac 6:2).
145 B.C.	Through alliance with Demetrius II, the Jews expand toward Samaria.
128 B.C.	John Hyrcanus destroys the temple on Mount Gerizim.
109 B.C.	His sons destroy Samaria. We know of a Samaritan diaspora, especially at Alexandria.
57–55 B.C.	Gabinius rebuilds Samaria.
ca. 30 B.C.	Herod beautifies Samaria and renames it Sebaste.
betw. 6 B.C. and 9 A.D.	The Samaritans defile the temple at Jerusalem with bones.
36 A.D.	Pilate massacres the Samaritans gathered at Mount Gerizim.
66–70 A.D.	The Samaritans take part in the war against Rome and lose 11,600 at Mount Gerizim.
	Vespasian builds Nablus (Neapolis) near the ancient Shechem.
131 A.D.	During the Second Jewish War the Samaritans suffer greatly and lose their sacred books.
	Herod has a temple of Jupiter built on Mount Gerizim.

When Samaria was captured in 722, about four percent of the population was deported. Pagans were settled in Samaria in their place. In the eyes of the Jews of Judah the inhabitants of the north then began to turn pagan (2 Kgs 17:29).

Hezekiah in the seventh century B.C. and Josiah at the end of the same century looked for the reunification of all Israel, as did the prophets Jeremiah and, later, Ezekiel (sixth century B.C.) and even Second Zechariah (fifth century B.C.).

The return of the exiled Jews created new barriers. Nehemiah refused Samaritan help in rebuilding the temple (437 B.C.); he was opposed to mixed marriages and, at the personal level, to Sanballat of Samaria (Neh 13:28–29).

In the fourth century B.C. Ezra continued a similar opposition to the Samaritans. Perhaps it was at this time that Jewish and Samaritan traditions regarding the Pentateuch began to diverge.

Around 333 B.C. there was a new factor creating separation: the building of the temple on Mount Gerizim. Shortly after came the flight of the Samaritans and their original documents to Jericho.

Around 200 B.C. Jesus son of Sirach is our first sure witness to the separation between Jews and Samaritans (50:25). The Samaritan canon of the Pentateuch was established.

Chapter 11
The Period of Hellenistic Domination

The appearance of Europeans in Asia represents a major turning point in the course of history. In 333 B.C. Alexander defeated Darius III at the battle of Issus in Syria. The road to Egypt was now open to him; it was a road that took him, of course, through Palestine.

On his way to Egypt Alexander had to spend seven months capturing the ancient maritime city of Tyre. On this occasion he accomplished a fantastic feat: the building of a causeway that joined the mainland to the fortified island. He then continued on through Palestine and conducted a two-month siege of Gaza. Once this city had been taken, he conquered Egypt, founded Alexandria, and, according to Josephus (*The Jewish War* 2:487–88), established the first Jewish community there, authorizing it to live in accordance with its own customs. Perhaps some Jews had fought under the command of Alexander; this would explain their receiving civil rights but also the name "Macedonians" which they apply to themselves in some papyri.

Our biblical sources say nothing about Alexander's passage through the country. We must therefore rely on Josephus' *Antiquities of the Jews* (= *AJ*). According to Josephus Alexander authorized the Samaritans to build their temple on Mount Gerizim. It is possible, however, that the temple had been built earlier; Gerizim is regarded as a holy place back in Deuteronomy (1:29; 27:12), and the Samaritans date the building of the temple to the fifth century B.C. (*AJ* 11:321ff.).

It is certain, on the other hand, that shortly after the visit of Alexander, the Samaritans revolted. They were quickly subdued and their city

166

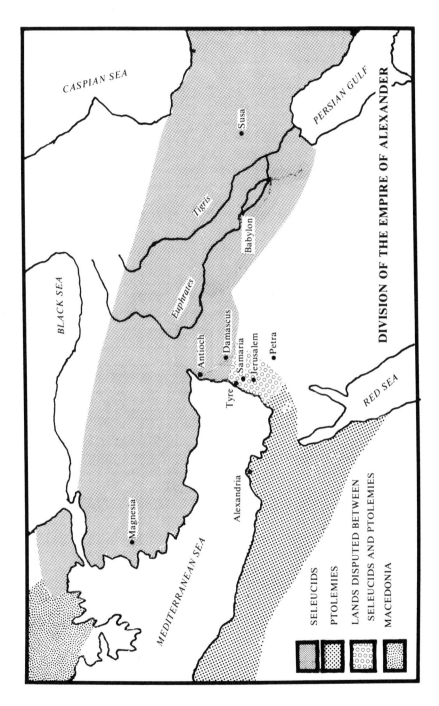

CASPIAN SEA

PERSIAN GULF

Susa

Tigris

Babylon

BLACK SEA

Euphrates

Antioch
Damascus
Samaria
Jerusalem
Petra
Tyre

RED SEA

Magnesia

Alexandria

MEDITERRANEAN SEA

SELEUCIDS

PTOLEMIES

LANDS DISPUTED BETWEEN
SELEUCIDS AND PTOLEMIES

MACEDONIA

DIVISION OF THE EMPIRE OF ALEXANDER

became once more a military colony. It was doubtless on this occasion that they fled to Jericho where their archives have been discovered (1962).

Josephus also reports that Alexander stopped at Jerusalem and visited the temple. The story is doubtless only a legend, but it attests to the fascination the man would have for later times.

Alexander seems to have obtained the submission of the Jews by peaceful means. He let them continue to have all the rights they had acquired under the Persians; to this extent he was a second Cyrus. At the same time, however, he prescribed a new concept of the world: all human beings are citizens of a single city, the cosmos; all are called to acknowledge the universal law that has its origin in God. He sought to communicate the idea of an oikumene and chose to believe that all his subjects, whether Macedonians or Persians (Paul would say: Jews or Greeks), were kin. Alexander even supposedly said that "all men were sons of one Father, and that his prayer was the expression of his recorded belief that he had a mission from God to be the Reconciler of the World."[1]

The characterization may be legend rather than fact, but it reflected the thinking of Zeno the Stoic, a Semite from Cyprus who taught at Athens beginning in about 315 B.C. Zeno dreamed of a world that was a single great city living under a single divine law, and in which all the citizens were united by the bond of love.

The first step to such a unification of the world took the form of a massive migration of Hellenes to all the regions of the east and in particular to Palestine where they founded Hellenistic cities for the purpose of spreading Hellenistic culture and the Greek language, that is, koine or common Greek, which did in fact reach the two extremities of India and Egypt. Everywhere they went the Greeks built their temples but also their stadiums and theaters. Everywhere their schools emphasized an instruction based on philosophy. Discussion became the accepted method of reflection. All this made a deep impression on Jews, who were fascinated by it but were also very certain that the universal law of the philosophers and the God of whom they spoke could only be Yahweh and his word.

This encounter of Jew and Greek could have led to a marriage based on love, to syncretism, or to total opposition. As a matter of fact, all three ways were traveled in succession and sometimes simultaneously.

The Successors

On the death of Alexander in 323 B.C. the Jews added political worries to these religious and cultural problems. Alexander's generals, known as the Diadochoi ("successors"), were at odds over the succession. Palestine became an apple of discord between the Ptolemies who occupied Egypt and the Seleucids who occupied Mesopotamia and Syria. At issue was control of the trade routes. Initially, Ptolemy took advantage of Seleucid difficulties with the Macedonian generals and gained the upper hand; at this time the Ptolemies consolidated their grip on Palestine and Phoenicia for a century to come.

Ptolemy I, who was victor in his last campaign of 302 B.C., deported some Jews to Alexandria (map, p. 167), where they would form a colony important both for its size and for its commercial and intellectual wealth. According to Josephus, this community numbered 100,000 by the time of Jesus; it was therefore one-sixth the size of the entire population of Jewish Palestine. Archeologists have uncovered a sizable Jewish quarter, a veritable city within the city, and one that had a government of its own. There, in the section of the city known as Schidra, the oldest synagogue presently known has been discovered; it dates probably from the time of Ptolemy III (246–221).

Within a short time, this community no longer spoke Hebrew or Aramaic; the Greek language had prevailed. It was therefore necessary to translate the sacred books. The Letter of Aristeas contains a fully developed legend: Ptolemy II Philadelphus wanted a translation of the sacred books of Judaism for his library. Were not the commandments of God in accord with the moral ideals of Greece? Were not the Greek philosophers worthy disciples of Moses?

In order to prove the profound harmony between Greek thought and Jewish thought Ptolemy invited (so the story goes) seventy-two Jewish scholars, six from each tribe, to translate all the books. To the astonishment of all they finished their task in seventy-two days. As a matter of fact, the original translation must have been only of the Pentateuch, and we are more or less certain that the entire task was not finished until into the first century B.C. The translation often turns into an interpretation; the need was to emphasize the agreement between Jews and Greeks, and therefore anthropomorphisms too offensive to the Greek mind were eliminated and God was made more conformable to reason. He no longer says of himself: "I am who I will be," but rather, in accordance with the philosophical ideal: "I am he who is." Similarly, the idea of resurrection disappears and is replaced by the Greek idea of the soul's immortality (see Wis 3:1–9).

In many instances the changes proved helpful to Christian thought later on. In Isaiah 7:14, for example, where the Hebrew text reads: "The young woman is with child," the Greek translation has: "The virgin is with child," thus making the passage a prophecy, for Christians, of the virgin birth.

333 Battle of Issus; end of the Persian empire (Darius III) At the death of Alexander his empire is divided:		

Egypt		Syria		Palestine
Ptolemy I	323–282	Seleucus I	311–282	Palestine is under Egyp-
Ptolemy II	282–246	Antiochus I	281–261	tian control
		Antiochus II	261–246	At Alexandria, beginning of the LXX
Ptolemy III	246–222	Seleucus II	246–225	Onias II high priest
Ptolemy IV	222–205	Antiochus III	223–187	
Ptolemy V	204–180	190 Roman victory at Magnesia		200 Antiochus III takes control of Palestine
Ptolemy VI	180–145	Seleucus IV	187–175	Onias III high priest
Antiochus IV must give up on conquest of Egypt. Roman warnings		Antiochus IV	175–164	Jason replaces Onias III Menelaus replaces Jason 167 Revolt of Mattathias
		Antiochus V	164–162	166–161 Judas Maccabeus Alcimus replaces Mene- laus Siege of Jerusalem
		Demetrius I	162–150	161–142 Jonathan Macca- beus Death of Alcimus Jonathan high priest
Cleopatra daughter of Ptolemy VI marries		Alexander Balas	150–145	
Ptolemy VII	145–116	Demetrius II	145–138	
		Period of conflicts		
		Trypho	142–138	142–135 Simon Macca- beus, high priest and viceroy
		Antiochus VII	138–128	135 Simon assassinated
		War with the Parthians		135–104 John Hyrcanus 128 Destruction of Geri- zim temple 108 Capture of Samaria 103–76 Alexander Janneus Conflict with the Phari-
		Decline of the Seleucid kingdom		sees 76–67 Salome Alexandra Hyrcanus II high priest 67 Aristobulus II king Hyrcanus II high priest Conflict among the broth- ers Hyrcanus supported by Antipater of Idumea 63 Appeal to Pompey

At times the Greek translation departs so much from the original Hebrew that it becomes simply a paraphrase; this is the case, for example, in the Book of Daniel. Furthermore, since the canon was not closed, the Alexandrians were able to add new stories, such as those of Susanna and of Bel and the dragon in Daniel. Or they quite simply added whole new books that would become part of the Greek canon: Judith, Tobit, Maccabees, Sirach, Wisdom and the Psalms of Solomon.

The encounter of Jewish and Greek thought sometimes went even further, and Jews did not hesitate to insert passages favorable to Judaism into Greek documents. Thus, for example, in the Sybilline Oracles the ancient Greek sybil becomes a witness to the God of Israel.

This favorable attitude to Hellenism was very important. Did it not reach the point of asserting that Jews and Greeks alike are descendants of Abraham, as can be seen from the letter of Areios of Sparta which is cited in 1 Maccabees 12:20–22?

To other writers of the time, however, this idyllic vision was a false one. Jesus son of Sirach and the redactor of the Greek version of Esther point out the danger of syncretism. The popular novel known as the Book of Tobit is openly hostile and urges the Jews of the diaspora to cultivate an inflexible respect for the law of Moses.

We do not know very much about what went on in Judea under the ptolemies. The country was still a small hyparchy, identical in extent with the Judea of the Persians. It was bounded on the north by Samaritis, on the south by Idumea which began north of Hebron, and on the west by Paralia, the coastal zone. In addition, the ptolemies carved out some private territories for themselves.

Luckily, excavators have found the correspondence of an Egyptian finance minister named Apollonius with Zeno, a regional administrator under the ptolemies. The latter had gone on a trip to negotiate the purchase of a little Sidonian slave girl in Ammanitis. There he met an important family, the Tobiads, perhaps the same family that had been hostile to Nehemiah. At this time the family doubtless lived in the citadel of Amman. The Tobiads were leaders of a clan, commanded a garrison that included Greek mercenaries, and had some cavalry at their disposal. They acted as prefect for the ptolemies. This wealthy and influential family owned some fine properties, one of them located at 'Arak el-Amir. From these estates Tobias sent Ptolemy Philadelphus II some rare animals as additions to his zoo.

This information is worth comparing with the results of excavations at Marisa, a town in Idumea and center of a sizable traffic in slaves with Egypt. The excavations have shown that at this period the town had a large Sidonian colony whose catacombs have been uncovered. In the main room of the catacombs the walls are covered with frescoes of giraffes, rhinoceri, hippopotami, and eagles; the ornamentation seems to show a dependence on the art of Alexandria.

The Tobiads of Ammanitis were convinced Hellenizers. In Judea, on the other hand, the devout orthodox Jews known as the Hasidim gathered under the leadership of the high priest Onias II in order to fight against the increasing influence of Greek culture.

During the reign of Ptolemy I Joseph, a son of the Tobiad family, greatly increased his fortune by becoming collector of taxes for southern Syria. Taking advantage of the third war between the Ptolemies and the Seleucids (246–241 B.C.) he had himself appointed ambassador of the Jews to the Egyptian ruler. He returned from there as the leading figure in the hyparchy of Judea and as farmer-general of taxes for Coele-Syria, Phoenicia, Judea and Samaria. By using and abusing his power he became one of the first great bankers in Jewish history.

But when Joseph reached the summit of his influence he had to reverse himself and side with the Seleucids, whose power he saw to be on the increase. He was unable to convince his son Hyrcanus to join him in this shift of alliances. Hyrcanus remained faithful to the ptolemies and withdrew to his estates at 'Arak el-Amir. From there he tried to direct the partisans of the ptolemies who were campaigning against the Arabs.

Seleucid Domination

Joseph's move was a prudent one, for Antiochus III, a Seleucid, allied himself with Philip V of Macedon and was victorious over Ptolemy V in a battle at the sources of the Jordan (200 B.C.). Judea changed masters once more; from now on it would be dependent on the province of Coele-Syria–Phoenicia.

The Seleucid party in Jerusalem had greatly helped Antiochus by overpowering the ptolemaic garrison there. As a result the arrival of the Seleucid troops and their elephants turned into a triumph (according to Josephus and an inscription at Bethshan). As a sign of his gratitude to the Jews for their welcome Antiochus ordered that all the Jews deported during the preceding wars might return home. Slaves were freed, taxes were reduced, and Antiochus even promised help in the rebuilding of the temple. Cultic personnel, the council of elders and the doctors of the law were all exempted from taxes (Dan 11:1–20). Above all, all Jews might henceforth observe their own national laws (AJ 12:138–46).

Antiochus continued his policy of peace, marrying his daughter Cleopatra to his old enemy Ptolemy V. Then he set out to help his ally, Philip V of Macedon, who was at war with the Romans. This move put an end to the period of prosperity: Antiochus was defeated at Magnesia (190 B.C.) and had to sign the humiliating peace treaty of Apamea. He had to pay such extensive war indemnities that he saw no way of honoring his debt except to loot the temples, which were the only banks of the time. While looting the temple of Bel at Susa he was assassinated.

His successor, Seleucus IV (187–175 B.C.), had the same financial problems; he therefore decided to loot the temple at Jerusalem. He ordered his treasurer, Heliodorus, to take possession of the temple treasure, but the high priest, Onias III, put up such strong resistance that Heliodorus had to withdraw (2 Mac 3:1–40). In this connection we learn that Hyrcanus of the Tobiad family had deposited funds in the temple.

This Hyrcanus, like his predecessors, was governor of Ammanitis. According to Josephus he was also a great builder. Near his residence at 'Arak el-Amir tombs have been discovered, one of which has the name Tobias inscribed on it in Aramaic letters. His house was called the "plaster house" because its walls were covered with white plaster on the outside and blue and red plaster on the inside. But the most interesting discovery is a fine building of white stone that is decorated with large statues of lions. This building, 132 feet by 60 feet, is located at the center of an esplanade that is in turn surrounded by water. A portico leads into an edifice that is divided into three rooms, which some archeologists regard as being the three parts of a temple.[2] If this be the case, then in about 175 B.C. Hyrcanus built a schismatic temple in the Transjordan.

Let us return to Heliodorus and his failure in dealing with Onias III. Since Heliodorus had all the power behind him, 2 Maccabees attributes his failure to miraculous resistance. It seems, however, that what people in Jerusalem regarded as a miracle was in fact to be explained by a political crisis at the Seleucid court; because of this, Heliodorus left Jerusalem in order to assassinate Seleucus. Nonetheless it was Antiochus IV, a brother of Seleucus, who seized power with the help of the Romans. Antiochus in his turn wanted to put his hands on the temple treasury. He therefore accused Onias of misappropriation of funds and especially of sympathy for the ptolemies, and deposed him. Onias was replaced by his brother, who took the Greek name Jason. He favored Hellenization and, as a faithful friend of the Seleucids, promised them a significant increase in the taxes due to the crown. Antiochus IV, however, wanted even more; he therefore abrogated the tax exemptions granted by Antiochus III as well as all the special privileges of the Jews.

1 and 2 Maccabees

These books tell the story of the period that begins here. The first book, after an introduction on Alexander and his successors, relates events beginning with the accession of Antiochus IV and in particular the rebellion of Mattathias and his sons down to the death of Simon in 135 B.C. It is a trustworthy document.

The second book covers the period from 180 to 161 B.C. It begins with two letters addressed to the Jewish community of Egypt, urging it to adopt a common calendar so that the feast of Booths and the feast of the purification of the temple may be celebrated at the same time in Jerusalem and in Egypt.

This second book is a resume of a work in five volumes by Jason of Cyrene that was written about 160 B.C. and is now lost. In its present form this second book was undoubtedly written in Pharisaic circles; the author adds to the resume of Jason the two introductory letters already mentioned. This addition suggests that the author did his work around 124 B.C. The Book of Esther is here mentioned for the first time (2 Mac 15:26).

In addition to describing events, the book reveals to us a new form of piety. The martyrs who died for their faith have forced the Jews of the day to rethink the problem of death. The idea of resurrection is indeed already present in Isaiah, but now Jews have a real hope that those who gave their lives for God will rise from the dead. The just who have died can intercede with God for the living, and conversely it is possible for the living to pray for the dead and thus make expiation for their sins.

There is a Third Book of Maccabees, but it is much later in origin and wholly legendary in content; it may, however, allude to one historical event: a massacre of Egyptian Jews which, according to Josephus, took place under Ptolemy VII (145–116 B.C.).

The Fourth Book of Maccabees is later still, and in part repeats 2 Maccabees or Jason. It attempts a philosophical treatise showing the accord between Greek philosophy and the law of God, between Jewish morality and Greek morality.

Daniel[3]

The Book of Daniel does not aim at being historical in the same way as 1 and 2 Maccabees. The book was in fact supposedly written four centuries earlier at Babylon. However, it confuses Nebuchadnezzar and Nabonidus to some extent, whereas it shows great familiarity with the Greek period and Antiochus Epiphanes, although it does not know of the tyrant's

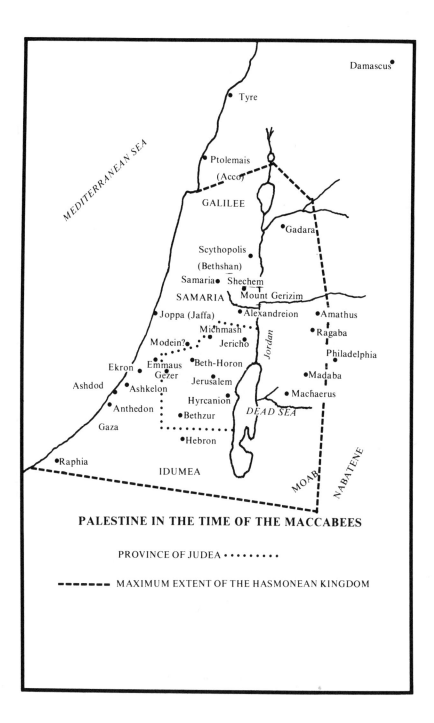

PALESTINE IN THE TIME OF THE MACCABEES

PROVINCE OF JUDEA ·········

- - - - - - - MAXIMUM EXTENT OF THE HASMONEAN KINGDOM

175

End of the Persian Period	Were the Nabateans Arabian tribes that had gradually infiltrated the territories of Moab and Edom? Or were they indigenous to the Negeb and specifically to the triangle marked by Nessana, Elusa and Oboda?
312	Campaign of Antigonus, a successor of Alexander, against the Nabateans.
259	Contacts between Ptolemy II and the Nabateans to arrange for supplies of grain.
200	Nabatean inscription at Eluse with the name of King Aretas in it.
168	Jason, the high priest, is imprisoned at Petra by Aretas the Nabatean.
163	Judas Maccabeus wages war on the Nabateans, then negotiates with them.
130	John Hyrcanus takes Medeba from the Nabateans.
100	Alexander Janneus takes the Nabatean port of Gaza from Aretas II.
93	Alexander Janneus is defeated at Garada by Obodas I.
85	Obodas I defeats Antiochus XII and is divinized.
84–62	Reign of Aretas III, who controls Damascus until 72, when the city passes into the power of Tigranes of Armenia.
66	Aretas III welcomes Hyrcanus II and besieges Jerusalem.
62	Scaurus, legate for Syria, undertakes to capture Petra; Aretas III, with the help of Antipater, pays tribute to have the siege lifted.
62–58	Reign of Obodas II?
58–30	Reign of Malichus I.
55	Malichus I is conquered by Babinius, proconsul of Syria.
47	Malichus I aids Caesar in Egypt.
34	Mark Antony despoils Nabatea to the advantage of Cleopatra.
30–9	Reign of Obodas III. Due to Roman action the Nabateans lose a part of the caravan trade which is henceforth diverted to Egypt.
9 BC–40 AD	Long reign of Aretas IV. He gives his daughter in marriage to Herod Antipas, then defeats the latter when this daughter is cast off.
40–70	Reign of Malichus II, who develops horse breeding as well as extensive irrigation-based farming in the Negeb. He provides Vespasian with 600 cavalrymen and bowmen in the war against the Jews.
70–106	Reign of Rabel II, Bozrah, south of Damascus, becomes the second capital.
106	The governor of Syria takes control of Nabatea, which becomes the province of Arabia with Bozrah as its capital.
130	Hadrian visits Petra.

death. We need hardly hesitate, therefore, to date the composition of it a little before 164 B.C.

The purpose of the Book of Daniel is to instill courage into the despairing faithful. God is not in fact failing to keep his promises, as contemporary events might suggest; on the contrary, he will fulfill all his promises at the end of time. All the empires will collapse, and the Son of Man will rise up (Dan 7:13). Daniel proclaims a new birth; the land will be cleansed once and for all, and God will establish his everlasting reign.

Just as in the time of Daniel Nebuchadnezzar was forced to humble himself before God, so today the just will emerge victorious. Antiochus too will have to bow down, because salvation is coming from God. As for the just who have already suffered persecution, they will experience the resurrection (Dan 12:1–3).

The Book of Daniel marks the beginning of the period of apocalyptic literature, which appears under the names of Ezra, Adam, Moses, Elijah, Baruch and Enoch. In the eyes of the Jews the period of prophecy was now ended, and it was no longer possible to write effectively without using one of the great names of the past. The writings focus no longer on preaching that bids Jews grasp the meaning of history, but on prediction. The writer speaks of future events, of what is coming, as if he were already seeing it. In his visions, which are always very elaborate and highly allegorical, he tells his readers what is going to happen, with precise details as to time and place. The apocalypses claim to describe the whole of history from its beginnings to the coming of God's reign.

Judith

The rise of Antiochus Epiphanes, who wanted all peoples to adore him as a god, also gave rise to another type of literature which is in the genre of the midrash. This literature includes the Book of Esther, which, as we saw earlier, is difficult to date, and the Book of Judith.

Here again, the story is supposed to take place in the time of Nebuchadnezzar. The heroine uses the same weapon as Esther—the appeal to sensuality—in order to seduce and then kill Holophernes, the general who is threatening to exterminate her people. But Judith resembles not so much Esther as Jael, the woman who in the time of the judges slew Sisera, another general (Jgs 4–5). Judith is the prototype of the national heroine who does not hesitate to sacrifice herself in order to save her people. Her patriotism is rewarded, for God comes to her aid in her undertaking.

The Book of Judith, like the Book of Esther, breathes national and religious hatred. This time the rabbis did not include it in the canon drawn up at Jamnia.

Chapter 12
The Maccabean Resistance
and the New Hasmonean Kingdom

Attempt To Hellenize Jerusalem

For the first time a high priest did not inherit his office but bought it, and this from a foreigner. The new high priest had but a single purpose: to make the Greek vision of the world prevail. His first actions pointed clearly in this direction: Jerusalem was to have its gymnasium, its training place for youth (2 Mac 4:9). It would thus resemble Samaria, which had become a military colony, Rabbah of the Ammonites which had become Philadelphia, and Acco which had become Ptolemais. Jerusalem was now to be known as Antiochia.

In addition to its political side, which was so hateful to the Jews, Hellenization was felt to be an abandonment of the Lord and a victory for syncretism. The Second Book of Maccabees expresses its horror of the idea in the statement: They "disguised their circumcision" (1 Mac 1:15). And in fact a number of priests abandoned their office, while Jews offered sacrifices to Hercules (2 Mac 4:18–20).

In 172 B.C. Antiochus IV deposed Jason and appointed Menelaus as high priest. Menelaus, too, was pro-Seleucid and was supported by the Tobiad family; his brother was administrator of the temple. He promised Antiochus that he could increase taxes on the Jews and the temple. As a result, he acted toward the Jews with "the hot temper of a cruel tyrant and the rage of a savage wild beast" (2 Mac 4:25). He was nonetheless unable to furnish the sums he had promised, and therefore he looted the temple treasury. His misdeed became known in Antioch where the deposed high priest Onias III was living. The latter, with the support of the Jewish community, accused Menelaus publicly. Menelaus' answer was to have Onias assassinated at Daphne (2 Mac 4:33–34). Menelaus then betook himself to Syria, leaving his brother Lysimachus in charge and with the financial responsibility. The people this time revolted against the religious scandal, the exactions of every kind, and the families who manipulated the priesthood without any concern for the people. Lysimachus was killed, but Menelaus returned with the backing of Antiochus.

Antiochus IV had new plans: he wanted to conquer Egypt. He launched a campaign in 170 B.C., with Alexandria as his destination, but the Romans sent him an ultimatum from the senate. Rome was a new and disturbing power on the scene; Antiochus abandoned Egypt. Meanwhile a report of his death had reached Jerusalem and became the occasion for Jason the high priest to incite a revolt among the people.

When Antiochus learned of this he was enraged, returned to Palestine, and ordered the "pacification" of Jerusalem. His general took the city by surprise on a sabbath day, sacked it and partially destroyed it (Dan 11:29; 1 Mac 1:29; 2 Mac 5). Many Jews were slaughtered; others fled, among them Jason who was for a time a prisoner of Aretas I, the Nabatean, before escaping to Egypt (2 Mac 5:8).

Antiochus now had a citadel, the Acra, built in the heart of Jerusalem. He stationed a Greek garrison there and peopled the city with Jews who had been won over to Hellenism. Jerusalem too now became a military colony.

Antiochus' plans went further. He wanted all the peoples of his kingdom to form but a single people; all special national customs therefore had to be eliminated. Consequently he withdrew from the Jews all the rights which Antiochus III had granted them; moreover he put an end to sacrifices in the temple and forbade sabbath practices. Circumcision and the holy books were outlawed; anyone disobeying the law was sentenced to death.

At the same time, he had temples of the Greek gods built in Jerusalem and, on December 6, 176 B.C., he had a pagan altar set up in place of the altar of incense; the temple of Jerusalem was rededicated to Olympian Zeus (2 Mac 6:2; Dan 11:31). This was "the abomination that makes desolate." In his own mind, Antiochus IV was identifying Zeus and Yahweh, just as a current of thought which believed in the possible unity of all religions had attempted to do. But while Antiochus was imposing ideas that might be interpreted as ecumenical, he did so through repression and slaughter. His action would leave its mark for good on orthodox Jews, whose attitude to pagans would always be one of distrust. A syncretist or perhaps simply liberal outlook would be discredited for a long time to come.

The Samaritan temple on Mount Gerizim suffered the same kind of fate, for it was rededicated to Zeus, Friend of Strangers. All Palestinians, Jews and non-Jews alike, were ordered to offer sacrifice to the Greek gods.

The Jewish Revolt

The Hellenizing Jewish party doubtless submitted to all this without too much difficulty. The population at large was afraid and accepted the new order of things, but this obedience hardly disguised a desire to revolt.

Mattathias and his five sons, members of a priestly family that had taken refuge at Modein, refused to offer sacrifice to the pagan gods and instead slew the officer in charge of carrying out the king's orders. This action marked the beginning of the resistance (1 Mac 2).

Mattathias and his family fled into the hills of Judah where it was difficult to follow him. A group of partisans was soon formed: devout men known as the Hasidim, who were so desirous of observing the law that many of them let themselves be killed rather than defend themselves on the sabbath (1 Mac 2:29–39). Mattathias had to abrogate the law of the sabbath in cases of military action.

Mattathias died in 166 B.C., but he left to his son Judas an army of about six thousand men. Because of his mighty deeds Judas became known as "the hammer" or, in Hebrew, Maccabee. He was in fact a great leader of men and military chieftain. He crushed a Seleucid detachment commanded by Apollonius, the man who had "pacified" Jerusalem. Then he defeated the governor of Syria at Beth-horon in northwestern Judea and pursued him as far as the coast.

Antiochus IV then sent a large army under the command of three generals: Ptolemy, Nicanor and Gorgias. By a clever maneuver Judas was again victorious, this time near Emmaus (1 Mac 3–4). Lysias, a lieutenant from the royal house, tried to take Judas from the south but he too was defeated.

According to 2 Maccabees 11 Lysias was anxious for peace and therefore appealed to Antiochus to reintroduce Jewish customs and allow Jews to offer sacrifice in the temple. Antiochus gave a favorable answer. But the version in 1 Maccabees is quite different: the authorization came from Antiochus V.

Judas' striking successes were certainly due to his ability but they also owed something to external factors. Antiochus IV was at this time involved in a war against the Parthians. This people, originally from the area of the Caspian Sea, had begun a slow expansion southward in the third century B.C.; they reached the apogee of their power under Mithridates I (171–138 B.C.).

In addition, Antiochus' hands were tied by the Romans. According to 2 Maccabees 11:34–38 the Romans sent a letter to the Jewish insurgents; this was the first link between Rome and Judea.

Judas was able to have a solemn purification of the temple in December 164 B.C. and then to rededicate it with a feast of dedication or Hanukkah. This was also the "feast of lights" and was associated with the eight-branched lampstand. The Jewish calendar was now complete: Passover was celebrated in the spring, Pentecost in the summer, Booths in the fall, and Hanukkah in the winter. The Jews of Egypt were urged to join in celebrating this new feast (1 Mac 4:36–59; 2 Mac 10:5–8).

But Judas' successes could easily be reversed. Jerusalem was still a Seleucid military colony, controlled by the Acra. In order to continue the resistance, Judas had to fortify the temple hill and Beth-zur,[1] south of Jerusalem. He then intervened in Galilee, while his brother entered Gilead, but the two men did not succeed in getting control of these regions, and so they urged the Jews of the area to join them in Jerusalem. They also moved southward, taking Hebron and destroying the pagan altars of Ashdod.

Judas now believed himself able to assault the Acra. But Lysias, accompanied by Antiochus V, set out against him, and Judas was defeated near Bethlehem. His citadel, Beth-zur, had to surrender because the garrison was starving. Jerusalem was besieged and was saved only by a palace revolt at the Seleucid court.

Antiochus V then signed a peace which was advantageous to the Jews (it is doubtless reflected in 1 Mac 6). Menelaus, who no longer exercised the office of high priest, was executed at Antiochus' order, being held responsible for all the evils in Judea. The high priest who succeeded him was once again a member of the house of Zadok, named Alcimus.

With peace restored the Jewish community became divided. The Hasmoneans, so called after an ancestor of Mattathias, were not satisfied with the degree of religious freedom they had regained. They wanted to continue the struggle and win national independence.

The Hasidim, or devout, however, were satisfied with the restoration of worship and the enthronement of Alcimus from the family of Zadok as high priest. The Hellenizing party, which was recruited essentially from the priestly aristocracy, wanted only peace and good relations with the Seleucids.

Although Alcimus belonged to the house of Zadok, he owed his authority to the Seleucids. Was this why the son of the high priest Onias III fled to Egypt? With the help of the ptolemies he there established a Jewish military colony known as the "Land of Onias," and built a schismatic Jewish temple at Leontopolis, near Memphis. In this way a Jewish mini-state was established within the Egyptian state.

This Jewish military colony rendered faithful service first to the Egyptian sovereigns, then to the Romans, until the latter decided to do away with the colony and its temple in 73 A.D.

Alcimus did not long enjoy the favor of his fellow Jews. Although close to the Hasidim at one time, he was above all else a pro-Seleucid and he turned against the Jews once they had gathered their forces. With the help of the Seleucid authorities he executed more than sixty of them.

At this Judas immediately launched a campaign, for the new Seleucid ruler, Demetrius I (162–150 B.C.), had sent Nicanor's army against him. Nicanor was defeated at Adasa near Jerusalem in 161 B.C. On this occasion Judas is said to have been aided by the Romans, who told the Seleucid king to leave Judea in peace. It was good policy for the Romans to have a wedge inserted between Egypt and Mesopotamia. Demetrius nonetheless continued his campaign, was victorious, and killed Judas (1 Mac 9). Alcimus was able to exercise his authority again with the help of Bacchides, a Seleucid general.

As a result of the wars the country was starving. Alcimus thought he could restore peace by putting pro-Hellenes in positions of influence everywhere.

Jonathan Maccabeus (161–142 B.C.)

After the death of Judas those Jews who could meet together took his brother Jonathan as their leader; he in turn sought help from the Nabateans. These were nomads who at the end of the fourth century B.C. began to build a kingdom on the eastern plateau that controls the area from the lower Arabah to the Red Sea. Their prosperity was based on control of the caravan routes between Arabia Felix, Yemen, the Persian Gulf and Greece (so Diodorus Siculus). Taking advantage of Seleucid weakness they also attempted to occupy the Transjordan.

Jonathan's brother, who had gone on a scouting expedition, was killed in an ambush. Because he lacked support, Jonathan himself had to take refuge beyond the Jordan. Bacchides now took possession of Judea and fortified the towns of Judah, especially Beth-zur and Gezer (which had become Gazara to the Greeks). Alcimus for his part removed the wall which prevented pagans from entering the temple. He died in 159 B.C., and we do not know who succeeded him.

Bacchides left Palestine but was recalled as early as 158 B.C. by the Hellenistic party. The latter were once again threatened by Jonathan's nationalists. Bacchides decided to encircle the Maccabean fortress of Bethbasi, but by a skillful maneuver Jonathan thwarted the siege. Probably because of new difficulties at the Seleucid court Bacchides was forced to sign a peace treaty with Jonathan. Jonathan then entered upon the functions of the judges of old, exercising them at Michmash, north of Jerusalem.

For five years things were quiet in Judea. The Seleucid court was the scene of rivalries between Demetrius I and Alexander Balas, the alleged son of Antiochus IV and the claimant supported by Rome. Each of the claimants sought Jonathan's help and he skillfully maneuvered between the two. Thus he obtained the freedom of all the Jewish prisoners housed in the Acra, and then received permission to fortify Jerusalem. When the time was ripe, he chose to support Alexander Balas.

In gratitude, Alexander offered him the position of high priest. On the feast of Booths in 152 B.C. Jonathan entered upon his priestly role. At the same time he donned the viceroy's insignia bestowed on him by Alexander. Thus by the favor of the Seleucids he exercised both priestly and governmental functions.

Who preceded Jonathan as high priest? Perhaps it was the man who would later be called the "Teacher of Righteousness" and who abandoned the Jerusalem temple and its cult in order to establish the Essene community whose members awaited the coming of a purified priesthood. If this hypothesis is valid, then in the eyes of these intransigent observers of the law Jonathan was the "wicked priest" referred to in the documents of the Essene community.[2]

In 150 B.C. Alexander won a definitive victory over Demetrius I. To celebrate it, he invited Jonathan to attend his marriage with Cleopatra, daughter of Ptolemy VI, the ruler of Egypt. Alexander also made Jonathan his associate in the government of the state. The latter, now at the peak of success, supported Alexander against the claims of Demetrius II, son of Demetrius I.

Jonathan was now free to attack the Hellenized cities on the coast. He therefore burned Ashdod, which had been renamed Azotus, and destroyed the temple of Dagon there; he attacked Ashkelon (Ascalon to the Greeks) and was offered the city of Ekron by Alexander Balas. Jonathan was for all practical purposes master of the coastal plain (1 Mac 10).

In 145 B.C. Alexander was defeated by Demetrius II. Jonathan took advantage of the crisis to besiege the citadel Acra. When summoned by Demetrius II, he managed to gain his favor and was confirmed in all of his offices. He even won control of three southern districts of Samaria whose inhabitants observed the cult of Jerusalem. There was, however, no question of allowing him to control the Acra.

Demetrius II in his turn had difficulties with Trypho, a former general of Alexander Balas. Jonathan supported Demetrius after being promised that the Acra would be handed over to him. Demetrius then repulsed Trypho, but reneged on his promise.

At this, Jonathan and his brother Simon switched camps. Trypho assigned them the task of subjugating the southern part of the province of Coele-Syria, from Tyre to the Egyptian frontier. The brothers carried out the task vigorously and took advantage of it to fortify the towns of Judah, especially Jerusalem (1 Mac 11–12). Simon even recaptured the fortress of Beth-zur, while Jonathan looked for support to Rome and Sparta. Disturbed by this growing power, Trypho managed to make Jonathan a prisoner by treachery and then moved against Judea.

Simon Maccabeus (141–135 B.C.)

Simon replaced his brother, repulsed Trypho, and captured Jaffa. Trypho then had Jonathan executed. Simon raised a monument at Modein in honor of his brother (1 Mac 13:25–30).

Simon now found himself siding with DemVeVus II who transferred to him the offices his brother had held: high priest, commander of the army, and ethnarch. Simon began to date his official documents according to the year of his government and to coin money; in these ways he was declaring the independence of the Jewish state.

He consolidated his power by seizing Gezer and especially by winning the return of the Acra in 141 B.C. For additional security he maintained alliances with Rome and Sparta.

According to 1 Maccabees 14 Simon was an excellent governor. The people made his offices as high priest and leader of the people hereditary, and the Hasmonean dynasty was founded. There was, however, one restrictive clause: "until a trustworthy prophet should arise" (1 Mac 14:41). The fact was that Simon was not the Hasidim's man, even though he persecuted the Hellenists and went so far as to ask Roman help in tracking down turncoat Jews. In this context we learn how extensive the diaspora was: there were Jews in Mesopotamia, at Pergamum, in Cappadocia, among the Parthians, along the Black Sea, on Cyprus, Rhodes and Crete, and at Cyrene (1 Mac 15).

Demetrius II was captured by the Parthians in 140. Antiochus VII, who succeeded him, continued the alliance with Simon against Trypho. But as soon as he was relieved of pressure in that area, he demanded that Simon restore Gezer, Jaffa and the Acra. Simon refused and was obliged to defeat the Seleucid army near Modein (1 Mac 16).

A short time later, Simon himself fell victim to a palace intrigue instigated by his son-in-law Ptolemy, governor of Jericho. During a banquet at Dok Simon was assassinated along with two of his sons, Mattathias and Judas (135 B.C.). What the Seleucids had been unable to accomplish by arms they obtained through treachery.

John Hyrcanus (135–104 B.C.)

Only one of Simon's sons, John, escaped the massacre. Once acknowledged as his father's successor, he forced Ptolemy to remain holed up in his fortress at Dok and then to take refuge at Philadelphia. But the greatest danger for John came from the Seleucids, as Antiochus VII began the conquest of Judea and laid siege to Jerusalem.

Once again, the internal affairs of the Seleucid state kept Antiochus from finishing the work he started, but he was nonetheless able to impose a burdensome peace on John. He required a large indemnity for Jaffa-Joppa and demanded that the Jews hand over their weapons to him, along with hostages whom he would turn into mercenaries. John Hyrcanus was once more a vassal of the Seleucids.

Meanwhile the war against the Parthians continued, and Antiochus was killed in 128 B.C.; from then on Antioch would be simply a theater for internal rivalries and would not again intervene in Judea. Was it in these circumstances that John Hyrcanus received a Parthian embassy (Jerusalem Talmud, *Berakoth* 7, 2)? If so, he was shifting alliances, since the Parthians were the most dangerous enemies of Rome.

Now that his hands were free, John Hyrcanus set about increasing his territory with the aid of a mercenary army. He took the town of Madaba from the Nabateans (map, p. 175). Then he entered Idumea (formerly Edom), whose inhabitants he forced to accept circumcision. In the north he captured Shechem and in 128 B.C. destroyed the temple on Mount Gerizim. During a second campaign his sons besieged Samaria; from this time on there would be a Samaritan diaspora in Egypt, Syria, Greece and Rome. Hyrcanus' troops advanced as far as Scythopolis, which they likewise seized in 107 B.C.; then they laid waste to the entire country south of Carmel (Josephus, *The Jewish War* 1:64–66).

The Maccabees were now no longer the champions of a religious cause; they were first and foremost nationalists. John Hyrcanus relied no longer on the people but on mercenaries. Jewish territory had been considerably expanded, trade was flourishing, and Jewish coins resembled those of the Seleucids: they were stamped with horns of plenty.

The Hasidim did not accept the combination of priestly and governmental functions in one person. This was doubtless the period that saw the rise of the Pharisaic party, which called for the purification of the role of high priest and demanded that John Hyrcanus give up this function. Since he did not go along with them, the Pharisees turned more and more to a messianic hope: they would wait for a descendant of David to come. They were strict interpreters of the law, but the law for them included laws transmitted orally. They aimed at a cleansing of the whole of life and a separation from the unclean and from people of evil life.

John Hyrcanus was therefore obliged to turn away from the Hasidim, the traditional supporters of his family, and to the Sadducees, the descendants of Zadok, who formed a religious aristocracy. Many of them had been converted to a degree of Hellenism; they were also sensitive to their immediate interests. In religious matters they opposed the Pharisees by denying any value at all to oral tradition and to such theological novelties as the immortality of the soul and the idea of rewards and punishments in an after-life (*The Jewish War* 2:162–66).[3]

John Hyrcanus died in 104 B.C. after thirty-one years of excellent government (in Josephus' opinion). Not only had he been ethnarch and high priest, but according to tradition he had also been a prophet and had even heard the voice of God when he ministered before him in the temple.

Aristobulus I (104–103 B.C.)

Aristobulus succeeded his father by imprisoning his brothers and mother, the latter of whom he allowed to starve to death. Only his brother Antigonus found favor with him; nonetheless he had him assassinated.

His short reign was marked by a campaign against the Itureans in the north; he forced them to accept circumcision, less for religious reasons than as a sign of submission to his authority.

Aristobulus would have been the first Hasmonean to wear a royal crown; in fact, however, this privilege was left for his successor (according to Strabo).

Alexander Janneus (103–76 B.C.)

When Aristobulus died (103 B.C.) his brothers were released. Alexander, surnamed Janneus (a diminutive of Jonathan), married Aristobulus' widow, Salome Alexandra, and took the title of king.

Alexander was an ambitious man and tried to conquer Ptolemais (Acco), which belonged to Ptolemy, king of Cyprus. He was conquered, however, and would have lost part of his own territory if Cleopatra of Egypt, the mother of Ptolemy, had not come to his rescue. Among the Egyptian troops there was a Jewish contingent under the command of the sons of Onias IV, the founder of the Jewish military colony called "Land of Onias."

Alexander then launched a campaign to the east, where he wanted to take possession of the territory beyond the Jordan. He first captured Gadara, the capital city of Perea, and the fortress Amathus (map, p. 175). He then turned back and attacked the coast, where he occupied the towns of Anthedon, Raphia and Gaza, which was the Nabatean port through which the main part of Nabatean trade passed.

His successes in the Transjordan were doubtless shaky ones, and he had to undertake a new campaign in Moab and Gilead and recapture Amathus. In all of these battles, including those on the coast, he was resisting the claims of the Nabatean king, Obodas I, who wanted control of the trade routes of the Transjordan and access to the Mediterranean.

It was Obodas who emerged victorious from the confrontation. He took possession of the Sinai area, the Negeb, and the northern part of the Arabian peninsula and advanced up the Transjordan as far as Damascus, where the Nabateans reigned from 84 to 72 B.C.

Alexander Janneus, after being thus conquered again, had difficulty in regaining Jerusalem, where he was met by internal opposition. During the feast of Booths the Pharisees roused the people against him. When he officiated as high priest, he was pelted with lemons. In revenge he used his mercenaries to execute six thousand Jews (Josephus, *AJ* 13:273).

The Pharisees would not admit defeat and appealed to the Seleucid king, Demetrius III, who defeated Alexander near Shechem (88 B.C.). It was then that, fearing a new Seleucid occupation, the Jews shifted allegiance to Alexander and repulsed Demetrius. In anger Alexander had eight hundred of his adversaries crucified and, to torture them further, he had their wives and children butchered before their eyes.

Eight thousand Jews were said to have then fled to Syria. Among them were doubtless the Essenes who composed one of their most important books in that country: the *Damascus Document*. This work explains in detail how the Community of the New Covenant interpreted the law.

Even though persecuted, the Pharisees came to play an increasingly important role in the country's life. They became the scribes who wrote down the explanations of the written and oral law. The men whom the Talmud calls the "fathers" were in part contemporary with Alexander Janneus. They regarded themselves as the successors of Ezra; their commentaries dealt at once with theological matters, customary law, and the defense of the poor. By using all the tools of Greek dialectic to refine their commentaries, they became the "doctors of the law."

After having eliminated internal opposition at the cost of fifty thousand lives, Alexander was able to resume his expansionist policies. He finally captured Golan in the east and took possession of the Transjordan as far as Moab. In the north he held Galilee as far as Tabor and in the west the Philistine plain; in the south, Idumea became subject to him.

In order to hold on to his conquests, he built fortresses: the Alexandreion facing Gilead, Machaerus facing the Nabateans, and a line of forts from Antipatris to Joppa in order to protect the port and its rich hinterland. Excavations at Joppa have uncovered a treasury of bronze coins with his name on them,[4] presses for wine and oil, and grain mills.

Alexander Janneus died in a final battle during the siege of Regaba near Gerasa (map, p. 193).

Salome Alexandra (76–67 B.C.)

On the death of Alexander Janneus, his wife, who had already been the widow of Aristobulus I, succeeded him as head of state. Being unable to exercise the functions of high priest she entrusted these to her son, Hyrcanus II.

According to Josephus, Alexander left her a last testament in which he advised her to make a change in his domestic alliances and to rely on the Pharisees, who had the support of the people. This she did.

Alexandra changed the composition of the council of elders in order to make room in it for the Pharisees. The latter were not in the majority, but their counsels prevailed nonetheless. The Sadducees gradually lost all real power.

The origins of this council of elders are rather obscure. The Scriptures speak of elders in connection with the investiture of the kings. We also find elders accompanying Ezra, but did they already form a council? According to Josephus, the establishment of a senate of the people was the work of Antiochus III (223–187 B.C.). According to 1 Maccabees Jonathan

(161–142 B.C.) was the first to make use of such a council. According to 2 Mac 1:10 the institution goes back rather to his predecessor, Judas Maccabeus.

There is reason to think that during this Hellenistic period there was a desire to imitate the organization of the Greek cities. If the high priest was leader of the nation, then he should have a council to assist him. Membership in this council was initially reserved to the priestly families; under Alexandra it became the place for the Pharisees to exercise authority. Their jurisprudence now became law. At the beginning of the Herodian period the council would become known as the Sanhedrin.

Once in power, the Pharisees sought to revenge themselves on the adherents of Alexander Janneus. The result was new tensions, as the Sadducees shifted their allegiance to Aristobulus, the second son of Salome Alexandra. With their support he made preparations to succeed his mother by occupying the fortresses which Alexander Janneus had built: Machaerus, the Alexandreion and the Hyrcanion (see map, p. 175).

Salome Alexandra also had to cope with an external threat. Tigranes, king of Armenia, seized possession of the Seleucid empire in 83 B.C.; continuing his advance, he drove the Nabateans from Damascus in 72 B.C. and threatened to invade the Hasmonean kingdom. The Hasmoneans managed to change his mind with money in 70 B.C.

Despite these difficulties the reign of Salome was celebrated by the Pharisees as a time of peace and domestic prosperity. "In her time, rain was so abundant that the grains of wheat grew as big as kidneys."

Aristobulus II

At the death of Salome (67 B.C.) Aristobulus immediately seized power and forced his brother Hyrcanus II to surrender all his functions in exchange for his life.

Hyrcanus II, however, received support from Antipater, governor of Idumea, who shared important interests with the Nabateans. On the advice of Antipater, Hyrcanus II signed a treaty with Aretas III, king of the Nabateans, who gave him asylum at Petra. Aretas III then joined forces with Antipater to reconquer Hyrcanus' kingdom for him in exchange for a promise to restore to Aretas the cities which Alexander Janneus had conquered east of the Jordan.

Aristobulus was defeated (65 B.C.) but he managed to make his way back to Jerusalem. There he secured himself in the temple, where Hyrcanus II, supported by Aretas and the Pharisee party, laid siege to him.

This division of the kingdom between brothers at odds provided just

A rock-cut temple at Petra, the capital of the Nabatean Kingdom.

the excuse the Romans wanted for intervening. Pompey ordered King Aretas to withdraw; then he summoned to his presence the two parties, Aristobulus and Hyrcanus, together with a delegation of Hasidim who wanted the restoration of the theocracy in an unmodified form. Pompey listened, promised to come to Jerusalem, and bade the parties keep the peace while waiting for him. Devout circles thought the messianic age was at hand (Ps 8).

Aristobulus, however, thought himself to be in strong enough a position that he could rebel. Pompey immediately marched on Jerusalem, where Hyrcanus opened the gates to him. Aristobulus was arrested and his followers took refuge in the temple. Pompey captured the temple in the autumn of 63 B.C. and entered it, making his way even into the holy of holies. This time the devout were scandalized. "In his pride the sinner knocked down solid walls with a battering ram. . . . Pagan foreigners mounted your altar and trod upon it in their arrogance; they profaned the gifts offered to God. . . . Lord, remove the heavy hand you have laid upon Jerusalem through the coming of the pagans" (*Psalms of Solomon, 2*).

Aristobulus and his two sons, Alexander and Antigonus, left for Rome where they were to be part of a triumph celebrated by Pompey. Hyrcanus was reinstated as high priest, but only over the territories of Judea, Perea and Galilee. The coastal cities once again became autonomous, while the cities of the Transjordan, from Damascus to Philadelphia, were joined in a federation, the Decapolis. Samaria and Scythopolis came under the control of the governor of Syria. The Hasmonean kingdom was now a thing of the past, and the devout, whose views are reflected in the *Psalms of Solomon*, were overjoyed; they now expected the coming of the Messiah descended from David (*Ps. Solom.* 17, 37–40).

Josephus gives a good summary of the situation:

> Pompey made Jerusalem dependent on the Romans, and took from the Jews the cities they had conquered in Coele-Syria, and placed them under the authority of the Roman governor. He thus forced the recently ambitious Jews back within their own borders. . . . Jerusalem owed all these woes to the dissension between Hyrcanus and Aristobulus. For practical purposes we lost our freedom and became subjects of the Romans. . . . Moreover, in a short time the Romans took from us more than a thousand talents, and the kingship, which had been hereditary in the family of the high priests, now became the prerogative of men from the people (*Antiquities of the Jews* 14, 74–79).

Chapter 13
The Roman Occupation

The first sign of Rome's presence in Asia[1] was the victory it won over the Seleucid sovereign, Antiochus III, at Magnesia in 190 B.C. From that point on the Romans were always on the scene. Thus Antiochus IV was halted on his expedition against Egypt by a warning from Rome. Again, the Romans are said to have intervened on the side of the Jewish insurgents in 164 B.C.; this would have been the first encounter of the two peoples. The Second Book of Maccabees mentions treaties made with the Romans by Judas, Jonathan and Simon.

Up to that time the Romans wanted it known that they had an interest in Asia, but there was no direct intervention until Pompey was put in charge of the war against Mithridates, king of Pontus, who was trying to defend the Greek cities against the Roman ascendancy. Mithridates was smart enough to ally himself with Tigranes of Armenia and with the Parthians.

After being appointed in 66 B.C. Pompey first defeated Mithridates. Then, profiting by intrigues within the Seleucid kingdom, he took possession of this realm and created the province of Syria in 64 B.C. It was at this time that the divided Jews appealed to him to arbitrate their differences. In pursuit of the same policy Pompey entered Jerusalem in 63 B.C. and was thus positioned at the gates of Egypt which, though it had long been in a weakened state, was still the last free kingdom.

After his conquest of Jerusalem, Pompey attached Judea to the province of Syria. He did however leave Hyrcanus II with authority over Judea, Perea and Galilee. This was now a divided territory, since Galilee and Judea were separated by Samaria, while part of southern Judea was de-

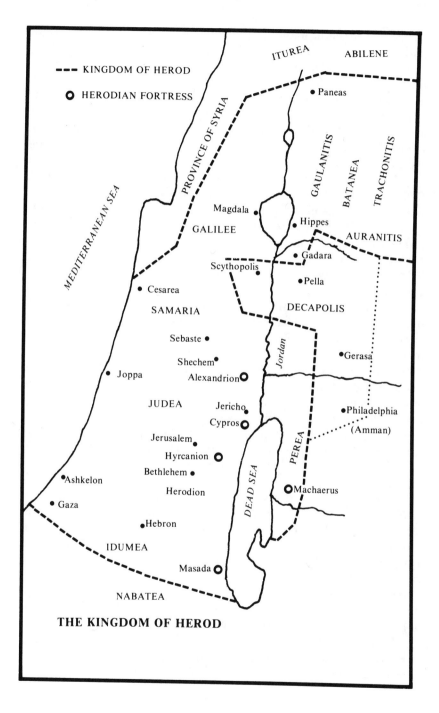

THE KINGDOM OF HEROD

- - - KINGDOM OF HEROD

O HERODIAN FORTRESS

ITUREA
ABILENE
• Paneas

PROVINCE OF SYRIA

MEDITERRANEAN SEA

GAULANITIS
BATANEA
TRACHONITIS

Magdala •
GALILEE
• Hippes
AURANITIS
• Gadara
Scythopolis •
• Pella
DECAPOLIS

• Cesarea
SAMARIA

Sebaste •
Shechem •
Alexandrion O

• Gerasa
Jordan

• Joppa

JUDEA
Jericho •
Cypros O
• Philadelphia
(Amman)

Jerusalem •
Hyrcanion O
Bethlehem •
Herodion

DEAD SEA
PEREA
O Machaerus

• Ashkelon
• Gaza
• Hebron

IDUMEA

Masada O

NABATEA

193

tached and added to Idumea. The coastal cities, Samaria and the Transjordan were all joined to the province of Syria.

Pompey took home with him some prisoners of war who would form the first sizable nucleus of the Jewish community at Rome.[2] Scholars think, however, that Jews had already been there since the second century B.C. Many of Pompey's prisoners must quickly have won their freedom, since as early as 59 B.C. Cicero speaks of the importance of the Jewish community. It was perhaps at this period that the catacomb of Monteverde, the oldest Jewish catacomb in Rome, was constructed.

On his return to Rome Pompey expected to celebrate a triumph in 62 B.C., but a distrustful senate made him wait a year. He therefore joined Caesar and Crassus in taking power; this was the first triumvirate. Pompey remained at Rome and entrusted the government of Syria to Scaurus, who had two legions at his disposal. Scaurus tried without success to take possession of Petra; at a cost of three hundred talents which were guaranteed by Antipater, King Aretas III persuaded Scaurus to cease pillaging the country.

Alexander, a son of Aristobulus II and one of those who were to walk in Pompey's triumph, managed to escape and reach Palestine where he attempted to raise a revolt against Hyrcanus. He was quickly defeated, but he and his followers succeeded in taking refuge in the fortresses built by Alexander Janneus: the Alexandreion, the Hyrcanion, and Machaerus. He doubtless hoped to revitalize Jewish nationalism and gather the people around him in the name of the Maccabees, but all he could do was put up a heroic resistance to the Roman troops led by Gabinius and Mark Antony.

The enterprise ended in the complete destruction of the three fortresses and, for Hyrcanus, in a loss of power. He was allowed to retain only an authority in matters spiritual, while Judea was divided into five districts in 57 B.C.

Hardly had this first uprising failed when Aristobulus II and his son Antigonus likewise managed to flee Rome. They undoubtedly had help in their escape, but we do not know who aided them or for what reason. Like Alexander, they looked forward to a war of resistance to the Romans, an epic struggle like that of the Maccabees, but instead they were defeated and sent back to Rome in 54 B.C.

On this occasion Antipater the Idumean proved himself an active supporter of the Romans. As a reward he received the title of administrator of Judea, the first step in a very successful career.

Licinius Crassus, the new governor of Syria, exploited the province of Judea and went so far as to plunder the temple (54 B.C.). Resentment against the Romans began to grow, and Licinius' successor, Cassius Longinus, had to deal with a Jewish revolt, which he crushed at Tarichaeae (Magdala)[3] on the western shore of Lake Tiberias.

All these were but convulsive moments of rebellion against the Romans. The truly important events were taking place at Rome, where Pompey gradually moved away from Caesar to become leader of the senatorial party. Caesar crossed the Rubicon in 49 B.C., and Pompey was not in a position to oppose him. Pompey therefore crossed to Greece where he was defeated at Pharsala in 48 B.C.; from there he fled to Egypt, where he was assassinated. Caesar had won, but he now had to reconquer the east, which belonged to the Pompeian party. Caesar thought he could rely on Aristobulus II and his son to reconquer Judea, but before they could take any steps they were assassinated by the Pompeians.

Caesar had to go to Egypt, and there he soon found himself in difficulties. It was then that Hyrcanus II and his Idumean adviser, Antipater, seized the opportunity to offer help to Caesar. Thanks to them, Caesar was able to link forces with Mithridates of Pergamum and defeat the followers of Pompey at Pelusium in the eastern delta.

Hyrcanus and Antipater, though former Pompeians, had won Caesar's favor. Hyrcanus was confirmed in his office as high priest and in addition was appointed ethnarch. The territory of Judea was augmented by the addition of Joppa.

The most important result, however, of the help given by Hyrcanus and, at his request, by the Jews of Alexandria, was that Caesar declared the Jewish religion to be a *religio licita* or legally recognized form of cult, and this throughout the empire. Jews were everywhere authorized to celebrate their own rites without hindrance; they might organize in communities, build synagogues, collect taxes from their co-religionists, and even establish their own markets for kosher food.[4]

Nor was Antipater forgotten: he became procurator of Judea and a Roman citizen. Henceforth the real power was in his hands. He was already a very rich man due to the extensive trade passing through the coastal ports; he was an ally of the Nabateans and had an excellent army of his own. Now he was able in addition to find places for his sons: Phasael became administrator of Jerusalem, Herod administrator of Galilee, and Joseph prefect of Masada.

Herod soon won himself a reputation by crushing the "brigands" led by a certain Hezekiah. Without seeking advice from the Sanhedrin he had Hezekiah executed along with a number of his followers. These "brigands" were undoubtedly rebels; their movement would continue under Hezekiah's son, Judas the Galilean.

People in Jerusalem were not so much gladdened by Herod's success as disturbed by his power. The Sanhedrin summoned him to appear before them, but Herod, supported by Sextus Caesar, governor of Syria, flouted them and even laid siege to Jerusalem without eliciting any intervention from Antipater. Not only was Herod acquitted of any fault; he even received a new Roman title: administrator of Coele-Syria and Samaria.

In Syria the Pompeians rose once more; Sextus Caesar was assassinated and was replaced by Cassius Longinus who had administered Syria in 53–51 B.C. and had crushed a Jewish rebellion. He set about plundering the province with the connivance of Antipater, whose one desire was to please the Romans. He also effected the destruction of Lydda and Emmaus and deported their inhabitants. Some Jews hatched a plot against him, and even Hyrcanus, disturbed by events, joined the plotters; Antipater was poisoned (43 B.C.). But the danger did not pass, since the sons of Antipater still held power and had the support of the Romans.

Antigonus, son of Aristobulus II, tried once more to win back his kingdom. He entered into an alliance with Marion of Tyre, who captured some towns of Galilee. Sensing the danger, Hyrcanus allied himself with Herod and offered his niece Mariamme in marriage (37 B.C.). Herod thus became a member of the Hasmonean family. He easily repulsed Antigonus once again, and the latter took refuge in Chalcis.

The Pompeians rose yet again, but this time they were definitively routed by Marc Antony and Octavian in the battle of Philippi in 42 B.C. Antony, who had conquered Alexander, son of Aristobulus II, was now master of the east. Various Jewish groups sent delegations to him; the Pharisees in particular sought to win the restoration of the theocracy and a scrupulous respect for Jewish law; they would pay for their courage with their lives.

Marc Antony listened instead to Hyrcanus, confirmed him in his offices of high priest and ethnarch, and offered him the freedom of Jews who had been condemned to slavery by Cassius. Hyrcanus interceded for Herod and Phasael, who received the title of tetrarchs. Then Marc Antony once again burdened Judea with highly unpopular taxes.

Marc Antony then went off to Cleopatra at Alexandria. The Parthians took advantage of his departure to invade Syria and reach Jerusalem. Antigonus once again offered them his services, for this was at last a real opportunity to regain his throne. He entered Jerusalem in 40 B.C. and imprisoned Phasael, who committed suicide. He also seized his uncle, Hyrcanus, and had his ears cut off so that he could not in the future claim to be high priest. Hyrcanus was then deported to Babylon.

Under the protection of the Parthians Antigonus reigned for three years (40–37 B.C.) and functioned as high priest under his Jewish name,

ANTIPATER (an Idumean)
supports Hyrcanus II and the Romans

PHASAEL
administrator of Jerusalem
d. 40 B.C.

JOSEPH
administrator of Masada
d. 38 B.C.

HEROD THE GREAT
tetrarch of Galilee
king 37–4 A.D.

SALOME
d. 10 A.D.

m. MARIAMME, niece of Hyrcanus

m. MARIAMME II

m. MALTHAKE

m. CLEOPATRA

ALEXANDER
d. 5 B.C.

ARISTOBULUS
d. 7 B.C.

HEROD PHILIP
m. HERODIAS

HEROD ANTIPAS
divorces daughter of Aretas
IV; m. Herodias; influenced
by John Bapt.; deported to
Lyons

ARCHELAUS
deported to
Vienne

HEROD PHILIP
tetrarch of Iturea
and Trachonitis

TIGRANES IV
of Armenia

HEROD OF CHALCIS

HEROD AGRIPPA I
favorite of Caligula, then
of Claudius; becomes king
of Herod's territory. D.
14 A.D.

HEROD AGRIPPA II
tetrarch of Philip's
tetrarchy, then of parts of
Galilee and Perea; takes
part with Vespasian and
Titus in war against Jews

BERNICE
with her brother
Agrippa receives
Paul

DRUSILLA
m. Felix,
procurator

Mattathias. The coins struck during his reign showed the menorah or seven-branched candelabrum.

Herod and the Reconquest of Judea (40 B.C.–4 A.D.)

Herod and his entire family managed to flee across the Dead Sea to the fortress of Masada. He put his family in the care of his brother Joseph and set about rebuilding alliances. He received no help from the Nabateans, but he believed that he could successfully plead his cause with the Romans. Was not Antigonus an enemy of Rome, whereas he, Herod, had aided Marc Antony?

Herod was a good diplomat and won the support of Marc Antony and Octavian, so much so that he was appointed king of Judea by the senate in 40 B.C.—a king without a kingdom. He then traveled to Syria where Ventidius, the Roman governor, was settling the business of the Parthians. Herod himself captured Joppa and freed his family, but he was unable to win any further advantage.

He set out once again on an embassy to Marc Antony who was besieging Samosata on the Euphrates in order to put an end to the Parthian problem. As a result of the embassy, a Roman army under the command of Sosius was joined to Herod's forces. This was a stroke of luck, since just at this time Antigonus conquered Herod's troops and killed his brother Joseph.

With the help of Sosius, Herod recaptured Galilee and then his entire territory except for Jerusalem. The faithful adherents of the Hasmonean dynasty had dug in there and continued to resist for five months. When the Romans finally captured the city, they embarked on such extensive pillaging that Herod had to give them presents in order to win their departure. They took Antigonus with them; at Herod's request he was executed in 37 B.C.

Once Antigonus was dead, Herod became king. At Jerusalem he undermined all opposition by executing forty-five men of prominence, probably Sadducees, friends of Antigonus and members of the Sanhedrin. Herod was now king of Judea, but not by the will of the Jews, who hated him, nor by his faith, for he was an Idumean, nor by reason of his family background (though Nicholas of Damascus claims he was descended from Jews left in Babylon), for only his wife Mariamme was a Hasmonean. No, Herod was the king appointed by the Romans because he was a friend of Marc Antony.

Paradoxically it was from this last-named fact that Herod's first difficulty arose. Antony had become the friend of Queen Cleopatra of Egypt, who demanded that she be given back all the ancient possessions of the ptolemies, especially the coastal towns as far as Joppa. She also demanded the splendid oasis of Jericho. Then, as she had supported the attempted rebellion of Alexander, son of Aristobulus, so now she requested the high priesthood for his son, Aristobulus III.

Herod regarded a Hasmonean high priest as too great a risk. True enough, he had brought Hyrcanus II back from Babylon, but the latter's mutilation prevented him from laying claim to the high priesthood, and Herod had given this to Hananel, another priest who had returned from Babylon. Herod cleverly pretended to accept the appointment of Aristobulus III, but then had him murdered at Jericho in 35 B.C.; he then turned around and won Antony's forgiveness.

A much greater danger now threatened him. His protector, Marc Antony, fell out with Octavian, and Herod sided with Antony. When the latter was defeated in the battle of Actium in 31 B.C., Herod immediately set out on an embassy to the new master and assured him of his fidelity. At the same time, however, he protected his rear by having the Hasmonean prince Hyrcanus II assassinated (30 B.C.). This remarkable diplomat succeeded in winning over Octavian and received back from him the territories which Cleopatra had taken, as well as Samaria, Gaza, Anthedon, Gadara, Hippus[5] and Strato's Tower.

Six years later Octavian stripped the Nabatean king, Obodas II, of Trachonitis and Batanea and offered these to Herod. Unlike Herod, Obodas had not managed to make Octavian forget his support of Marc Antony.

Herod was now safe as far as the Romans were concerned, but he remained obsessed with the Hasmoneans, seeing in every descendant of the Maccabees the possible author of a plot against him. He was not satisfied therefore to have gotten rid of Aristobulus III, who had claimed the high priesthood; he also had the elderly Hyrcanus assassinated, then Alexandra, the scheming mother of Aristobulus. He even went so far as to have his wife, Mariamme, executed in 29 B.C. despite the fact that he loved her.

These were only the most prominent among those who disappeared during his reign, for in fact Herod was obliged to be constantly putting down revolts among the people, who refused to accept him as their legitimate king. His violence and brutality, though terrifying, won for the kingdom a period of peace that allowed for expansion and building.

Herod was henceforth able to take advantage of his position. He was a king allied with Rome and dependent no longer on the governor of Syria but only on Octavian and the senate. From now on he even appointed the high priest in Jerusalem.

In the furtherance of his own commitments and interests Herod helped eliminate bands of looters everywhere in his part of the world. By way of recompense, once Octavian became emperor, he offered Herod Auranitis. As a result Herod's kingdom now had the same boundaries as in the time of David, except for the south which was in the possession of the Nabateans and for the Decapolis in the west. (The Decapolis was a federation of cities which were to keep an eye on both Jews and Arabs. They were centers for the spread of Hellenistic culture. The number and names of the cities included changed frequently,[6] but here are some worth recalling: Scythopolis was located west of the Jordan and was in contact with Samaria; of the other cities, all in the Transjordan, Philadelphia was the southernmost; Hippus controlled the Golan area; Damascus was the most important center in the north.)

On the domestic scene Herod had to expect opposition from the Pharisees whom he had harshly repressed. He was unable to obtain an oath of allegiance from the Essenes, but he did not therefore persecute them, since he did not think them to be much of a political threat. He felt however that he had to rally to his side the people at large who were sympathetic to the outlook of the Pharisees. He attempted to win them over by magnificent edifices erected to honor the tomb of the patriarchs at Hebron and by building an enclosure around the sanctuary at Mamre.[7]

His greatest undertaking, however, was the rebuilding of the temple in Jerusalem, the esplanade of which he extended considerably. He undertook this colossal work in 20 B.C.; it would be completed only in 62 A.D. The construction gave permanent work to ten thousand men; included were a thousand priests who would see to it that the temple was not defiled. The desired quality of the work, its architectural style, and the required stonecutting made it necessary to bring in Roman technicians. Herod dealt with them as Solomon had dealt of old with the Phoenicians.

The outermost area was the court of the Gentiles, which was surrounded by a battlemented wall, and each of its four sides had an elaborate gateway in the Hellenistic style.

At the center of the court was the temple proper. First came the court of the women, each corner of which was occupied by rooms (storage space for wood and oil; residences for lepers and for nazirites). Then came the court of Israel, which was reserved for men and was separated by a fence from the court of the priests. In the latter court were the great altar and also the slaughterhouses. Around this area there were once again gateways and rooms, one of these being doubtless for the Sanhedrin.

The new temple imitated the temple of Solomon: a vestibule with a magnificent entryway; the building proper with a table for the loaves of offering, the great seven-branched candlelabrum, and the altar of incense (all these would one day be depicted on the triumphal arch of Titus). Fi-

The temple rebuilt by Herod.

nally, separated by a double veil, came the holy of holies into which the high priest alone entered once a year on the great Day of Atonement.

Even though covered with gold, this temple was the work of Herod alone and did not meet the demands of Jewish piety. Herod had blundered by erecting statues and had even attached a great golden eagle to the most beautiful of the gates, while on another gate he had inscribed the name of Marcus Agrippa as a compliment to the great man. All these were offensive to Jewish piety. Some young Pharisees tried to destroy the eagle with axes; Herod had them burned. At Qumran meanwhile the Essenes were writing, in the Temple Scroll, their ideal of a holy city closed to the wicked and in which the very birds might not fly over the temple. Their dream was very much in the line of Ezekiel.

Herod sought to combine a degree of fidelity to the Jewish faith with an openness to Greco-Roman culture. In Jerusalem he had a palace built which he dedicated to Antony; its tower, which became famous as the Antonia, looked down on the esplanade of the temple. It seems, however, that he never resided in this palace, which was reserved for the high priest Hananel. In accordance with his guiding policy he had a hippodrome built in Jerusalem and, outside the walls (in order not to offend Jewish piety), a theater and an amphitheater. In 27 B.C. he organized the first Olympic games at Jerusalem.

In Samaria, where he could act with less constraint, he built a real Roman city with a theater, forum, hippodrome and, towering over all else, a temple in which the cult of Augustus could be celebrated. Alongside the temple of Augustus there was a temple of the local goddess, Kore. The new city was named Sebaste and its residents were six thousand Gallic, Thracian and German settlers.

After receiving from Augustus the ancient Phoenician port of Strato's Tower, Herod turned it into an entirely new city named Caesarea. He built a completely artificial harbor by having lakes dug out of the sandy shore and protected by two seawalls of from 750 to 1,800 feet in length; the whole was overlooked by the temple of Augustus. Excavations have also brought the theater to light. When this was reconstructed one of the pieces that had to be fitted in was a stone with the name of Pontius Pilate on it. But the finest remains are doubtless those of the aqueduct that brought water from the slopes of Carmel to Caesarea.

Herod's court was a thoroughly Hellenized affair, with an extensive domestic staff made up of slaves and freedmen. Herod spoke Greek, knew Greek literature, and surrounded himself with men of letters, the most famous of whom was his biographer Nicholas of Damascus. Josephus would make use of Nicholas' work. The young princes had Greek tutors; Alexander and Aristobulus, the sons of Mariamme, a Hasmonean, were sent to Rome to complete their education but probably also to get them out of the way. When they returned they were accused of plotting against Herod, found guilty and strangled in 7 B.C. Antipater, who had denounced them and called for their death, fell under suspicion in turn and was executed in 5 B.C.

Perhaps it was the continual fear of plots against him that inspired Herod's most extraordinary architectural masterpieces, his fortresses

An ornamental movable basin for ritual washing in the temple.

(map, p. 193). Masada, which towered 1,500 feet above the Dead Sea, was doubtless the most impressive of them. It was a hill-top building in the shape of a ship and surrounded by a double wall with thirty-eight towers. At the northern end, suspended over the abyss, was a three-level palace and remarkable baths. In the storehouses archeologists have found all sorts of things, including winejars from Italy and a synagogue. The water problem was solved here as it was in all the other fortresses. Two dammed up watercourses made it possible in the periods of torrential rain to fill cisterns that were plastered to make them leakproof. There was storage room for 32,000 cubic meters of water in the rock of Masada.

Opposite lay the magnificent fortress of Machaerus, a full-blown city planned to withstand a siege. According to Josephus, its palace was a magnificent one; baths have been discovered there.

Six miles north of Jerusalem Herod built a memorial to himself: the Herodion. This was at once a fortress, a luxurious summer residence, and Herod's tomb. The whole covered two hectares and drew all eyes with its stepped towers that were inspired by the lighthouse at Alexandria. These towers gave a view of a splendid panorama and also served for surveillance. The whole structure was magnificent; the stucco decorations imitated marble, while the colonnades were modeled after those of palaces in Alexandria.

Also to be mentioned are the building of the citadel of Cypros near Jericho and the restorations of the Hyrcanion and the Alexandreion, where Mariamme and her sons were buried.

Herod's talents as a builder also found an outlet in his splendid residence at Jericho. He built there a complex intended for his amusement during the winter season. Excavators have discovered not only numerous frescoes but the layout of extraordinary gardens with ponds for boat rides and aquatic contests.

Palestine had never seen so many monuments built in so short a time. Herod's talent accounted for all this luxury, which he financed by extorting money from the people but also by a judicious use of alliances. As a faithful ally of Rome he could guarantee peace on the frontiers and a consequent agricultural prosperity. And yet this touchy tyrant was willing to strip his palaces during the crisis of 25 B.C. in order to buy needed wheat from Egypt. This meant that the population, which is estimated at a million or a million and a half at that time, could be fed and seed provided for the following year.

This agricultural prosperity, the trade in palm and balsam products from Jericho and En-gedi,[8] and the opening of the port of Caesarea also contributed to Herod's renown. He was a man who knew how to profit by his Idumean and Nabatean origins.

But Herod also wanted his name and his people to be respected throughout the Roman empire. And so, like every Hellenistic prince, he gave endowments to cities with Jewish colonies: Tripoli, Damascus, Tyre, Byblos, Pergamum, Rhodes, Antioch, Athens. The Jewish diaspora, estimated at several million through the empire, was of some consequence; its role in trade and culture was already beginning to be noticed. Horace was an amused and somewhat irritated witness to the part played by Jews at the imperial court.

Like Antiochus III, Herod called upon the Jewish family of the Zamarises to establish a military colony in the Golan area. This gave Jewish pilgrims a supporting way-station between Babylon and Jerusalem (*AJ* 17, 25–27).

In Eastern eyes Herod's reign was a magnificent one, and he was called Herod the Great. In Israel, however, he was spurned: because of his origins as an Idumean and non-Jew; because he wanted to Hellenize the country; because of his bloodthirsty nature. He reigned in isolation, massacring his own family and stripping the Sanhedrin of all political authority.

Being deprived of political power, the rabbis turned their energies to a deeper knowledge of Scripture. It was from this period that the authority of Hillel and Shammai dated; these two interpreters of the law established the rules governing Jewish exegesis and their schools became famous. Paul, for example, came from Tarsus in order to study under Hillel's grandson, Gamaliel the Elder, the man who persuaded the Sanhedrin to release Peter when the latter had been arrested for preaching the resurrection. Christian legend embroidered the incident and turned Gamaliel into a convert.

The Herodian Succession

Herod died in 4 B.C., leaving behind him considerable accomplishments and an unforgettable reputation for both cruelty and greatness.[9] It was doubtless this reputation that influenced Matthew the evangelist to tell the story of the massacre of the innocents which occurred after the birth of Jesus under Herod the Great.

Herod had changed his will so often that when he died it gave rise to disputes. Who was to inherit the kingdom: Achelaus or Antipas? It was up to Augustus to approve the will.

The two brothers who were the claimants therefore betook themselves to Rome, along with their aunt Salome. But the Jews hostile to the Herodians also sent a delegation to oppose them and to ask for an end to

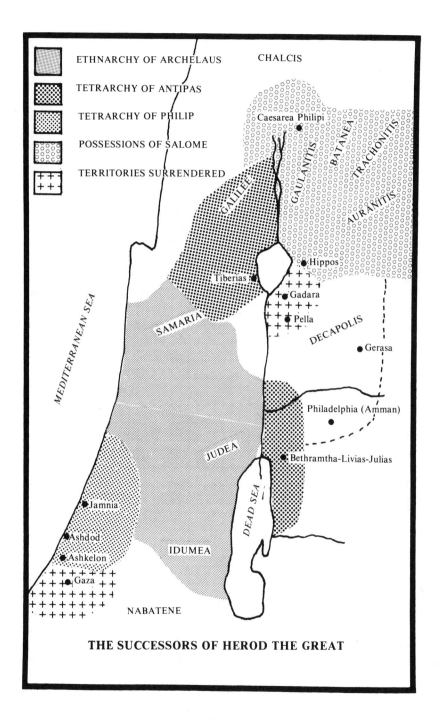

ETHNARCHY OF ARCHELAUS

TETRARCHY OF ANTIPAS

TETRARCHY OF PHILIP

POSSESSIONS OF SALOME

TERRITORIES SURRENDERED

CHALCIS

Caesarea Philipi

GALILEE

GAULANITIS

BATANEA

TRACHONITIS

AURANITIS

Hippos

Tiberias

Gadara

Pella

SAMARIA

DECAPOLIS

Gerasa

MEDITERRANEAN SEA

Philadelphia (Amman)

JUDEA

Bethramtha-Livias-Julias

DEAD SEA

Jamnia

Ashdod

Ashkelon

IDUMEA

Gaza

NABATENE

THE SUCCESSORS OF HEROD THE GREAT

their rule and exactions. These Jews asked to be governed by the high priest and the Sanhedrin.

Augustus sent a procurator, Sabinus, as his emissary to Palestine, but this man behaved so badly there that he caused the Jews to revolt. The latter had three leaders who took royal titles in keeping messianic expectations in Israel. The three were a shepherd named Athronges, a slave named Simon, and, above all, Judas of Galilee, a son of the Hezekiah who had rebelled under Herod the Great. Since each of the three claimed the kingship against the others, Varus, the legate of Syria, had no trouble in overcoming them. But this did not put an end to the matter, since Judas the Galilean and his descendants would continue to harass the province.

As a result of these disturbances and despite the efforts of Nicholas of Damascus, Augustus decided not to give the kingship to Archelaus. Instead he appointed him ethnarch of Judea, Idumea and Samaria; but Archelaus had to surrender Gaza, which was attached to the province of Syria. Herod Antipas was appointed tetrarch of Galilee and Perea, two territories which were separated from each other by the Decapolis, to which the cities of Hippus and Gadara were added. Herod Philip was appointed tetrarch of Gaulanitis, Batanea, Trachonitis and Auranitis. Salome received the cities of Ashdod and Jamnia and a palace at Ashkelon. At her death her possessions reverted to the imperial family.

Archelaus

Archelaus was not to reign very long. His despotism and his habit of appointing and deposing high priests caused the Jews once more to petition Augustus. Augustus exiled Archelaus to Vienne in Gaul in 6 A.D. There is only one positive achievement to record: Pliny was to remember him for the groves of palm trees he planted north of Jericho.

Herod Antipas

Herod Antipas retained his tetrarchy until 39 A.D. His reign is known to us chiefly for his scandalous marriage to Herodias, wife of his half-brother, Herod Philip (Mk 6:17–29).

Herodias was the granddaughter of Mariamme the Hasmonean and she longed for a glorious destiny. She persuaded Antipas to divorce his first wife, who was the daughter of Aretas IV, the Nabatean king. The latter was then at the height of his economic and cultural power; he therefore immediately declared war on Antipas and would have utterly destroyed him were it not for the intervention of Vitellius, governor of Syria. According to Josephus, the Jews attributed the defeat of Antipas to the latter's execution of John the Baptist.[10]

Herodias wanted to be queen. She was a bad counselor, however, when she urged Antipas to claim this title from Caligula, who had just become emperor (in 37). Not only did Antipas not receive a crown, but he was deported to Lyons in 39. These unfortunate dealings with his wife should not cause his accomplishments to be forgotten, for like his father he was a great builder. For example, he constructed the fortress of Bethramtha in Perea, to which he gave the successive names of Julias and Livias in honor of his patrons.

But his greatest work was his new capital on the shore of the Sea of Gennesaret; he gave it the name of Tiberias in honor of Emperor Tiberius (14–37 A.D.). Thanks to its hot springs the city boasted baths; yet despite the luxury of the place Antipas had trouble populating his new capital. Tiberias was bult near a cemetery, which was unclean ground for Jews. Antipas was forced therefore to import paupers, freedmen, and exiles. In order to attract devout Jews, he built a synagogue, but at the same time he offended these same Jews by adorning his palace with statues. According to the Gospels, he was interested in Jesus, because he was afraid that Jesus might be John the Baptist returned to life (Mk 6:14–16); he demanded a miracle of him (Lk 9:9), and, at the end, took part in his trial (Lk 23:6f).

Herod Philip

According to Josephus, Herod Philip was a good ruler. Like his brother, he built a capital for himself on the site of the ancient Paneas and, as a sign of respect for Rome, named it Caesarea (Caesarea Philippi: the Caesarea of Philip). It is there that Peter is said to have confessed Jesus as Messiah (Mk 8:37).

Herod Philip died childless in 34 A.D.

Judea as a Roman Province (6–41)

After Archelaus was deposed in 6 A.D., Judea became dependent on Quirinius, the legate governing Syria. According to the Gospel of Luke, Quirinius was in charge of the census of Palestine. Josephus confirms this statement, but not the date, since according to him the census was conducted in 6 A.D. The legate had three legions at his disposal, and to these could be added auxiliary forces, making thirty-six thousand men in all. But the legate of Syria was not governor of Palestine, and he intervened there only in case of need.

Judea was an independent province and was ruled by a procurator or prefect. The latter had at his disposal auxiliary forces which he recruited exclusively from the non-Jewish sectors of the population. He did this in order to obey the edict of Caesar that Jews be exempt from military service. Since, however, the troops consisted exclusively of pagans, they often acted with great brutality toward the Jews. These forces were stationed at Caesarea and Sebaste, two cities in which there were few Jews. When they entered Jerusalem they were to enter without their colors, out of respect for the Jews.

The governor too resided in Caesarea, which thus became the administrative capital at the expense of Jerusalem, the city of worship and the city of the Jews. He lived in the palace which Herod had built; it became the pretorium. When he visited Jerusalem, he doubtless lived in Herod's palace there, for it occupied a strategic position overlooking the entire city. This palace was in all likelihood the pretorium where the trial of Jesus was held.

The task of the governor of Judea was an especially difficult one, since he had to maintain peace among four segments of the population whose aspirations were often in conflict: the Jews, the Samaritans, the newly converted Idumeans, and the residents of Hellenized cities like Caesarea and Sebaste where the population was predominantly pagan.

To these difficulties there was added the collection of numerous and heavy taxes. There was, to begin with, the poll tax as established by the census. This affected all men between fourteen and sixty-five and all women between twelve and sixty-five. The Jews regarded any census as the work of Satan (1 Chr 21). A second tax was levied on the harvests. In addition to these two main taxes, there were many others, in particular those levied on the circulation of goods; these were collected by the "tax collectors," whom the Jews hated as being collaborators and robbers. Finally, the governor could also impose forced labor on the occasion of major building operations.

Coponius was the first procurator. The levying of a poll tax spurred a revolt under the leadership of Judas the Galilean.[11] He claimed that such a tax turned the Jews into slaves, and he urged them to claim their freedom. The Romans, however, regarded this nationalist hero as a mere brigand; Josephus sees in him the philosopher of a new sect which he does not name but which greatly resembles the Zealots. Judas was killed and the rebellion crushed. In order to calm the people, the high priest who had been deposed in 4 B.C. was restored at this time or else by Quirinius in 6 A.D. Josephus contradicts himself on this point.

When Augustus died in 14 A.D., the senate entrusted the empire to his adopted son, Tiberius. The latter appointed Valerius Gratus as procurator of Palestine (15–26). Valerius Gratus was in constant conflict with the high priests. He deposed three of them in succession before appointing Caiaphas, who would hold the office from 18 to 37. This procurator also began a practice that would be continued until the reign of Claudius: he kept the vestments of the high priest in fortress Antonia. These vestments possessed a great deal of symbolic value for the Jews. When a high priest was invested with his office, he received its insignia which consisted of eight pieces of clothing, each of them having the function of expiating certain sins of the people. When the high priest donned these garments, he was aureoled with holiness and played a supremely important role in the Jewish world.

Valerius Gratus was succeed in 26 by Pilate.[12] The first event reported in which he was involved was his attempt to bring into Jerusalem by stealth certain images of Caesar which, in the Jewish mind, suggested emperor worship. The Jews pleaded with Pilate to remove them from Jerusalem. In response, he threatened to massacre them; whereupon "as if a command had been given, the Jews prostrated themselves like one man and bared their necks, shouting that they were ready to surrender their lives rather than violate the law. Astonished at such an intransigent faith, Pilate ordered that the standards be immediately removed from Jerusalem" (*The Jewish War* 2, 169–74).

The Jews were involved in a second revolt when Pilate took possession of the temple treasury and emptied it in order to build an aqueduct that would bring water to Jerusalem. In this matter he certainly had the support of Caiaphas, but the people rebelled. Was not the temple treasury sacred? Had not Caesar and Augustus guaranteed that taxes would be collected for the temple in all Jewish communities? This time Pilate ordered the soldiers who had mingled with the crowd to strike. There were many victims, as the soldiers perhaps exceeded their orders.

The period when Caiaphas was high priest and Pilate was governor was the time when Jesus did his preaching, but we have no proof of it except for the Gospels. Josephus does speak of Jesus as active in the time of Pilate, but the passage has long been recognized as a Christian interpolation.

There can be no doubt that Jesus was a native of Nazareth; the story of his birth at Bethlehem, on the other hand, has strong theological overtones. It is quite likely that his influence over the crowds made him appear a dangerous agitator in the eyes of the authorities. Had he not chased the tradesmen from the temple? Were there not some Zealots among his disciples: Simon the Zealot and perhaps Judas Iscariot, that is, Judas the Dagger-man? Did Jesus regard himself as the Messiah, as so many other men of his day regarded themselves? Did the crowd not want to make him a king both at the time of the multiplication of the loaves (Jn 6) and on the day of palms?

In any case, at the time of Passover, which was an especially favorable moment for popular uprisings, the authorities thought it necessary to silence him. The priestly circles saw their interests and authority threatened; the Pharisees were afraid the people would turn away from their teachings and follow a supposed descendant of David, a Messiah. The Romans for their part feared a possible revolt more than anything else.

It is true that according to the Gospels Pilate tried to protect Jesus, in whom he found no guilt. Such an attitude on his part seems highly implausible; according to all the other sources on this man, he seems never to have been one bothered by his conscience. It is likely on the other hand that a missionary concern led Christian apologetes to excuse Pilate who was a Roman. The apocryphal literature even has a story of his being converted (see Tertullian, *Apologeticum* 21, 24).

According to the Gospels Jesus was crucified after a slapdash trial. The Sanhedrin condemned him without calling witnesses and then asked the Roman governor to carry out the execution. According to the Babylonian Talmud, on the other hand, the trial lasted for forty days; a herald publicly announced the reasons for the condemnation: sorcery and the intention of leading the people astray; despite repeated requests no witness came forward to declare Jesus innocent.

A final testimony, of a later date, comes from Tacitus. When a defamatory rumor went abroad that Rome had been burnt on orders (in 63 A.D.), "Nero tried to dispel it by supplying guilty parties and subjecting to refined torments a group of people whose abominations had already made them detested and whom the crowd called 'Christians.' Their name was derived from one Christ whom the procurator Pontius Pilate had condemned to execution in the reign of Tiberius" (Tacitus, *Annals* 15, 44).

Let me call attention here to the following indirect testimony from a Syrian Stoic at the end of the first century or the beginning of the second, who compares the deaths of Socrates, Pythagoras and Jesus:

> What did the Athenians gain by putting Socrates to death, when the price they paid for their crime was famine and plague? And what did the Samians gain by burning Pythagoras? In a short time their land was covered with sand. What did it profit the Jews to execute their wise king, when from this time on their kingdom was taken from them? God justly avenged these three wise men: the Athenians died of hunger; the Samians were over-

whelmed by the sea; the Jews, once united, were hounded from their land, to live as an utterly scattered people. Socrates did not die, because Plato came after him; Pythagoras did not die, because of the statue of Hera; nor did the wise king die, because of the precepts he set down.

This text is quite remarkable because it confirms that the death of Jesus was caused by the Jews and regards the destruction of 70 A.D. as a punishment from God; it is a first manifestation of the polemics that would rage between Jews and Christians.

The steps taken against the Jews did not originate in Pilate's personal feelings. Tacitus, Suetonius and Dio Cassius tell of an expulsion of Jews from Rome under Tiberius in 19. This incident introduces a new theme:

The Testimony of Flavius Josephus

(The Antiquities of the Jews 18, 64)

"During this same period there lived a certain Jesus, who was a wise man, if indeed he is to be called simply a man, seeing that his works were so astounding. He used to teach those whose delight it was to be instructed in the truth, and not only many Jews but many pagans as well became his followers; he was the Christ, the Anointed One. When some leaders of our nation accused him to Pilate, the latter had him executed.

"Those who loved him during his lifetime did not abandon him after his death. He appeared to them and rose from the dead on the third day, as the holy prophets had foretold, while adding that he would perform many other miracles. It is from him that the Christians, who are still around today, derive their name."

We do not know what the original text of Josephus at this point was. We can only infer the way in which it was revised by comparing the text in its present form with the same passage as reported by Agapius, an Arab historian of the tenth century and himself a Christian:

"During that period there lived a wise man named Jesus. His manner of life was good and he was renowned for his virtue. Many moreover, from among both the Jews and other peoples, became his disciples. Pilate condemned him to crucifixion and death. But those who had become his disciples did not abandon his teaching. They claimed that he had appeared to them three days after his crucifixion and that he was now alive; he was therefore perhaps the Messiah of whom the prophets told such astonishing stories."

Since Agapius was a Christian, he had no reason for removing from his source statements which expressed the very object of his faith. Yet he does not report the words: "if indeed he is to be called simply a man." His source, then, does not assert the messiahship of Jesus nor his resurrection, but simply reports what the disciples of Jesus believed. Finally, responsibility for the condemnation of Jesus rests entirely with Pilate and is not shared by the Jews.

the emperor was supposedly rendered uneasy by the success of Jewish proselytism in Roman circles and even in high society (Fulvia, an aristocrat, is named).

Later on, in 28–31, Sejanus vented his fury against the Jews, demanding not only a local expulsion but even a persecution throughout the empire (Philo, *The Embassy to Gaius*, 159–61).

Given this context, it is understandable that Pilate thought to honor Tiberius by dedicating gilded shields to him in the governor's palace. But it meant provoking the Jews by manifestations of the imperial cult. Eminent Jews asked Pilate to reverse himself. When he refused, they sent an embassy to Tiberius, who disavowed his governor.

One last incident was to cause Pilate's downfall. The Samaritans were restless. They gathered in large numbers at their sacred place, Mount Gerizim; they too were doubtless looking for a restoration of a messianic kind. They hoped to discover the sacred vessels which Moses had buried—the ark, the jar of manna, the rod of Aaron—so that a purified authentic worship could be celebrated on Gerizim. The person who discovered these sacred emblems would restore the cult and would also win recognition from the pagans.

Pilate acted quickly and massacred a large number of Samaritans. In his eyes, the issue here as in the case of Jesus was one of nipping messianic rebellions in the bud. He had all of the leaders executed.

The Samaritans lodged a complaint with Vitellius, the legate for Syria; the latter, who was very careful to respect the peculiar ways of each ethnic group, sent Pilate to Rome to explain himself. When he arrived, Tiberius was dead; we know nothing of what happened to Pilate. (According to Tertullian, *Apologeticum* 5,2, some *Acts of Pilate* were sent to Tiberius who was convinced by them of the divinity of Christ.)

The next year (37), Vitellius went to Jerusalem for the Passover; there "he released the inhabitants from the taxes they had to pay on the sale of their crops" (*Antiquities of the Jews* 18, 90). He also deposed Caiaphas and appointed Jonathan high priest, but then dismissed him in turn and replaced him with Theophilus. He gave the priestly vestments back into the care of the high priest.

Caligula

At the death of Tiberius, his nephew Caligula succeeded him (37–41) and committed many extravagant acts. He may have been insane. Among these excesses was his decision—doubtless urged on him by his courtiers—to have himself recognized as a god while he was still on earth.

At the time of Caligula's accession one of his close friends was Agrippa, the grandson of Herod the Great. The emperor honored him by making him king of Abilene, a province north of Damascus. The royal title excited the jealous desire of Herodias, who urged her husband, Herod Antipas, to ask the same title for his tetrarchy, a title Augustus had refused him. Caligula listened to his request and then, on the advice of Agrippa, exiled him to Lyons. Agrippa later inherited Antipas' tetrarchy of Perea and Galilee, in 39.

In 38 Agrippa left Rome to take possession of his kingdom. On the way he stopped at Alexandria where the luxury of his retinue won admiration. The Greeks of Alexandria, however, being hostile to the Jews, made fun of him, to the point of turning him into an object of ridicule. They set a paper crown on a madman's head and put a reed in his hand; then they greeted the poor fellow as king. On this occasion, Flaccus, the Roman governor, did not intervene to establish order. According to Philo of Alexandria, Flaccus was violently anti-Jewish.

According to Josephus, "there were repeated clashes between Jews and Greeks; in vain did the magistrates daily punish many representatives of the two communities, for the riots only became worse" (*The Jewish War* 2, 489).

The Jewish community in Egypt was a very large one; Philo estimated it to be a million, with 100,000 living in Alexandria itself. Here the Jews completely filled two of the five quarters and amounted to perhaps thirty to forty percent of the population. Their community had enjoyed official recognition since the time of the ptolemies; it was governed by an ethnarch and a gerousia or council of seventy-one elders. The city had many synagogues, which were places of both worship and instruction. Ever since the edict of Caesar the Jewish religion had been a *religio licita*, an officially recognized form of cult.

These Jews were engaged in all the varied tasks found in society: they were farmers and soldiers, but also craftsmen, traders, importers and exporters, and bankers. Despite Exodus 22:25, "If you lend money to any of my people with you who is poor, you shall not be to him as a creditor, and you shall not exact interest from him," Alexandrian Jews, like the Marashu family at Babylon, did lend money at interest, and a papyrus from that time advises a borrower: "Avoid the Jews."

These Jews spoke only Greek, and frequently they adopted the Greek code of law. Thus a papyrus tells us that in Alexandria Jews could divorce by mutual consent. They now read only the Septuagint Bible, and a commemoration of the translation was part of the festal calendar of the Alex-

BC 63–56	Pompey in Jerusalem	Hyrcanus II high priest dependent on province of Syria	Aristobulus II brought to Rome Abortive attempt of Aristobulus II and ethnarch	
		Hyrcanus II high priest		
49	Caesar emperor		Herod administrator of Galilee	
44	Caesar assassinated		Herod tetrarch of Galilee	
42				
40	Peace between Octavian and Antony	Hyrcanus II deposed Antigonus high priest	Parthian invasion Antigonus king Herod king of Judea	
37		Hananel II		
35		Aristobulus III, assassinated in same year		
30	Antony & Cleopatra killed Octavian supreme			
4			Death of Herod Kingdom divided into 3 tetrarchies	
		Judea, Samaria, Idumea	Gaililee Perea	
		Archelaus 4–6 exiled at Rome	Herod Agrippa 4–39 exiled in Rome marries Herodias, divorced wife of Herod	Herod Philip 4–34 Tetrarchy is attached to province of Syria

andrian community. These people therefore regarded themselves as citizens; some of their writings even speak of them as the "Macedonians," in memory of their entering upon the scene there with Alexander. The Greeks, on the other hand, had a different view: they regarded the Jews as foreigners.

		Roman governors from 6–41	Philip
		Quirinius 6?	
		Coponius	
14	Death of Augustus	Valerius Gratus 15–26	
	Tiberius emperor	Annas high priest 6–15	
		Then sons and sons-in-law of Annas 18	
26		Pontius Pilate 26–36	
37	Caligula emperor		Herod Agrippa tetr.
39			Herod Agrippa king of the
41	Claudius emperor	Herod Agrippa king of Herod's kingdom	two tetrarchies
			Death of Herod Agrippa
		Cuspius Fadus governor 44–46	
		Tiberius Alexander 46–48	Herod Agrippa II
		Ventidius Cumanus 48–52	King 50–53
		Felix 52–69, marries Drusilla, sister of Herod Agrippa II	
53			Herod Agrippa II
54	Nero emperor	Festus 60–62	tetrarch 53–100;
		Albinus 62–64	also rules parts
		Florus 64–66	of Galilee
		Jewish revolt 66	
		Fall of Jerusalem 70	
68	Galba		
69	Otho; Vitellius		
70	Vespasian		
79	Titus		
81	Domitian		
96	Nerva		
98	Trajan		
117–138	Hadrian		

Since Flaccus was standing aside, the Greeks thought they could push their advantage further. To please Caligula, they claimed the right to set up his statues in the synagogues, and the Jews were bidden to practice the imperial cult. When they refused their synagogues were closed; they were declared to be foreigners, and lost all the rights peculiar to their community. From this point on, the Jews were forced back into their own quarters as into a ghetto. Philo's description allows no mistake:

> After driving all these many myriads of men, women, and children like herds of cattle out of the whole city into a very small portion as into a pen, they expected in a few days to find heaps of dead massed together. . . . And if any were caught in the other parts of the city before they could escape . . . they experienced manifold misfortunes, being stoned or wounded by tiles or branches of ilex or oak in the most vital parts of the body and particularly in the head, the fracture of which proved fatal. . . . A close watch was kept for those attempting to slip through and when any were caught they were at once dispatched by their enemies.[13]

After they had been slaughtered, burned, crucified, and forced to eat pork under penalty of death, the Jews' luck turned when Caligula ceased to have confidence in Flaccus and had him arrested and brought back to Rome. The Jews took advantage of the respite to send a delegation to Rome under the leadership of Philo.

Philo[14]

Philo was born into a wealthy Jewish family of Alexandria. His brother, Caius Alexander, owned large estates, doubtless had Roman citizenship, and was one of the wealthiest Jews of the city. He is said to have given gold and silver with which to cover the doors of the Jerusalem temple. In addition, he had the office of alabarch or chief magistrate of the Jewish community.

Two of Philo's nephews also became famous. The first, Tiberius, was a son of Caius; he renounced Judaism and in 45 became procurator of Judea where he put down a nationalist rebellion. He subsequently became prefect of Egypt and finally chief of staff to Titus during the latter's war with the Jews.

The second seems to have been none other than the great Alexandrian exporter, Marcus Julius Alexander, who, together with some Greek firms, carried on trade with India and Arabia. He was the first husband of Bernice, the daughter of Herod Agrippa.

Like all the other members of his family, Philo received a full Greek education, and he doubtless spoke only Greek. As one open to Greek thought, he introduced the ideas of the "divine Plato" into Jewish thinking.

Throughout his life he was to be a zealous commentator on the law. He tried to distinguish between the soul of the text and its letter, and in so doing provided the letters patent of nobility for the allegorical exegesis that would later be the glory of the Christian school of Alexandria. To take but one example, he interpreted the migration of Abraham as a process of initiation which gradually led the patriarch into the intelligible world of which God is the crown.

His aim was to show, in a language understood by the Greeks, the holiness of the patriarchs, the dignity of Jewish customs, and the grandeur of Jewish monotheism as contrasted with the cult of the gods and the emperor. He compared Greek and Jewish thought, not with a view to a syncretistic fusion of the two, but in order to develop a Jewish philosophy that would set the God of Israel apart from the other gods who are only approximations to the divine.

While he was the first Jewish philosopher and one of the greatest commentators on the law, he was also a formidable apologist who answered all the scurrilous pamphlets circulated against the Jews, whether at Alexandria or at Rome. Paradoxically, this vast production, intended for the glory of the Jews, was to be forgotten in Judaism but would provide models for Christian apologists.

Philo seems to have been a preacher as well. Many of his writings, in particular the *Allegorical Interpretation of Genesis,* sound to us like a series of homilies and were doubtless read when the law was being commented on during the sabbath evening. Similar writings flourished in Palestine: *The Book of Wisdom,* for example, or *The Testaments of the Twelve Patriarchs.* Once again, it was the Christians, rather than the Jews, who would carry on the tradition of Philo's homilies.

Though an eminent man of letters and one close to the centers of power through his family, Philo was also a man of great piety who seems at times to have gone into retreat among the Egyptian Jewish mystics known as the *Therapeutae* ("physicians," "devotees"). He tells us of their village and of the sacred chamber or "monastery" in each house, of their life of prayer, their allegorical reading of the Bible, and their meal in preparation for Passover, a meal consisting of pure water, bread and salt. In this context he also tells us that many women "preserved their virginity out of love for wisdom." In addition, he describes their singing: "They form two choirs, one of men, the other of women, which sing either together or alternately and dance until dawn, drunk with a holy intoxication."

The Embassy to Rome

It was Philo, then, who was chosen to lead the delegation of Alexandrian Jews to Rome. He had to confront Caligula, a man increasingly convinced of the necessity of the imperial cult and very much influenced by the anti-Jewish intrigues of Apion. When Caligula agreed to receive Philo, he is said to have addressed him thus: "Are you not the people who are enemies of the gods and who scorn me, preferring to my cult the cult of your nameless God?"

Furthermore, even though Caligula had dismissed Flaccus, he had been carrying out the plan Flaccus had conceived. As a result, news reached Rome that he had ordered his statue set up in the temple at Jerusalem. He even ordered the legate of Syria to commit suicide if he did not succeed in carrying out the emperor's wishes.

Philo had little chance of being heard, but at this same time Herod Agrippa had also come on an embassy to his friend Caligula. According to Josephus, Agrippa succeeded in changing the emperor's mind.

Philo himself reports Agrippa's courageous speech, which at the same time lets us know how widespread Judaism was in the empire.

> Jerusalem is my native city, but she is also the capital not of the land of Judea alone but of most other countries as well. She is this by reason of the colonies she has sent at various times to neighboring lands: Egypt, Syria, Phoenicia and especially Coele-Syria, but also to peoples in more distant regions: Pamphilia, Cilicia, and the greater part of Asia as far as Bithynia and the very end of Pontus. She has also sent them to Europe: to Thessaly, Boeotia, Macedonia, Aetolia, and Attica, as well as to Argos, Corinth, and most of the best parts of the Peloponnesus. Nor is it only the continents that are filled with Jewish colonies; the same is true of the most highly esteemed islands: Euboea, Cyprus, and Crete. And I say nothing of the colonies beyond the Euphrates, for Babylon and, in the other satrapies, all the cities with belts of fertile land around them, have Jewish residents.

This impressive panorama is confirmed by Josephus, the Book of Acts, and the Pauline letters. At the same time, however, the fact remained that this Jewish world was a turbulent one and in many places—Antioch, Jerusalem, Alexandria—hostile to the Greeks. What decision did Caligula come to? We do not know, for he died at an assassin's hand, and the Jews who had thus been saved slaughtered the Greeks. Only under Claudius would calm be restored.

Let me make a detour outside the empire and say something about the Jews living beyond the Euphrates, the Jews in the kingdom of the Parthians.

The Jews under Parthian Domination

In his *The Antiquities of the Jews* (Books 18 and 20) Josephus tells two stories that deserve to be better known. They are among the few documents we have on the diaspora in Mesopotamia.

The first story is of two brothers in Babylonia, Anileus and Asineus by name, who rebelled against their employer. They were able to gather around them other impoverished young men and to conquer a small territory between the rivers, where they built a fortress. They then established an illegal Jewish military colony and exacted ransom from their neighbors.

The king of the Parthians came to fight them but was conquered; Asineus even broke the sabbath in order to carry on the fight. The king of the Parthians then proposed a treaty. Like Antiochus III of old, he commissioned them to protect Babylonia for him. According to Josephus, Asineus "became more powerful than any of those before him who had dared to usurp power after such lowly beginnings. . . . Henceforth all the affairs of Mesopotamia depended on him, and his happiness only increased for fifteen years" (18, 20–35).

Unfortunately, the accord between the brothers did not last, and the king of the Parthians came against them and was victorious, until he was captured and slain by the Babylonians. As in Elephantine, so here in Mesopotamia the Jews allied to the Parthians were not regarded as friends. The death of the two brothers became the occasion for a massacre of Jews. Josephus says that fifty thousand of them died. The survivors took refuge at Nehardec in Babylonia and Nisibis in northern Mesopotamia.

The second incident also took place in the Parthian empire, in Adiabene, a small kingdom on the Upper Tigris. Izates, king of Adiabene (36–60), enjoyed great freedom because he had rendered service to the Parthians during a succession crisis. He and his mother Helena asked to be received as converts to Judaism. This is evidence of Jewish proselytism but also of the attraction which the monotheism and the community life of the Jews had for many pagans. The major difficulty attending his conversion was the demand of the strict Jews that he be circumcised; the matter comes up again in Paul's missions to the pagans. He was also asked to set aside the death penalty as a tool of government (20, 17–52).

Helena came to Jerusalem with gifts for the temple, and troops from

David and Goliath in Parthian dress from a 10th century A.D. church.

Adiabene would later serve as reinforcements for the Jewish resisters in their war against Rome (*The Jewish War* 2, 520, and 6, 536).

Judaism was solidly established in Adiabene until the end of the second century, the time when the Christian mission to this first nucleus of converts to Judaism would gain the day.

Emperor Claudius (41–54)

When Claudius succeeded Caligula he endeavored to restore peace. He gave back to the Jews all the rights they had under Augustus; at the same time, however, he warned them not to lay claim to further privileges.

> I call upon the Alexandrians to behave in a gentle and humane way to the Jews who have so long resided in the same city with them; not to hinder any of the traditional practices by which they honor the divinity; and to allow them to follow their own customs, as these existed in the time of the divine Augustus and are now confirmed by me. On the other hand, I expressly order the Jews not to seek to extend their ancient privileges nor to think in the future of sending an embassy in competition with yours (a thing unheard of in the past), nor to seek to take part in the competitions organized by the gymnasiarchs or the cosmetes, but rather to be content to live on their revenues and, as residents in a foreign city, to profit from the abundance of all goods.

According to the terms of this letter the Jews became "strangers" once again. It seems that Claudius even sought to end Jewish emigration to Alexandria.

Claudius adopted the same attitude toward Jerusalem. He guaranteed the high priest the right to keep the priestly vestments in his possession, because of the symbolic power these had in the eyes of the people.

In Rome, however, Claudius adopted a different policy, probably because the Jewish community there was divided. Was there opposition between orthodox Jews and Christianized Jews? We are told of disturbances caused on the initiative of a certain Chrestus. Claudius expelled at least some of the Jews from Rome (Suetonius; Acts 18:2); thus at Corinth Paul met Priscilla and Aquilla, Jews expelled from Rome.

Agrippa I

For a long time Agrippa had the advantage of the friendship of Claudius, who added Judea, Idumea, and Samaria to his possessions. For practical purposes, Agrippa now ruled over the territory once held by Herod, along with Abilene (map, p. 227).

Agrippa betook himself to Jerusalem and was received like a brother (he was fifty years old at the time). People forgot his light-hearted youthful days and admired his piety. On all points he conformed to the rules of the Pharisees. Sure now of support from Rome, he thought himself in a position to rebuild the walls of Jerusalem, but he was forced to stop the work on the orders of the legate of Syria (Mishnah, Tr. Bikkurim 3, 4).

In order to show his agreement with the Jewish authorities and to check the spread of the new sect known as the "Christians," Agrippa had James, son of Zebedee, executed and Peter jailed (Acts 12:2–9).

Nonetheless, like all the Herodians, Agrippa remained a Hellenistic prince. He surrounded himself with extreme luxury; he encouraged gladiatorial fights and even organized solemn games at Caesarea. He wanted to display his royal magnificence there and be acclaimed as a living god.

He was to die shortly after, laid low by violent pain. The Book of Acts sees in this a punishment for his wickedness (Acts 12:23; see *The Antiquities of the Jews* 19, 343–52). His death was followed by a revival of the antagonism of the Hellenized cities toward the Herodians. The inhabitants of Caesarea and Sebaste expressed public joy at his death and thereby outraged the royal family. In memory of his own friendship for Agrippa, Claudius decreed sanctions which were not applied (*The Antiquities of the Jews* 19, 364–66).

Judea to 66 A.D.

When Agrippa I died, Claudius did not grant the kingdom to his son, Agrippa II. Instead it was once again made a dependency of the governor of Syria, Palestine being under the command of procurators residing at Caesarea.

Cuspius Fadus, the procurator at this time (44–46), began by respecting Jewish customs, but he wanted to take back control of the high priest's vestments. The people were aroused, and he did not insist. He already had to deal with armed bands, described as brigands, which were in fact commanded by nationalist prophets such as Thaddeus, a man subsequently beheaded.

Cuspius was succeeded by Tiberius Alexander (46–48). Tiberius was a grandnephew of Philo of Alexandria, but this did not make him more acceptable to the Jews, who regarded him as a renegade. Like his predecessor, he had to put down a nationalist uprising that was headed, it seems, by the sons of Judas the Galilean. The leaders were crucified.

Ventidius Cumanus, who was procurator from 48 to 52, had to put down a much more extensive revolt. The obscene gestures which some Roman soldiers directed to the Jews who had gathered for Passover set in motion a rebellion that had been quietly simmering since the reign of Herod. This first major attempt was crushed, but it cost twenty thousand lives, according to Josephus.

A new incident narrowly failed to light the powder keg once again. A Roman courier was attacked, and the order was immediately given to plunder the village where the guilty man lived. During the pillage, a soldier added the final straw to Jewish hatred by publicly destroying a Torah scroll. In order to stop the insurrection the Roman soldier had to be executed.

Then came a more serious incident: a group of Galilean pilgrims passing through Samaria were massacred by the local population. The procurator of Judea did not intervene. As a result it was the Zealots who took it upon themselves to launch a punitive expedition. The Roman army then had to intervene, and it took a great deal of diplomacy on the part of the young Agrippa II to convince Claudius of the necessity of executing the Samaritan leaders and replacing the Roman procurator.

After this incident it was no longer possible to talk of the schemes of brigands. The Zealots had now come out into the open as a party which had for its purpose to overthrow, by any means possible, both the foreign overlords and their collaborators.

The Zealots drew their inspiration from the nationalist and religious ideology of the Maccabees, but also from a body of literature represented by the Book of Jubilees. This book doubtless originated among the Pharisees, for it gives an important role to angels and demons, is concerned with the future life, and assigns a pre-eminent place to oral tradition.

The Book of Jubilees takes the form of a commentary, an apocalyptic midrash on Genesis and the beginning of Exodus. It claims for its content the status of a revelation received by Moses on Sinai; it carefully dates each event from the beginning of time to the end of the forty-nine weeks of years.

The book as a whole seeks to show that an impassable barrier exists between Jews and pagans. It features a tradition according to which Abraham destroyed the idols of the pagans. Simeon and Levi are no longer blamed but honored for having treacherously killed the Shechemites (Gen 34), while Jacob is depicted as having slain his brother Esau, the ancestor of Edom.

The hope associated with the end of time is the hope that God will come with his angels and fight at Israel's side in order to defeat her enemies once and for all, the latter being led by demons. The ideology of Jubilees was not that of the Zealots alone; it was also that of the Essenes, but these did not play a part in public life.

The Zealots seem to have originated in Galilee, the province that had already seen the revolt of the priest Hezekiah against Herod and then the revolt of Judas in 6 A.D. against the levying of taxes but also against submission to any earthly master. God alone was to be acknowledged as Lord.

The Zealots were joined by many disinherited and debt-ridden Jews as well as by slaves; Josephus the historian later scorned them as robbers. During the revolts, these groups would try to burn the record-offices in which evidence of debts was filed; the Zealots (still according to Josephus) set poor against rich.

Claudius accepted the advice of Agrippa II and appointed a new procurator named Felix (52–60). Unfortunately, he outdid all his predecessors in greed and baseness. Tacitus says of him: "He gave free rein to his cruelty and capriciousness and exercised royal power in the spirit of a slave" (*Histories* 5, 9).

Felix began with a striking success: he arrested Eleazar, leader of the Zealot party that had attacked the Samaritans; this put an end to the organized armed bands. The Zealots ceased to attack openly; henceforth they would mingle with crowds and assassinate men with a dagger or *sica* (whence their nickname *Sicarii* or "Daggermen"). They even assassinated the high priest Jonathan whom they regarded as a collaborator of the Romans (*The Jewish War* 2, 254–57).

This period of insecurity, rebellion and mystical exaltation heightened the Jewish expectation of the Messiah. It is not surprising, therefore, that when Paul preached the Messiah he was arrested and confused with a rebel known as "the Egyptian" (Acts 21:38). He was transferred to Caesarea to the residence of Felix the procurator and received by the latter in the presence of his wife Drusilla, the sister of Agrippa II.

Agrippa II

Though Agrippa had been kept from the kingship by Claudius, he nonetheless became the emperor's confidant and adviser; as a reward, in 48 he received the kingdom of Chalcis,[15] located between the Lebanon and Antilebanon ranges. In 49 he was also given the right to oversee the appointment of the high priest and to govern the temple. In 59, he was moved from the kingdom of Chalcis to Abilene, the old tetrarchy of Philip, and was given in addition some territories in the Lebanon.

In 54 Claudius, Agrippa's patron, was assassinated by his own wife, Agrippina, and the empire passed to Nero. The latter continued to show favor to Agrippa, bestowing on him the cities of Tiberias, Magdala, and Julias (Bethsaida), together with their surrounding territories.

In 60 Nero recalled Felix, who had been accused by the Jews, and in his place appointed Festus, a man of integrity, as procurator. Was Nero influenced in this by his Judaizing concubine, Poppaea? We do not know very much about the period when Festus held office, except that he had to deal with the accusations of the Jews against Paul. He had Paul brought before him and presented him to Agrippa II and his sister Bernice, who passed for experts on Jewish matters, but when Paul invoked his Roman citizenship, Festus had no choice but to send him on to Rome.

When Festus died in 62, Annas was high priest; he was the son of the Annas who presided over the Sanhedrin when it condemned Jesus. This later Annas doubtless took advantage of the absence of any procurator to attack the Christians and have James, the brother of the Lord, executed. This mention of the martyrdom of James, leader of the Jerusalem Christian community, is the first attestation to the existence of Christians as an organized community.

According to Josephus (*The Antiquities of the Jews* 20, 200–202), the populace strongly disapproved of the stoning of James. Other excesses of Annas were to lead his deposition by Agrippa II.

The governors who succeeded Festus once again set out to plunder Judea. Rebellions multiplied, the Daggermen resorted to taking hostages, the office of high priest became an object of dispute in the streets, and priests were thrown into prison. Greeks and Jews engaged in violent conflict in Caesarea, but Florus the procurator did not intervene. The moderates tried to achieve peace by sending an embassy to Rome; among its members was a man named Josephus. He was from a priestly family and had engaged in rabbinical studies; he also spent three years in the wilderness as a hermit before joining the Pharisee party. When sent to Rome as a diplomat, he established solid friendships there.

The First Jewish War

When Josephus returned to Palestine, the people were ready to revolt. Nero made mistake after mistake. In the wake of conflict between Jews and Greeks in Caesarea, the government of the city was entrusted to the Greeks. In Jerusalem, Florus the procurator (whom Josephus says was a hangman sent to execute the condemned) claimed the right to deduct seventeen talents from the temple treasury. The crowd then organized a mock collection for Florus, who responded by sending his troops against them; the soldiers pillaged and killed 3,600 people. Agrippa II tried to act as a go-between but was forced to flee; the anger of the Jews had reached the point of no return.

It was at this point that the Zealots captured Masada and slaughtered its Roman garrison. A young captain of the temple named Eleazar immediately adopted Zealot ideas and rallied the priestly classes to their side, but with difficulty. The priestly classes had, after all, a good deal to lose since they had long since compromised with the enemy, to the point of conducting a daily service of worship of the emperor. But now that the rebellion had become widespread, the priests took the side of the people and organized the resistance.

A group of moderates under the leadership of Ananias (high priest, 47–55) tried to intervene, because they did not believe it possible to achieve a lasting success against the Romans. But the crowd got out of control, invaded the city, captured Fortress Antonia and began to burn the property archives and with them all evidence of their debts. Ananias and the moderates could only take refuge in the palace of Herod.

Josephus

The period now beginning is especially well-known to us thanks to Josephus' book, *The Jewish War*. This work covers the period from Antiochus IV to the fall of Jerusalem. Unfortunately, the book was written in Rome at the court of Vespasian, shortly after 70. It is a defense of the moderate Jews, the Zealots being held responsible for all the troubles, and Josephus does not hesitate to see the Romans as God's agents in punishing a wicked generation.

This first work was supplemented by a second, *The Antiquities of the Jews*, which was written around 95. This time the writer's purpose was to rewrite the whole of Jewish history from its beginnings. It is a very pro-Hellenistic history; in Josephus' eyes the Stoics and the Pharisees are identical in their ideas.

We have still another work from Josephus' pen, the *Against Apion*, which is a defense of the Jews against accusations circulating in the diaspora. Josephus seeks to show the very great antiquity of Judaism, to praise its morality as being conformed to reason in every detail, and to glorify the Jews as a people who have always tried to make immortality their spiritual goal. Finally, the author praises their form of government, theocracy.

Josephus' work was to be rejected by the Jews, who considered him a traitor to his country. Christians, on the other hand, adopted it; they had no scruples about revising it and introducing into it the famous "Testimony of Flavius [Josephus] (*Testimonium Flavianum*), which I cited earlier. This

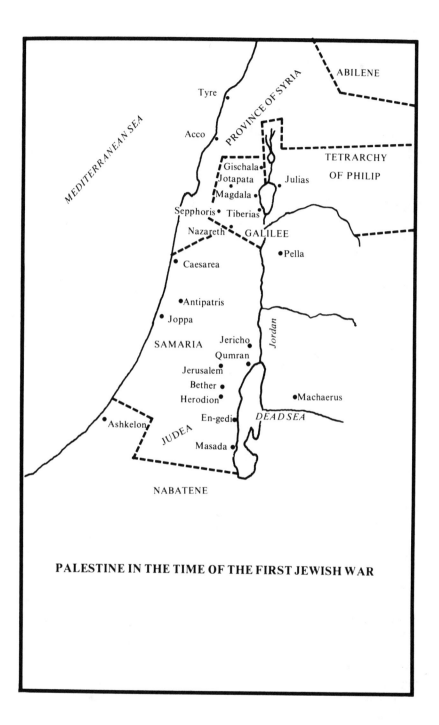

PALESTINE IN THE TIME OF THE FIRST JEWISH WAR

Money of the First Jewish Revolt.

"Jerusalem the Holy" with a pomegranate in the center.	"Shekel of Israel: year 2" with the cup of salvation.

document has Josephus saying of Christ that he was a wise man, "if indeed he is to be called simply a man." It even has Josephus professing that Jesus is the Christ or Messiah and that he rose on the third day. Such statements could not have come from a Jew who remained a Pharisee.

Organization of the Rebellion

The entire Jewish people rose in rebellion, but it was a divided people. On the one hand, there were the committed Zealots who unreservedly professed the ideals of the Maccabees. Their position was that the Romans and all their collaborators had to be forced out. The Zealots had all the poor on their side, but many adventurers as well.

On the other hand, the priestly classes and the Pharisees would have preferred to take a much more moderate course. They were very conscious of the power of the Romans and would have been satisfied to see Jewish worship fully respected.

In the beginning, the Zealots carried the day. Under the leadership of Menahem, who according to Josephus was a grandson of Judas the Galilean, they captured Masada and distributed the weapons from Herod's arsenals. Menahem embodied the messianic hopes of the people. He was a skillful politician and succeeded in isolating the Roman garrison and having his chief Jewish opponents, among them Ananias, put to death. He then donned royal garb and went up to the temple, doubtless hoping to be king and high priest like the Maccabees.

Waiting for him in the temple was Eleazar, captain of the temple police and son of Ananias. Eleazar killed Menahem. Was his intention to assassinate one whom he regarded as a tyrant? Was he opposed to the linking of religious and civil offices? Did he want the power for himself?

The obvious result of the assassination was to deprive the Jewish rebellion of the only leader who had trained troops at his disposal throughout the entire territory. From this point on, the Zealots did not trust the priestly classes. They withdrew into their fortress at Masada under the leadership of Eleazar son of Jairus, another relative of Judas the Galilean.

Eleazar son of Ananias continued the rebellion and freed Jerusalem from the Romans. The whole of Palestine arose against the Greek settlers and their Jewish collaborators. The disturbances are said to have reached even Alexandria, where they led to the death of thousands of Jews.

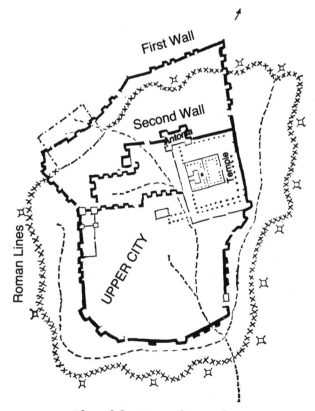

Plan of the Siege of Jerusalem.

Cestius Gallus, legate of Syria, marched on Jerusalem, but after some easy successes failed to capture the temple and had to withdraw. During his retreat he was harried by Jews under the leadership of Simon bar Gioras. At this point he suffered a real defeat near Beth-horon, losing six thousand men and the Roman artillery. The Jews thought they had regained their independence. They struck coins with triumphal inscriptions: "Jerusalem the Holy!" "To the Freedom of Israel!" "To the Ransoming of Zion!"

This success gave the moderates an opportunity to introduce organization into the country. Jerusalem was put in charge of the former high priest Annas. Eleazar was sent to Idumea, probably to get rid of him. John the Essene was put in charge of the highland of Ephraim; it is in this way that we learn of the participation of the Essenes, who believed that the hour had struck for the eschatological war of the sons of light against the sons of darkness. Josephus, the future historian, was put in charge of Galilee. Everywhere the moderates tried to channel the enthusiasm and to calm passions. They wanted to prepare for possible negotiations with the Romans.

Josephus certainly represented this current of moderation, and this won him the unyielding opposition of John of Gischala, who was for war to the death. John regarded Josephus as simply a traitor ready to compromise with the Romans.

Finally, by way of completing this survey of Palestine, we must not forget the cities which had long since been Hellenized. These had nothing in common with the rebels and resisted them or at least quickly went over to the Roman side. Among the cities that would not yield were Sepphoris and Ashkelon (map, p. 227).

The Galilean Campaign

Josephus attempted to restore order in Galilee. He united the scattered bands of fighters into a regular army, fortified the towns, and put down the insurrections in Sepphoris and Tiberias. These, however, were but a derisory kind of preparation for facing the Romans.

In 67, Vespasian, conqueror of the Germans and Britain, debarked at Antioch. He was joined there by Agrippa II and his troops, by a Nabatean army of Malichus II, and then by his son Titus. As a result they had sixty thousand men available at Ptolemais (map, p. 227). Sepphoris, which was hostile to the rebels, immediately rallied to the imperial side.

Josephus' troops disbanded, and he had no choice but to take refuge in the fortress of Jotapata. During a two-month siege of the place he demonstrated first-rate qualities as a general. But reinforcements from Jerusalem never came, and a traitor handed the city over to the Romans.

The Zealots, faithful to their ideal, called for a collective suicide. They hoped in this way to do something meritorious in the eyes of God whose cause they were defending. They would call for the same action at the fall of the temple and the capture of Masada. When Josephus was urged to commit suicide, he managed very cleverly to be the final survivor. As a prisoner of Vespasian he turned prophet and predicted that the general would soon be emperor.

Vespasian believed he could now go and take a rest at Agrippa's palace in Caesarea Philippi. Meanwhile Tiberias surrendered, and Titus captured Magdala. Thus Galilee was pacified, and John of Gischala alone was left to continue the struggle, but he had to flee toward Jerusalem.

At Tiberias the Romans organized some games during which many Jews died. Others were sent as slaves to work in the building of the canal at Corinth.

Jerusalem

When John of Gischala reached Jerusalem with his little band of Zealots, he massacred the Jews who were in authority there. Power passed once more into the hands of the Zealots. The high priest was replaced through a drawing of lots by the members of an ancient priestly family; the choice fell on Phinehas ben Samuel, a simple man and laborer.

This appointment, along with the ideals of the Zealots and their determination to fight to the death, caused new divisions among the Jews. The moderates and the priestly class joined forces around the deposed high priest, and the Zealots had to take refuge in the temple.

The Zealots then appealed to the Idumeans, claiming that the priestly circles were ready to hand Jerusalem over to the Romans. The Idumeans assembled twenty thousand men and marched to Jerusalem, to which the Zealots gave them entrance. They then proceeded to massacre all dignitaries, beginning with the high priest, the leader of the opposition. But things did not stop there. The Zealots organized a real revolutionary tribunal in order to cleanse the city through killing. If someone happened to be declared innocent and was set free, as was the case with a certain Zechariah, two Zealots rose up right in the court and "liberated him through death." Terror reigned. The Idumeans grew weary of the horrors and withdrew.

Vespasian took his time. He knew that divisions among the Jews were weakening the resistance to him. He occupied Perea and then stationed the fifth legion at Antipatris to the northeast of Joppa. The moment had come for the Samaritans to suffer: sixteen thousand of them were slaughtered at Mount Gerizim (Josephus, *The Jewish War* 3, 302ff). In 68 Vespasian captured Jericho. The trap was closing around Jerusalem, when operations were interrupted by news of the death of Nero in 68. Titus was immediately sent to greet the new emperor, Galba. On the way, however, he learned that Galba had already been assassinated, and so he returned to Caesarea.

Then began a period of difficulties for both the Jews and the Romans. A new Idumean army under the command of Simon bar Gioras reached Jerusalem, and the inhabitants of the city were so wearied of John of Gischala and his tribunals that they opened the gates to Simon. The Zealots once again took refuge in the temple.

In Rome two claimants, Otho and Vitellius, were disputing the imperial title. At this point the legions in Egypt, and then all the legions in the East, proclaimed Vespasian emperor. The latter then took up residence at Alexandria while waiting for an opportunity to go to Rome, where he would plot against Vitellius, who by now was sole emperor. Meanwhile Vespasian contented himself with reducing Idumea to submission, except for the Herodian fortresses.

In the spring of 70 Vespasian was finally able to sail to Rome. He became emperor in accordance with the prophecy of Josephus, who was given his freedom in honor of the occasion. Meanwhile Vespasian's son Titus received responsibility for finishing the war against the Jews.

The Capture of Jerusalem

When Titus turned his attention to Jerusalem in 70, the city was rent by fierce divisions. Eleazar ben Simon held the temple, but he was besieged by John of Gischala who occupied the outer precincts. Finally, both were besieged by Simon who held the city. Terror reigned everywhere and famine began to rage. The story is told of Rabbi Johanan ben Zakkai who was able to escape from the city by passing himself off as a corpse.

Even though Simon and John were reconciled, the Roman earthworks, protected by catapults, moved rapidly forward. In fifteen days the first rampart of the city was captured. Five days later the second rampart yielded.

From above in the Antonia the Jews bombarded the Romans, and John managed to undermine and collapse the nearest earthwork. The Romans then built a 21 foot wall around the city and began their earthworks anew. They sent Josephus to urge the people to surrender, but in vain.

The Arch of Titus.

The Romans succeeded in entering the Antonia by night, and the Jews there retreated to the temple. Once again, earthworks had to be erected, but so well had Herod built that the edifice resisted all the battering rams.

During a final assault, the temple was set on fire, despite the orders of Titus. The Jewish fighters laid aside their weapons and made an effort to save the temple, which was the symbol that sustained them in all their struggles. For the second time a collective suicide took place. The fighters cast themselves into the flames or cut one another's throats or threw themselves on the swords of the Romans. Only a small group fled into the city. Now that the Romans had gained control of the temple esplanade they offered a sacrifice to their gods.

The upper city then offered to surrender, on condition that its inhabitants might leave with their families. Titus refused, began the assault and set fire to the city. According to Josephus the siege of the city cost a million lives in all.

Some of the survivors were sent to participate in the circus games; others went to Egypt as slaves. Titus meanwhile set seven hundred Jews aside for his triumph. Among these was Simon bar Gioras, who was scourged the entire length of the procession and then executed at the crowning moment of the festivities.

On this occasion a memorial arch was erected at Rome in honor of Titus. On it are represented some of the most valuable objects taken from the temple in Jerusalem: the seven-branched candelabrum, the table for the loaves of offering. In celebration of their victory the Romans also struck coins with the image of the emperor and, on the reverse side, the trophies taken from the Jews or Judea represented as weeping beneath a palm tree, with the inscription *Judea Capta* (Judea a Prisoner).

The Jewish population of Rome increased to a notable degree; soon those deported there would become freedmen and join the classes lowest in the economic scale. Latin writers such as Martial, Juvenal and Persius Flaccus were contemptuous of these people. They claimed that Jewish children were trained as beggars by their mothers, while the latter themselves earned a living by telling fortunes. Their homes were despicable, the windows dirty, the only furnishings a basket and some straw. Persius Flaccus speaks with disgust of their earthen vessels and their food. They ate, he says, only tuna, a very common fish, and even then bought only the tail which was sold very cheaply.

Juvenal's satire of the Jews (*Satire* XIV) is a more serious matter, because it betrays a great deal of misunderstanding of Jewish practices and a contempt for them. The Jews, he says, are sectarians, and their sabbath encourages laziness:

> Some who have had a father who reveres the sabbath, worship nothing but the clouds and the divinity of the heavens, and see no difference between eating swine's flesh, from which their fathers abstained, and that of man; and in time they take to circumcision. Having been wont to flout the laws of Rome, they learn and practice and revere the Jewish law, and all that Moses handed down in his secret tome, forbidding to point out the way to any not worshiping the same rites, and conducting none but the circumcised to the desired fountain. For all which the father was to blame, who gave up every seventh day to idleness, keeping it apart from all the concerns of life.[16]

The Jewish catacombs of Rome also bear witness to how the Jews lived. For, with the exception of a few sumptuous sarcophaguses, the tombs on the whole are very modest. They are decorated with a few Jewish objects: the seven-branched candelabrum, the palm branch, the knife of circumcision.

The Final Resistance in Palestine

Jerusalem had fallen and Palestine had been reduced to subjection, but the Jewish war was not therefore over. Three Herodian fortresses still held out: the Herodion, Machaerus, and Masada (map, p. 227). We know almost nothing about the first two of these fortresses, but archeology and Josephus tell us a great deal about Masada.

Masada, the greatest of the Herodian citadels, had room on its summit for crops; as a result it did not lack for food, while its remarkable cisterns provided it with water. The insurgents meanwhile transformed the Herodian palaces into lodgings for their families, without regard for works of art that were damaged beyond repair.

Masada was a religious citadel; ritual baths have been found there, as well as the jars for cultic offerings. Fragments of biblical texts have also been discovered: Psalms, Deuteronomy, Ezekiel, and, above all, chapters 39–44 of the original Hebrew text of Jesus son of Sirach. In addition to these biblical texts the Book of Jubilees and a song for the sabbath sacrifice have also been found. These last two texts are close in spirit to those discovered at Qumran; it is an easy inference that the Essenes took part in the defense of Masada.

It is once again the archeologists who have thrown light on the steps taken by the Romans to capture the fortress. The digs have uncovered the wall circling the crag, the dams built across the water-courses, and the serpentine road that gave access to the fortress itself. On the hill opposite Masada the Romans set up an observation camp. The Roman army brought into action at Masada numbered around ten thousand men.

Silva, the Roman general, built an access ramp starting from a spur of rock. On this spur itself he built a tower one hundred and fifty feet high. Then his men breached the wall with a battering-ram. The defenders tried to repair the breach with wood, but the Romans set this on fire. Then Eleazar gathered everyone together at night. He reminded them that they had never been slaves and that they desired to belong to God alone. Therefore they decided to burn everything but the food, for they wanted to make it clear that they had not been conquered by hunger. Then, to keep the women from being dishonored and the children from being enslaved, all these were slain. Ten men were then appointed to kill all the other men, and the last of the ten set the palace on fire before killing himself. In the morning the Romans learned of the collective suicide; they found nine hundred and sixty bodies. The only survivors were two women and five children who had taken refuge in an underground cavern. The Jewish resistance had come to an end (May 73).

Qumran[17]

Among the important ruins of Judea are those of Qumran. This community center was built under John Hyrcanus (135–104) and extended under Alexander Janneus and Alexandra; after extensive damage from the earthquake of 31 it was inhabited once again beginning in the reign of Archelaus and seems to have been destroyed by the tenth Roman legion when it conquered Jericho in 68.

Before the excavations the Essenes were already known from a number of documents. There are, to begin with, two passages in Philo. The first is in his book *Every Good Man Is Free*, where he describes the Essenes as perfect Jews. In fact, he takes the word "Essene" to mean "holy." According to him, these people live in communities apart from the world, contenting themselves with the essential necessities of life. They reject personal property and slavery. Daily they study the law and put it into practice, take their meals in common, care for the sick, and overcome all tyrants by their virtue. These "saints" offer no sacrifices; Philo regards this as a sign of advanced spirituality. His information is accurate, but the refusal of sacrifices represents in fact a break with the Jerusalem priesthood.

The second passage from Philo has been preserved for us by Eusebius of Caesarea; it is from a lost work entitled *Defense of the Jews*. This passage hardly differs from the first, except that it perhaps lays greater stress on the work done in common: farming, stockbreeding, beekeeping, crafts. Here too it is not only lands, the fruits of labor, and meals that are held in common, but even clothing. To meet the needs of the community the Essenes have excluded marriage, and accept only mature men into their ranks.

We also have two passages in Josephus. The first is in *The Jewish War*. Like Philo, Josephus speaks of the life of the community, but according to him the Essenes accept very young children in order to teach them the Essene way. Josephus describes the community's day as lived in a framework of prayer and emphasizes in particular the organization of the common meals, the dining hall being a sacred place. He tells us that in addition to reading the ancient texts the Essenes study the properties of plants and stones so as to use these to help their neighbors.

Josephus also reports the conditions for acceptance among the Essenes. Candidates must have studied the books of the sect and must promise to live in conformity with the rule. They may then be introduced to the ritual baths. Josephus emphasizes the unswerving fidelity of the Essenes, even under torture by the Romans. This courage had its source, among others, in their belief that their souls would be raised up into the heavenly world.

Plan of the Monastery of Qumran.

In *The Antiquities of the Jews* Josephus also speaks of the estrangement of the Essenes from the temple, although they continued to take part in its worship by their offerings, sacrifice being part of their liturgy. He speaks too of their rejection of marriage, although he knows a group of Essenes who have opted for marriage, not for the sake of pleasure but because children are a necessity.

Philo and Josephus have knowledge therefore of more than one group of Essenes and even of notable differences among the groups. The only documents of the Essenes themselves that have been discovered are those relating to the community at Qumran, which Pliny the Elder has described.

On the west side of the Dead Sea, but out of range of the noxious exhalations of the coast, is the solitary tribe of the Essenes, which is remarkable beyond all other tribes in the whole world, as it has no women and has renounced all sexual desire, has no money, and has only palm-trees for company. Day by day the throng of refugees is recruited to an equal number by numerous accessions of persons tired of life and driven thither by the waves of fortune to adopt their manners. Thus through thousands of ages (incredible to relate) a race in which no one is born live on for ever: so prolific for their advantage is other men's weariness of life![18]

But the excavation of the ruins and the neighboring caves was to produce a harvest of documents which made it possible to identify the residents of Qumran with the Essenes.

Many biblical texts have been found which are the oldest we have in Hebrew. These make it possible to determine the value of the various versions already known to us: the Masoretic text, the Septuagint, the Samaritan text. The differences among them are almost all attested at Qumran.

In addition to texts of Scripture there are collections of hymns, psalms in greater number than in the canon (the canon was not yet closed at this time), commentaries on Scripture including a Targum on Job, and liturgical compositions peculiar to the community. Furthermore, there are a number of writings that make known the composition of the community and its manner of life: the Rule of the Community, the Rule of the Congregation, the Damascus Document, the War Scroll, the Temple Scroll.

Along with texts of Scripture and other texts dealing with the community, the library of the group contained some of the Jewish apocrypha: the Book of Jubilees and the Book of Enoch, which became known for the first time in their original Hebrew version.

The harvest was immense and enabled us for the first time to reexamine our ideas on the origin of the canonical text and on Jewish belief not only at the time of Jesus but going back to the time of John Hyrcanus. Finally, these documents raised questions on the relations between Essenes and Christians.

What, for example, was the relation between the baptism of John and the baptism of the Essenes? Between Jesus and the Teacher of Righteousness? What were the messianic expectations of the Essenes? What passages of the Old Testament did they use in order to proclaim him? Did Christians draw on the same sources? What was the relation between the messianic banquet of the Essenes and the Last Supper of Jesus? Is there a similarity between the eschatological expectations of the two communities? Was John the evangelist inspired by the writings of the Essenes when he adopted the language of darkness versus light, lies versus truth?

In his special chronology of the passion did John use the Essene calendar which differed from the official temple calendar? All these questions need to be discussed in the light of a careful study of the Qumran texts; such questions will, in any event, introduce a fresh slant into our reading of the Scriptures.

Alexandria

Some Jews managed to flee to Egypt where they attempted to incite a rebellion. But the Jewish authorities—the gerousia or council of elders with its seventy-one members—had them arrested and handed over to the Roman authorities. The Jewish revolt did not extend to the diaspora: on the contrary, the diaspora now became the center of the Jewish faith.

From the Destruction of Jerusalem to the Revolt of Bar Kokhba

For this period we have no continuous source such as the history of Josephus. We do find scattered items of information in the Talmud. The work of Dio Cassius, which covers this period, is known to us only through an abstract by a monk of the eleventh century. As a result, our best information comes from the documents discovered at Murabba'at that deal with the period of Bar Kokhba.

Titus settled his legions in Jerusalem and built places of worship for them; an inscription to "Jupiter Best and Greatest" had been found there. In theory Vespasian financed these new places of worship by turning the tax which every Jew had to pay to the temple into a tax paid to the capital instead. This was the fiscal punishment for the revolt and it affected all Jews both in Judea and in the diaspora. It soon became a very heavy burden not only financially but also and above all morally; it turned the Jews into a people apart throughout the empire. Titus gradually authorized Jewish prisoners and even the former rebels to take up residence again. Little by little, Jews from the diaspora found their way back to Jerusalem, and the population of the city grew; but the newcomers brought with them the danger of syncretism, which the rabbis pointed out. The latter tried to keep the faithful from wearing any ring that depicted the moon, the sun, or a dragon.

The Talmud says that Rabbi Aqiba was even given permission to visit the ruins of the temple and to undertake excavations. But the temple was no more and the sacrificial cult was a thing of the past. The Apocalypses of Baruch and Ezra describe the distress of the people but also their hope that God would intervene once more and that a time of rebuilding would come. This hope seems hardly to have affected the diaspora. Liturgical life there had long since become centered on the worship of the synagogue.

The central figure in Palestinian Judaism was Rabbi Johanan ben Zakkai, who had escaped from Jerusalem by pretending to be a corpse. He founded a school of rabbinical studies at Jamnia, and established a new Sanhedrin that was composed solely of doctors of the law; its president was given the title of patriarch. The aim was to pursue the study of the law and in particular to apply the laws concerning the temple, now gone, to everyday life. Henceforth the laws governing the cleanness of priests were applied to the entire people; the ceremonial of the temple was shifted into daily life. Henceforth it was daily life and no longer the temple that would be treated as sacred.

At Jamnia, in the year 90, the Sanhedrin established canon of the Scriptures. In fact this canon already existed in part, since the Pentateuch had been given its final form in the fourth century B.C. at the latest and the canon of the prophets had been closed in the second century B.C. But there had still been disagreement about accepting Ecclesiastes and the Song of Songs into the canon. A number of books that were part of the Septuagint were not accepted, since they allowed too much to Hellenistic thinking.

Also undertaken was a codification of oral law and the commentaries of the fathers. This work, begun by Rabbi Aqiba, produced the most sacred part of the Talmud, the Mishnah, which was to be assimilated through repeated reading of it.

To all this were added commentaries or midrashim, examples of which we have already seen at Qumran—for instance, the commentaries on Habakkuk or Nahum, or the Book of Jubilees.

Hebrew had become a purely liturgical language and was no longer spoken by the people. To meet the needs of worship, therefore, more or less free translations were made that were at times studded with explanations. These translations were known as Targums; the Targum on Job, found at Qumran, is an example. This activity continued for several centuries and gave rise to two major recensions: the Targum of Onkelos or Babylonian Targum, and the Jerusalem Targum. This work had made great progress before the second Jewish war and was carried on simultaneously in several places, Samaria being one of them.

The products of all this labor spread to the synagogues of Palestine, Egypt and Babylon, and even beyond into those of Greece and Italy. It was in such communities as these that Paul the Apostle would preach, meeting there not only Jews but a good many pagans attracted by the Jewish faith and known as "God-fearers."

Christians and Jews

Alongside the Jews there now existed a Christian community. These Christians did not take part in the Jewish war but fled from Jerusalem to Pella.[19] Since they had not taken up arms against Rome, they were soon able to return to Jerusalem where their community grew rapidly. They also spread to the rest of the empire, although it was not always easy to distinguish between the new religion and the Jewish religion. Christians were often looked upon as simply a more or less dissident Jewish sect and as desirous of profiting by the privileges given to the Jews. Pagans leveled the same objections against the Christians as they did against the Jews: they spoke of hatred of the human race, of impiety, of absurd practices, and even of ritual murders.

When a pesecution arose, it was not always easy to say at whom it was aimed. Hegesippus, for example, speaks of a persecution of Christians by Domitian. The emperor was said to be hunting for the grandsons of James, brother of the Lord, because he feared that these descendants of David could be a source of trouble for him. But when he realized that they were simple peasants awaiting a spiritual Messiah, he let them go. The story smacks somewhat of legend.

But other persecutions in the same reign, though often regarded as directed at Christians, seem to have included Jews. The latter were persecuted for two reasons: one was active proselytism, in which they resembled the Christians, and the other had to do with the payment of the Jewish tax instituted by Vespasian. According to Suetonius,

> besides other taxes, that on the Jews was levied with the utmost rigor, and those were persecuted who without publicly acknowledging that faith yet lived as Jews, as well as those who concealed their origin and did not pay the tribute levied on their people. I recall being present in my youth when the person of a man ninety years old was examined before the procurator and in a very crowded court, to see whether he was circumcised.[20]

This practice was a prelude to what would be done for centuries to come.

Similarly, when Trajan (98–117) crushed the Jewish revolt in Judea, we learn that he had Simeon, a Christian bishop, executed, because he was of the race of David. This is an indication of the importance of the Christian community in Jerusalem, a point confirmed by the list of its first fifteen bishops as drawn up in the reign of Hadrian (117–138).

But while pagans confused them with one another, Jews and Christians made every effort to distinguish themselves from each other. Every point became a subject of dispute and even of violence; this was true in particular of the rights which the Jewish community had acquired, but also of the fact that Jewish and Christian proselytizing activity was directed at the same circles, as is abundantly clear from the Acts of the Apostles and the Pauline missionary journeys.

Controversy between the two communities was extremely bitter when it came to the method of interpreting the Scriptures and especially the texts about the Messiah. We find traces of these disputes in the Talmud but also in Justin the apologete's response to Trypho the Jew. In his polemic Justin makes use against the Jews of the allegorical exegeses of Philo, one of their own. The climate of tension found expression in a prayer of Gamaliel II: "May the Nazarenes and the Minim [Christians] perish in an instant; may they be erased from the book of the living and not be counted with the righteous!" We are far here from the tolerance of Gamaliel I (Acts 5:34ff). The same tension finds expression in this passage of the Jerusalem Talmud (II, 1), which is applied however to Jesus himself: "If anyone tells you, 'I am God,' he is a liar; if he says, 'I am the Son of God,' he will regret it at the end; if he says, 'I shall ascend to heaven,' he may say it but he cannot do it." Of course, while there is a Jewish anti-Christianity at the outset, there will also be increasingly a Christian anti-Judaism that will take its place alongside the ancient curses directed by pagans at the Jews.

The Final Jewish War

This final war was quite different in character from the first war. This time there was a revolt which gradually spread to the Jewish communities of Cyprus, Egypt, Mesopotamia and Judea.

Eusebius of Caesarea, at the end of the third century, records the facts in his *History of the Church* IV, 2, 1–6:

> When the emperor [Trajan] was about to enter his eighteenth year another rebellion broke out and destroyed vast numbers of Jews. In Alexandria and the rest of Egypt, and in Cyrene as well, as if inflamed by some terrible spirit of revolt they rushed into a faction fight against their Greek fellow-citizens. . . . From the first encounter they emerged victorious. But the Greeks fled to Alexandria, where they killed or captured the Jews in the city. But though deprived of their aid, the Jews of Cyrene went on plundering the territory of Egypt. . . . Against them the emperor sent Marcus Turbo with land and sea forces, including a contingent of cavalry. He pursued the war against them relent-

lessly in a long series of battles, destroying many thousands of Jews, not only those from Cyrene but others who had come from Egypt to assist Lucuas their king.

The emperor, suspecting that the Jews in Mesopotamia also would attack the people there, instructed Lucius Quietus to clear them out of the province. Lucius deployed his forces and slaughtered great numbers of the people there.[21]

It seems that the Jews of Cyrene took advantage of Trajan's campaign against Mesopotamia in 115 to rebel against the Greeks. The opposition between these two groups was unfortunately of long standing, as events under Caligula had shown. But in addition to this cultural hostility there was a nationalist element as well. The Jews were led by a king named Lucuas. The rebellion moved from Cyrene to nearby Egypt where, according to papyri that have been discovered, the Jews engaged in many atrocities and destroyed Egyptian temples. Rome intervened and there was a war from 115 to 117. According to Dio Cassius, 220,000 Jews perished. The communities of Egypt and Cyrenaica were completely wiped out.

But the rebellion did not remain contained. The Jews of Mesopotamia also revolted and launched an attack from the rear on Trajan's army as it was attacking the Parthian empire. Once again, the rebellion was put down with great ferocity.

Jerusalem also saw a revolt against Quietus; it is mentioned in the Mishnah. At Trajan's command Quietus had attempted to set up in a temple there an idol named "Caesar." We know nothing of the incident, ex-

Bar-Koziba money.

Symbols of the feast of Tabernacles.

The temple with a star over it.

cept that the Talmud speaks of a "Day of Trajan" on which Jews are not to fast, so great is Israel's joy. The Jewish uprising was therefore successful.

In order to end the Jewish revolt in Judea, Hadrian, Trajan's successor, had Quietus executed. This spirit of appeasement toward the Jews did not last. Hadrian required all his subjects to pay him worship and forbade circumcision, which pagans always looked upon with horror.

In 130 Hadrian came in person to Jerusalem; moved by the sight of the ruined city he ordered it rebuilt. But his intention was to make it a Hellenistic city that would bear his own name, Aelia. The threat of the Hellenization of Jerusalem initially led to only a passive resistance. Dio reports that the Jews forged inferior weapons for themselves; when permission for these was refused, they retained them nonetheless for future use.

It was at this point that a man arose whose name, Bar Koziba, has been made known to us by the excavations at Murabba'at. The name is explained by reference to Numbers 24:17: "A star shall come forth out of Jacob." He claimed to be the Messiah whom the Jews were awaiting and used the text just cited, which was interpreted as messianic both at Qumran and among Christians. Christians rejected his claim and refused to join him; for this they were cruelly persecuted. Devout Jews, on the other hand, saw in him the divinely promised Messiah who renews the ideals of the Maccabees. In the official documents found at Murabba'at he is called the Prince. Later on, when he had failed, his name was reinterpreted as based on the root *kazab,* and he became known as "Simon the Deceiver."

Simon was a nationalist and religious warrior. He demanded a strict observance of the sabbath; even caravans had to be halted on that day. Even in the midst of war, he had citrons, palm branches and myrtle brought in so that the feast of Booths might be celebrated. In the caves used by the insurgents the scroll of the minor prophets has been found. Religious vessels taken from the Romans were carefully hammered out in order to remove the images of pagan divinities. Among the rabbis, Rabbi Aqiba, of whose high reputation I have already spoken, rallied to him, but he was unable to obtain the support of the Pharisees as a group, because they were, once again, made uneasy by messianic claims. Simon also appointed a new high priest named Eleazar.

Initially, the insurgents gained control of the fortified places in the territory of Judea and outfitted caves like those that have been found. Bar Koziba or Bar Kokhba set up everywhere an administrative system like that of the Romans. He knew that the provisioning of fighting forces was an absolute necessity in time of war. The whole of Jewish territory was quickly drawn into the revolt. Bar Kokhba succeeded in freeing Jerusalem, as is attested by coins that have been discovered. He undoubtedly managed even to rebuild the temple, since Hadrian was compelled to raze it once again before erecting a sanctuary in honor of Jupiter.

The war that began at the departure of Hadrian (131) soon brought sixty-five thousand Romans into the field and, it seems, even the emperor himself. The architect Apollodorus of Damascus was asked to design machines of war that would be adapted to attacks on eagles' nests. The fortresses were recaptured one by one, a thousand or so villages were destroyed, and 580,000 people were killed, not counting, it seems, those who succumbed to hunger, sickness and fire. Once again, part of the population of Jerusalem was deported.

The fortress of Bether, southwest of Jerusalem, is said to have held out for three and a half years. Archeology does not confirm this report, but on the contrary suggests a very short siege. As a matter of fact, these remaining Jewish resisters became the subject of legend. In the view of some, the Prince was a mighty hero and must have resisted to the end. But in circles hostile to him the story was that a serpent was found on his corpse. In any event, the insurgents were tortured and killed. Aqiba is said to have recited liturgical prayers while being tortured and to have given his final teaching: "In the past I did not know how to love God with all my soul, but now I know: I shall love God with all my soul by giving it back to him." He died saying, "The Lord God is the only God." This attitude of Aqiba became the ideal for persecuted communities in time to come.

With the death of these last Jewish resisters around a man who claimed to be the Messiah, history took a decisive turn. The Jewish nation ceased to exist; it would not enter the stream of history as a nation again until the morrow of the Second World War.

When the nation disappeared, the Sadducees too left the scene once and for all. In the Talmud their name is synonymous with heretic. Without a temple and without a nation there could no longer be an aristocracy.

No strong apocalyptic or messianic movements arose from the ashes of this second defeat. The Essenes seem to have been erased from the map in 70; the last of the messiahs of Israel is remembered in the Talmud as a liar who deceived Israel with false promises of national restoration.

Just as Josephus, rejected by the Jews, found a place in the history of the Christian Church, so too Jewish apocalyptic literature was preserved and handed on by this Church which translated and interpreted it or introduced into it interpolations that make it proclaim the messiahship of Jesus.

All that was left to represent Judaism was the rabbinical schools. The only party that survived was the Pharisees, who were henceforth the trustees of the community's history. This group remained very active throughout the diaspora and especially in Babylon which has for centuries been a cultural center.

The Jewish community of Judea was for all practical purposes exterminated. But under the leadership of Gamaliel II the Sanhedrin were able to migrate to Beth-shearim, west of Nazareth, where excavations have revealed the existence of a synagogue and catacombs. The synagogue is of more recent date, but the building of the catacombs began as early as the second century and provide us with many inscriptions in Greek and in Hebrew. These are invaluable witnesses to the history and the piety of the community.

The Sanhedrin is said to have migrated later on to Sepphoris, south of Nazareth. There, under the leadership of two Pharisees, Simon and in particular Judah Hanassi, the immense task of codifying the traditions was undertaken. The fruit of this first labor was the Mishnah, published by Rabbi Judah the Holy in about 220. This first nucleus was then supplemented by the rabbinical school of Tiberias, until the Palestinian Talmud was completed in about 350.

This literary and spiritual work instilled new life into the Jewish community of Galilee, which down until the sixth century built magnificent synagogues in accordance with the instructions in the Mishnah. The political disturbances of the sixth and seventh centuries caused the disappearance in turn of these Galilean communities.

The Jewish nation had disappeared, but there were Jews everywhere in the Roman empire; in these early centuries they may have made up as much as seven percent of the population. They enjoyed an exceptional legal status, since Judaism was a legally recognized form of worship. This meant that in each town Jews could organize as an association and have not only a synagogue but schools, libraries, ritual baths, canteens and poorhouses. The Jewish authorities had the right to levy taxes directly on their brothers in the faith; this was an important source of funds that kept the community united in its expansion and its care of the poor.

This Jewish organizational structure and sense of community, together with monotheism and its concrete applications in everyday life and in celebrations, impressed the ancient world. The Jews exerted an attraction, and Flavius Josephus could write: "Even among the masses there has long been felt a keen desire for our religion, and there is not a single Greek or foreign town into which the practice of the seventh day as a day of rest has not made its way and in which fasting and the use of lights and many of our dietary practices are not observed."

Josephus deserves credence here, for, according to Acts 2, Jews from all the nations came together on Pentecost. Paul would later travel to the Jewish communities of Asia Minor, Greece and Rome in order to speak of Christ to them. Even the Roman poets—Ovid and Horace, for example—speak of the influence of the sabbath, although Horace, it is true, is offended by it.

Even apart from Jewish faith and practice, there is some interest in following the course of this community that was scattered throughout the empire. The Jews gradually appear as traders and as preferred ambassadors. For even though they cultivated all the trades and professions wherever they gathered, the bonds between the communities favored these new roles in particular.

But there were also shadows on this richly detailed picture. Jewish monotheism was not always understood but appeared to some to represent a desire to remain apart or a fanatical outlook that was scornful of other religions.

Philostratus, a Sophist at the beginning of the second century, could sum up the commonly leveled accusations and write: "This people has long been in rebellion not only against the Romans but against the entire human race. People who can conceive of a life apart from society, and who share with their fellow human beings neither table nor libations nor sacrifices, are farther removed from us than Susa or Bactria." We are far here from the apologies of a Philo or a Josephus, who make Moses the ancestor of all the philosophers.

A further source of danger for the Jews of the diaspora was the Christians. The Christians were initially confused with the Jews by the pagans who rejected them both (Tacitus believed they shared the same accursed superstition; the rumor was about that they adored a God with an ass' head), but very soon the God-fearers and many pagans were turning to the new religion.

These people rejected Judaism with its difficult rites, especially circumcision and the dietary laws, and its multiplicity of commandments that had to be followed daily. By becoming Christians they could remove from themselves the opprobrium attached to the Jews in the Greek world. They did not have to accept those Jewish ideals that were connected with the promised land; they did not have to suffer the harsh financial burdens placed on Jews. On the other hand, they could enter a religion that followed comparable principles of community life and practiced monotheism, but in its missionary outlook recognized no distinction between Jews and Greeks. Finally, these people were touched by the mystery of the dead and risen Christ who sends his Spirit upon every human being.

From the time of Hadrian on, the two communities seem to have been clearly distinct. Christians increasingly made their way even into high Roman society and persuaded people there that Christ is the true Messiah for the nations. They survived harsh persecutions and achieved toleration and then recognition as an official religion under Constantine. From that point on, Jews were only too often subjected to pressures of all sorts that were brought to bear on them by Christians.

These difficulties between Jews and Christians were not found outside the Roman empire. Except for the persecutions under Trajan, the Jewish community of Babylon lived in peace for centuries. After being cut off from Palestine in a definitive way by the war of 70, the community in Babylon was organized, probably from as early as the second century, under the government of an exilarch. He was an important personage at court, generally being the fourth-ranking official. Under his authority the schools of Babylon produced the Babylonian Talmud between the third and fifth centuries.

The center of Judaism subsequently shifted to the Jewish academies of Sura and Pumbadita, which were directed by the gaonim, the men of rank from the sixth to the eleventh centuries. Jews anywhere in the world who aspired to an academic degree came to study under their direction; the Babylonian Talmud had triumphed.

Notes

Introduction

1. *Bible et Terre Sainte*, no. 123.
2. *Le monde de la Bible*, no. 20.
3. The Hebrew expression "River of Egypt" probably referred to different things at different periods: (a) The easternmost arm of the Nile; (b) the Wadi Ghazzeh which debouched near the town of Gaza; (c) the Wadi el-'Arish (according to the Septuagint).

2. History

1. S.N. Kramer, *History Begins at Sumer* (Garden City, N.Y.: Doubleday Anchor Books, 1957); A. Parrot, *Sumer,* tr. by S. Gilbert and J. Emmons (London: Thames & Hudson, 1960); *Bible et Terre Sainte*, no. 17.
2. G. von Rad, *Genesis: A Commentary,* tr. by J.H. Marks (rev. ed.; Philadelphia: Westminster, 1972); J. Briend, "Une lecture du Pentateuque," *Cahiers Evangile,* no. 15 (1976).
3. H. Cazelles, *Les Patriarches* (Paris: Cerf, 1979); R. Michaud, *Les Patriarches: Histoire et théologie* (Coll. *Lire la Bible*; Paris: Cerf, 1975).
4. A. Alt, "The God of the Fathers," in his *Essays in Old Testament Religion and History,* tr. by R.A. Wilson (Garden City, N.Y.: Doubleday, 1967; Doubleday Anchor Books, 1968).
5. R. Martin-Achard, *Actualité d'Abraham* (Neuchâtel: Delachaux et Niestlé, 1969); A. Parrot, *Abraham et son temps* (Neuchâtel: Delachaux et Niestlé, 1962).
6. *Bible et Terre Sainte*, no. 17.
7. Ibid., no. 80.
8. Ibid., no. 84.

9. Ibid., nos. 6, 16, 20, 25, 156.

10. E. Jacob, *Ras Shamra Ugarit et l'Ancien Testament* (Neuchâtel: Delachaux et Niestlé, 1968–69).

11. F. Michaeli, *L'Exode* (Neuchâtel: Delachaux et Niestlé, 1974); G. Auzou, *De la servitude au service* (Coll. *Connaissance de la Bible;* Paris: Ed. de l'Orante, 1963); *Bible et Terre Sainte,* no. 185.

12. A. Neher, *Moses and the Vocation of the Jewish People,* tr. by I. Marinoff (New York: Harper Torchbooks, 1959); H. Cazelles, *A la recherche de Moïse: Histoire et théologie* (Coll. *Lire la Bible;* Paris: Cerf, 1979).

13. *Le monde de la Bible,* no. 10.

14. These fortresses are clearly depicted on the wall of the temple at Karnak, where the story is told of the campaigns of Seti I. Gaza is especially recognizable.

3. The Age of the Conquest

1. G. Auzou, *Le don d'une conquête* (Paris: Ed. de l'Orante, 1964).

2. We may note here that the Samaritans, who do not regard this book as canonical, have their own version of it.

3. *Bible et Terre Sainte,* no. 167: "Les Philistins."

4. Ibid., nos. 14, 187.

5. Ibid., no. 151.

6. Ibid., nos. 18, 26, 35, 56.

7. Ibid., no. 125.

8. Laish is already mentioned in the Egyptian execration texts (nineteenth century B.C.) as well as in the Mari correspondence. Later, under the Hyksos, it was fortified like Hazor.

9. *Bible et Terre Sainte,* no. 124.

4. The Age of the Judges

1. G. Auzou, *La force de l'Esprit* (Paris: Ed. de l'Orante, 1965).

2. In the story as I have told it a mystery remains: How could a group of semi-nomads so quickly become a sedentary agricultural society?

I pointed out earlier that groups which had emerged from Egypt certainly fused with groups which had never left Canaan. But is it possible to go further and think that the groups from Egypt took part in a rebellion of Canaanite peasants against the kings of the city-states?

Israel would thus be made up not only of semi-nomadic groups from Egypt along with their semi-nomadic brothers already more or less settled in Canaan. It would also be a union in rebellion with a Canaanite peasantry that wanted a more egalitarian society and one free of slavery. This idea was probably the specific contribution of the tribes from the wilderness.

Daniel Lys, in *Etudes théologiques et religieuses,* 1982, suggests the hypothesis that this Canaanite peasantry in rebellion against the cities may represent the posterity of Seth, the first worshipers of Yahweh (Gen 4:26), as opposed to the accursed posterity of Cain, who were rejected by Yahweh but who built towns and developed technologies.

5. Samuel and the Establishment of the Monarchy

1. G. Auzou, *La danse devant l'arche* (Paris: Ed. de l'Orante, 1968); H.W. Hertzberg, *I and II Samuel. A Commentary*, tr. by J.S. Bowden (Philadelphia: Westminster, 1964); P. Gibert, *La Bible à la naissance de l'histoire* (Paris: Fayard, 1979).

6. The Reigns of David and Solomon

1. *Le monde de la Bible*, no. 7.
2. S. Amsler, *David, Roi et Messie* (Neuchâtel: Delachaux et Niestlé, 1963); *Bible et Terre Sainte*, no. 167: "David et Goliath"; *Le monde de la Bible*, no. 7.
3. J. Gray, *I and II Kings. A Commentary* (Philadelphia: Westminster, 1963); F. Michaeli, *Le livre des Chroniques* (Neuchâtel: Delachaux et Niestlé, 1967).

7. Schism: 933 B.C. (?), 1 Kings 12

1. A Parrot, *Samaria, Capital of the Kingdom of Israel*, tr. by S.H. Hooke (Studies in Biblical Archaeology 7; London: SCM, 1958); *Bible et Terre Sainte*, nos. 28, 120, 121, 184.
2. Exegetical notes of the Société des Ecoles du dimanche (Paris).
3. The most beautiful of the jasper seals found in Palestine undoubtedly dates from the time of Jeroboam II; it was discovered at Megiddo and bears the inscription: "Shema, servant of Jeroboam."
4. S. Amsler, *Amos* (Neuchâtel: Delachaux et Niestlé, 1965).

8. Assyrian Domination and the End of Israel

1. A. Parrot, *The Arts of Assyria*, tr. by S. Gilbert and J. Emmons (New York: Golden Press, 1961); J. Deshayes, *La civilisation de l'Orient Ancien* (Paris: Arthaud, 1969).
2. *Bible et Terre Sainte*, nos. 37, 47.
3. J.M. Assurmendi, *Cahier Evangile*, no. 23; P. Auvray, *Esaïe 1–29* (Paris: Gabalda, 1972).

4. E. Jacob, *Osée* (Neuchâtel: Delachaux et Niestlé, 1965).

5. R. Vuilleumier, *Michée* (Neuchâtel: Delachaux et Niestlé, 1971); A. Maillot and L. Lelievre, *Actualité de Michée* (Geneva: Labor et Fides, 1976).

6. *Le monde de la Bible*, no. 11.

7. *Bible et Terre Sainte*, no. 194.

8. Ibid., no. 63.

9. Babylonian Domination and the End of Judah

1. *Bible et Terre Sainte*, no. 162.

2. Several of the many ostraka found at Arad seem to be from this period. One of them conveys a command to send reinforcements from Arad to Ramah of the Negeb in order to resist a threat from Edom.

An extensive correspondence has also been discovered, containing instructions from Eliashib, last governor of the citadel. He orders that he be supplied with rations of bread and wine, particularly for the Kittim. Judah doubtless had Greek mercenaries in its service.

3. *Bible et Terre Sainte*, no. 112.

10. Persian Domination and Return from Exile

1. *Bible et Terre Sainte*, no. 153.

2. There is evidence that during the entire Persian period desert tribes slowly infiltrated, gradually occupied and finally put an end to the kingdoms of Moab and Edom. The first of the new settlers were the tribes of Kedar.

Later would come the Nabateans, but there is less agreement on their origin. Were they Arabs migrating westward or very ancient inhabitants of the Negeb who finally began to expand?

At the end of the Persian period the kingdom of Moab no longer existed. As for the Edomites, some moved northward and even occupied Hebron; they were henceforth called Idumeans.

3. The first Jewish coin was struck during the period of Nehemiah: a half-shekel with the head of a woman on the face, and the head of a bearded man on the reverse side. Was the coinage motivated by a desire to pay the temple tax with Jewish money?

4. At Tell el-Far'ah a tomb has been found that is enclosed within a brick wall. It contains rich furnishings: a bronze stool, a silver bowl and a matching ladle, the handle of which is in the form of a naked girl.

5. According to the chronicles of the Samaritans the break between them and the Jews goes back much further: back to the beginning of the tenth century B.C. when the priest Eli, Samuel's tutor, transferred the ark from Gerizim to Shiloh.

6. According to the Samaritans, Moses alone was inspired; after him there

would be no other prophet until one came who was like him (Dt 18:15). This successor would be the Messiah.

Being more conservative than the Jews, the Samaritans did not recognize the 613 commandments of Moses and allowed no place for the oral commentaries so dear to the Pharisees. We may note that according to the Samaritans the tenth commandment given to Moses ordered worship to be offered on Mount Gerizim. As a result, the Passover sacrifice is celebrated there even today.

They regard their text of the Pentateuch as superior to the Hebrew text, on the grounds that they had it directly from a descendant of Aaron.

7. A. Lacocque, *Commentaire de 2. Zacharie* (Neuchâtel: Delachaux et Niestlé, 1979).

11. The Period of Hellenistic Domination

1. W.W. Tarn, cited in M. Eliade, *A History of Religious Ideas*, tr. by W.R. Trask (2 vols.; Chicago: University of Chicago Press, 1978–82), 2:204.

2. The recent excavations begun in 1976 raise doubts that this building can be regarded as a temple: the plan would seem to be completely different and would suggest rather a country villa of two stories. Due to Hyrcanus' brilliant foresight, the villa had an artificial lake at its service, which at the same time provided water for the horses of the garrison.

The whole estate was doubtless located within the agricultural domain of the Tobiads, and probably included gardens and orchards which justified the historian Josephus' description of it as "the paradise of Tyre."

This monumental work, which was doubtless built by the labor of Arabian slaves, was never completed. Hyrcanus is said to have committed suicide, fearing reprisals from Antiochus IV after the death of Seleucus IV (Josephus, *AJ* 12:236). (See: *Le monde de la Bible*, no. 22.)

3. G. Gaide, *Le livre de Daniel* (Paris: Mame, 1969); A. Lacocque, *Le Livre de Daniel* (Neuchâtel: Delachaux et Niestlé, 1976).

12. The Maccabean Resistance and the New Hasmonean Kingdom

1. During this entire period as well as the following period of Roman occupation Beth-zur was one of the most important fortified places in Judea. It had been fortified long ago by the Hyksos, by Rehoboam at the time of the schism, and by Nehemiah after the return from exile. Excavations at Beth-zur have turned up the oldest Jewish coins we have; they bear the name "Yehud" and were perhaps struck by Nehemiah.

2. The Damascus Document opens with an accusation against the whole of that faithless Jewish community, but then it announces that God visited them 390 years later (the number doubtless comes from Ezekiel 4:4–6). At that time people

were converted but then experienced twenty years of troubles: "They were like blind men and like men who groping seek their way for twenty years. And God considered their works, for they had sought Him with a perfect heart; and He raised up for them a Teacher of Righteousness to lead them in the way of His heart and to make known to the last generations what He would do to the last generation, the congregation of haters" (in A. Dupont-Sommer, *The Essene Writings from Qumran*, tr. by G. Vermes [1961; repr. Gloucester, Mass.: Peter Smith, 1973]). Since Josephus speaks of the Essenes for the first time in connection with the pontificate of Jonathan, the Teacher of Righteousness was perhaps a contemporary of Jonathan.

3. Josephus has this to say about the differences between Pharisees and Sadducees: "The Pharisees had introduced among the people many customs which they had inherited from the ancestors. These, however, were not written in the laws of Moses, and on this account the Sadducees rejected them, maintaining that only what was written should be regarded as law and that what was purely a matter of tradition should not be observed" (*Antiquities of the Jews*, 13, 297).

Elsewhere he notes: "The Sadducees will have nothing to do with the idea of fate. They claim that God can neither do nor foresee evil and that individuals follow their own wills in turning the one way or the other. They deny the continued existence of the soul after death as well as any rewards and punishments in another world" (*The Jewish War*, 2, 164–66).

4. In addition to the name and title of the king the coins bear other symbols: anchor, star, palm branch, cornucopia, pomegranate flower.

13. The Roman Occupation

1. J. Jeremias, *Jerusalem in the Time of Jesus*, tr. by F.H. and C.H. Cave (Philadelphia: Fortress, 1969); M. Simon, *Jewish Sects in the Time of Jesus*, tr. by J.H. Farley (Philadelphia: Fortress, 1969); E. Lohse, *The New Testament Environment*, tr. by J.E. Steely (Nashville: Abingdon, 1975); A. Paul, *Le monde des Juifs à l'heure de Jésus* (Paris: Desclée, 1981).

2. *Le monde de la Bible*, no. 18.

3. *Bible et Terre Sainte*, no. 192.

4. Josephus often refers to the decree of Caesar. According to him Augustus said: "In view of the fact that the Jewish people has been recognized as having proper feelings toward the Roman people, not only at the present time but in the past as well and especially in the reign of my father, Emperor Caesar, I have decided that the Jews may observe their own customs in conformity with the law of their ancestors, just as they did in the time of Hyrcanus . . . that their contributions to their religion are to be regarded as sacrosanct and sent to Jerusalem to be put in the hands of that city's tax receivers; that they are not to be forced to go bail on the sabbath. . . . If anyone is caught in the act of stealing their sacred books or the money collected for religious purposes, such a one is to be considered a sacrilegious thief."

Dolabella, a Roman general, says: "I follow my predecessors in granting the Jews exemption from military service, and I authorize them to observe the customs of their nation, as well as to assemble in order to celebrate their cult and ceremonies, as their law bids them do."

A proconsul writes in the same spirit to the inhabitants of Paros who want to force the Jews to observe the common customs: "When Caius Caesar issued a decree forbidding the formation of associations at Rome, the Jews were the only ones he did not include in the prohibition. I too, while forbidding all other associations, authorize the Jews alone to live according to the customs and laws of their nation and to assemble for their banquets."

These privileges were, of course, rarely honored in their totality. At the same time, however, they turned the Jews into a race apart, making it possible for them to live according to their own laws but at the same time laying them open to the hostile attention of all the other inhabitants of the empire. The privileges cut two ways, since they often provided food for anti-semitism.

5. Hippus gave Herod control of the Golan Heights.

6. Pliny the Elder gives a list of ten cities: Damascus, Raphanea, Canatha, Dion, Hippus, Gadara, Scythopolis, Gerasa and Philadelphia.

7. According to Josephus, Herod had no difficulties with the Sadducees: "Their teaching is accepted by only a small number, although these are men of the first rank. They are able to do practically nothing, however, for when they become magistrates unwillingly and against their wishes, they conform to the views of the Pharisees since otherwise the people would not support them" (*Antiquities of the Jews* 18, 17). Josephus was himself a Pharisee, of course, but it is quite clear that for practical purposes the Sadducees had now only an honorific role.

8. *Bible et Terre Sainte*, no. 162.

9. According to Josephus, *The Jewish War* 1, 665, Herod died of an intolerable itch over the entire surface of his body and of continual intestinal pains. He tried to obtain a cure in the hot springs of Callarhoe, near the Dead Sea. The site of these springs is marked on the mosaic map found at Madaba and dating from the sixth century A.D.

10. Josephus speaks of the event as follows in *Antiquities of the Jews* 18, 116–19: "There were Jews who believed that the destruction of Herod's army was caused by the divine will in just revenge for John the Baptist. Herod had had John put to death, even though he was a good man and was urging the Jews to practice virtue, to be just in their dealings with one another and devout in relation to God, to receive baptism. . . . Some people had gathered around John, for they were deeply moved by his words. Herod was afraid that John's ability to persuade people would lead to an uprising, inasmuch as the crowds followed his advice on all matters. Herod therefore thought it better to seize John before any disturbance could be caused than to be sorry later on at having exposed himself to danger should a movement in fact arise. Because of these suspicions of Herod, John was sent to Machaerus and executed there. The Jews, as I said, believed that the catastrophe which fell on the army was in revenge for the killing of John, since God decided to punish Herod in this manner." The story of John the Baptist as told by Josephus

differs notably from the Gospel version of it. It does, however, shed light on the thinking of Caiaphas when he had Jesus arrested before it was too late and before the crowd realized what was happening.

11. Josephus writes: "A man known as Judas the Galilean plunged into rebellion. He claimed that this census entailed nothing less than a complete enslavement of the Jews, and he called upon the people to assert their freedom. Judas the Galilean was the founder of the fourth sect of Jewish philosophy. His followers were in general agreement with the teaching of the Pharisees, but they had an invincible love of freedom, because they maintained that God is the only ruler and master. Even the most extraordinary kinds of death inflicted on them, or the tortures to which their relatives and friends were subjected, left them indifferent, as long as they did not have to give any human being the title of "master."

12. J. Blinzler, *The Trial of Jesus*, tr. by I. and F. McHugh (Westminster, Md.: Newman, 1959); F. Bovon, *Les derniers jours de Jésus* (Neuchâtel: Delachaux et Niestlé, 1974); J.P. Lemonon, *Pilate et le gouvernement de Judée* (Paris: Gabalda, 1981).

13. *The Embassy to Gaius*, nos. 124, 127–28, tr. by F.H. Colson (Loeb Classics, Philo 10; Cambridge, Mass.: Harvard University Press, 1962), 63, 65.

14. J. Daniélou, *Philon d'Alexandrie* (Paris: Fayard, 1957).

15. *Bible et Terre Sainte*, no. 139.

16. Juvenal, *Satires* XIV, 97–106, tr. by C.G. Ramsey, *Juvenal and Persius* (Loeb Classics; Cambridge, Mass.: Harvard University Press, 1940), 271, 273.

17. A. Dupont-Sommer, *The Essene Writings from Qumran*, tr. by G. Vermes (1961; repr. Gloucester, Mass.: Peter Smith, 1973); *Cahier Evangile*, no. 13; *Le monde de la Bible*, no. 4.

18. Pliny, *Natural History* V, 15, tr. by H. Rackham (Loeb Classics; Cambridge, Mass.: Harvard University Press, 1950), 2:277.

19. According to Eusebius, *The History of the Church* III, 5, 3, tr. by G.A. Williamson (Baltimore: Penguin, 1965), 111: "The members of the Jerusalem church, by means of an oracle given by revelation to an acceptable person there, were ordered to leave the city before the war began and settle in a town in Peraea called Pella. To Pella those who believed in Christ migrated from Jerusalem . . . as if holy men had utterly abandoned the royal metropolis of the Jews and the entire Jewish land." According to Epiphanius they returned to Jerusalem after its destruction and worked great signs there.

20. Suetonius, *Life of Domitian* 12, in Suetonius, *Writings*, tr. by J.C. Rolfe (Loeb Classics, 2 vols.; Cambridge, Mass.: Harvard University Press, 1940), 2:365–67.

21. Eusebius, *The History of the Church* IV, 2, 1–6 (Williamson, 154–55).

Bibliography

General

A. Lods, *Histoire de la littérature hébraïque et juive* (Paris: Payot, 1950)
G. von Rad, *Old Testament Theology*, tr. by D.M.G. Stalker (2 vols.; New York: Harper & Row, 1962, 1965)
R. de Vaux, *Ancient Israel: Its Life and Institutions*, tr. by J. McHugh (New York: McGraw-Hill, 1961)
Dictionnaire encyclopédique de la Bible (Paris: Brépols, 1960)
M. Eliade, *A History of Religious Ideas*, tr. by W.R. Trask (2 vols.; Chicago: University of Chicago Press, 1978, 1982)

Archeology

Bible et Terre Sainte
Le monde de la Bible (Paris: Bayard-Presse)
Cahiers d'archéologie biblique (Neuchâtel: Delachaux et Niestlé)
Dictionnaire archéologique de la Bible, ed. by A. Negev (Paris: Fernand Hazan, 1970)
F. Michaeli, *Textes de la Bible et de l'Ancien Orient* (Neuchâtel: Delachaux et Niestlé, 1961)
J. Briend and M.J. Seux, *Textes du Proche Orient Ancien et histoire d'Israël* (Paris: Cerf, 1977)

Atlases

L.H. Grollenberg, *Atlas of the Bible* (New York: Nelson, 1956)
H.G. May, *Oxford Bible Atlas* (London: Oxford University Press, 1976)

History of Israel and Judah

M. Noth, *The History of Israel*, rev. tr. by P.R. Ackroyd (New York: Harper & Row, 1960)

R. de Vaux, *The Early History of Israel*, tr. by D. Smith (Philadelphia: Westminster, 1978)

A. Neher, *Histoire biblique du peuple d'Israël* (Paris: Maison-neuve, 1974)

J.H. Hayes and J.M. Miller (eds.), *Israelite and Judaean History* (Philadelphia: Westminster, 1977)

A. Lemaire, *Histoire du peuple hébreu* (Paris: Presses Universitaires de France, 1981)

Prehistory

A. Parrot, *L'aventure archéoloique* (Paris: Laffont, 1979)

———, *Sumer*, tr. by S. Gilbert and J. Emmons (London: Thames and Hudson, 1960)

W.F. Albright, *The Archeology of Palestine* (Baltimore: Penguin, 1949)

S.N. Kramer, *History Begins at Sumer* (Garden City, N.Y.: Doubleday Anchor Books, 1957)

The Patriarchs

A. Parrot, *Abraham and His Times*, tr. by J.H. Farley (Philadelphia: Fortress, 1968)

R. Martin-Achard, *Actualité d'Abraham* (Neuchâtel: Delachaux et Niestlé, 1969)

G. von Rad, *Genesis: A Commentary*, tr. by J.H. Marks (rev. ed.; Philadelphia: Westminster, 1972)

J. Briend, "Une lecture du Pentateuque," *Cahier Evangile*, no. 15 (1976)

R. Michaud, *Les patriarches* (Paris: Cerf, 1975)

H. Cazelles, *Les patriarches* (Paris: Cerf, 1975)

A. Alt, "The God of the Fathers," in his *Essays in Old Testament Religion and History*, tr. by R.A. Wilson (Garden City, N.Y.: Doubleday, 1967)

J. Deshayes, *La civilisation de l'Orient Ancien* (Paris: Arthaud, 1969)

The Sojourn in Egypt

P. Montet, *L'Egypte et la Bible* (Neuchâtel: Delachaux et Niestlé, 1959)

E. Jacob, *Ras Shamra et l'Ancien Testament* (Neuchâtel: Delachaux et Niestlé, 1960)

F. Daumas, *La civilisation de l'Egypte Pharaonique* (Paris: Arthaud, 1967)

R. Michaud, *Joseph le Makirite* (Paris: Cerf, 1976)

Oppression in Egypt and the Exodus

M. Noth, *Exodus: A Commentary*, tr. by J.S. Bowden (Philadelphia: Westminster, 1962)

———, *Numbers: A Commentary*, tr. by J.D. Martin (Philadelphia: Westminster, 1968)

G. Auzou, *De la servitude au service* (Paris: Ed. de l'Orante, 1974)

F. Michaeli, *L'Exode* (Neuchâtel: Delachaux et Niestlé, 1974)

A. Neher, *Moses and the Vocation of the Jewish People*, tr. by I. Marinoff (New York: Harper Torchbooks, 1959)

H. Cazelles, *A la recherche de Moïse* (Paris: Cerf, 1979)

R. Michaud, *Moïse: Histoire et théologie* (Paris: Cerf, 1979)

Age of the Conquest

G. Auzou, *Le don d'une conquête* (Paris: Ed. de l'Orante, 1964)

J.A. Soggin, *Joshua: A Commentary*, tr. by R.A. Wilson (Philadelphia: Westminster, 1972)

The Judges

G. Auzou, *La force de l'Esprit* (Paris: Ed. de l'Orante, 1965)

Establishment of the Monarchy

H.W. Hertzberg, *I and II Samuel: A Commentary*, tr. by J.S. Bowden (Philadelphia: Westminster, 1964)

G. Auzou, *La danse devant l'arche* (Paris: Ed. de l'Orante, 1968)

S. Amsler, *David Roi et Messie* (Neuchâtel: Delachaux et Niestlé, 1963)

P. Gibert, *La Bible à la naissance de l'histoire* (Paris: Fayard, 1979)

Le monde de la Bible, no. 7.

The Monarchy

J. Gray, *I and II Kings: A Commentary* (Philadelphia: Westminster, 1963)

F. Michaeli, *Le livre des Chroniques* (Neuchâtel: Delachaux et Niestlé, 1967)

A. Parrot, *Nineveh and the Old Testament*, tr. by B.E. Hooke (New York: Philosophical Library, 1955)

———, *Samaria, Capital of the Kingdom of Israel*, tr. by S.H. Hooke (London: SCM, 1958)

————, *Babylon and the Old Testament,* tr. by S.H. Hooke (New York: Philosophical Library, 1958)

————, *The Arts of Assyria,* tr. by S. Gilbert and J. Emmons (New York: Golden Press, 1961)

Le monde de la Bible, no. 15

The Prophets

W. Vischer, *Les premiers prophètes* (Neuchâtel: Delachaux et Niestlé, 1951)

Elie (Paris: Société des Ecoles du Dimanche, n.d.)

A. Neher, *Amos* (Paris: Vrin, 1981)

S. Amsler, *Amos* (Neuchâtel: Delachaux et Niestlé, 1965)

E. Jacob, *Osée* (Neuchâtel: Delachaux et Niestlé, 1965)

P. Auvray, *Esaie 1–39* (Paris: Gabalda, 1972)

J.M. Asurmendi, *Cahier Evangile,* no. 23.

C. Westermann, *Isaiah 40–66. A Commentary,* tr. by D.M.G. Stalker (Philadelphia: Westminster, 1967)

R. Vuilleumeir, *Michée* (Neuchâtel: Delachaux et Niestlé, 1971)

A. Maillot and L. Lelievre, *Actualité de Michée* (Geneva: Labor et Fides, 1976)

C.A. Keller, *Nahaoum, Habacuc, Sophonie* (Neuchâtel: Delachaux et Niestlé, 1971)

O. Bogaert, *Le livre de Jérémie* (Louvain: 1981)

A. Neher, *Jérémie* (Paris: Stock, 1980)

W. Eichrodt, *Ezekiel. A Commentary,* tr. by C. Quin (Philadelphia: Westminster, 1970)

S. Amsler, *Jonas* (Neuchâtel: Delachaux et Niestlé, 1965)

P. Buis, *Le Deutéronome* (Paris: Beauchesne, 1969)

The Persian Period

F. Michaeli, *Esdras et Néhémie* (Neuchâtel: Delachaux et Niestlé, 1967)

T. Chary, *Aggée, Zacharie, Malachie* (Paris: Gabalda, 1968)

S. Amsler, R. Vuilleumier, and A. Lacocque, *Aggée, Zacharie, Malachie* (Neuchâtel: Delachaux et Niestlé, 1981)

Hellenistic Domination

Josephus, *The Antiquities of the Jews*

G. Gaide, *Le livre de Daniel* (Paris: Mame, 1969)

A. Lacocque, *Le livre de Daniel* (Neuchâtel: Delachaux et Niestlé, 1976)

A. Paul, *Le monde des Juifs à l'heure de Jésus* (Paris: Desclée, 1981)

F. Chamoux, *La civilisation hellénistique* (Paris: Arthaud, 1981)

Roman Period

J. Daniélou, *Philon d'Alexandrie* (Paris: Fayard, 1957)

M. Simon, *Jewish Sects in the Time of Jesus*, tr. by J.H. Farley (Philadelphia: Fortress, 1967)

————, *La civilisation de l'Antiquité et le christianisme* (Paris: Arthaud, 1972)

J. Blinzler, *The Trial of Jesus*, tr. by I. and F. McHugh (Westminster, Md.: Newman, 1959)

J. Jeremias, *Jerusalem in the Time of Jesus*, tr. by F.H. and C.H. Cave (Philadelphia: Fortress, 1969)

E. Lohse, *The New Testament Environment*, tr. by J.S. Steely (Nashville: Abingdon, 1975)

F. Bovon, *Les derniers jours de Jésus* (Neuchâtel: Delachaux et Niestlé, 1974)

J.P. Lemonon, *Pilate et le gouvernement de la Judee* (Paris: Gabalda, 1981)

Jewish War

Josephus, *The Jewish War*, tr. by G.A. Williamson (Baltimore: Penguin, 1970²)

P. Prigent, *La fin de Jerusalem* (Neuchâtel: Delachaux et Niestlé, 1969)

A. Dupont-Sommer, *The Essene Writings from Qumran*, tr. by G. Vermes (Cleveland: World, 1961)

Cahier Evangile, no. 13

Le monde de la Bible, no. 4.

Index

A

Aaron, 45, 212
Abdon, 73
Abiathar, 91, 92
Abilene, 193, 213, 224
Abimelech, 79–80
Abner, 89
Abraham, 25–9
Absalom, 90–1, 97
Acco (Acre), 12, 33, 41, 55, 178, 187
Acra, 179, 181, 184
Adadnirari, 113
Adasa, 182
Adonijah, 92
Adoram, 91, 99
Aelia, 244
Agrippa I, 221–2
Agrippa II, 224–5
Ahab, 4, 104–6
Ahaz, 117, 120, 128
Ai, 4, 21, 51, 63
Ain Mellaha, 14
Akh-en-aten, 34, 40
Alcimus, 181–2
Alexander Balas, 183–4
Alexander Janneus, 187–8
Alexander the Great, 166–8
Alexandra Salome, 188–9
Alexandreion, 188, 194

Alexandria, 167, 169, 179, 195, 196, 213, 218, 239, 242–3
Amalekites, 46, 54, 78, 82
Amathus, 187
Ammon/Ammonites, 7, 9, 10, 29, 58, 71, 73, 78, 82, 90, 119, 129, 139
Amorites, 22–4, 26, 30, 32, 58, 64
Amos, 110, 113–5
Ananias, 226
Annas, 225, 230
Antigonus, 186, 191, 198
Antioch, 167, 204, 218, 230
Antiochus III, 172–3, 192, 204
Antiochus IV, 177–81, 183, 192
Antiochus V, 181
Antiochus VI, 185
Antipater, 189, 194–5
Aphek, 7, 33
apocalypse, 177, 239–40
Arabah, 4, 9, 10, 19, 54, 113
Arad, 8, 88, 93, 131
Arameans, 10, 30, 58, 71, 82, 102, 104, 113
Archelaus, 206–7
Aretas I, 179
Aretas III, 189, 194
Aristeas, letter of, 169
Aristobule I, 186
Aristobule II, 189–92
Aristobule III, 199

Arnon, 9, 58
Artaxerxes I, 156–8
Artaxerxes II, 160–4
Artaxerxes III, 162
Ashdod, 53, 118, 124, 126–8, 135, 156, 181, 183, 206
Asher, 61, 67, 76, 78
Ashkelon, 32, 42, 53, 230
Astarte, 53

B
Baal, 10, 37, 46, 49, 53, 78, 79, 93, 108, 131
Babylon/Babylonians, 6, 22–3, 39, 50, 51, 82, 128-30, 135–45, 204
Baruch, 137, 177, 239
Bashan, 9, 11, 59
Bathsheba, 90–2
Beersheba, 10, 26, 29, 40, 101
Benjamin/Benjaminites, 23, 59, 62–4, 67, 68, 71, 76–8, 85, 92
Bethel, 8, 12, 25, 26, 30, 63, 69, 76, 81, 100–1, 114, 132, 151, 155
Bethlehem, 10, 73, 87, 181, 209
Bethshean, 12, 21, 53, 55, 89, 172
Bilhah, 65, 67
Booths (Tabernacles), feast of, 183, 187, 244
Byblos, 16, 21, 31, 32, 129, 158, 204

C
Caesar, 194–5
Cain, 3, 37, 44, 77
Caleb, 56, 75
Caligula, 212–6, 221, 243
Cambyses, 153–4
Canaan/Canaanites, 10, 23–6, 29–31, 33–8, 43, 48, 51, 55–9, 63–4, 68, 71, 76, 78, 93, 101
Carmel, 7, 13, 53, 108, 186
Cicero, 194
Claudius, 221–4
Cypros, 193, 203
Cyrus the Great, 147–53

D
Dagon, 37, 53, 183
Damascus, 16, 33
Dan, 64–5, 67–8, 71, 76, 78, 80, 100–1
Daniel, 143, 149, 171, 174–7
Darius I, 154
Darius II, 158–60
Darius III, 166
David, 25, 55, 56, 68, 86–91, 97
Dead Sea, 4, 9, 10, 13, 18, 54
Debir, 56
Deborah, 65–6, 75–8
Deborah, song of, 59–61, 67
Decalogue, 48–50
Delilah, 80
Demetrius I, 183
Demetrius II, 183–4
Demetrius III, 187
Deuteronomistic tradition, 49, 51, 55–6, 68–70, 97, 100–1, 131–3
Dibon, 55
Dinah, 58
Dothan, 10

E
Ebla, 4, 29, 31
Edom (Esau), 9, 10, 25, 30, 43, 55, 56, 67, 68, 71, 82, 90, 106, 140, 223
Ehud, 77
El, 26, 29
El Amarna letters, 36, 38, 52, 66
Elephantine, 141, 150, 153, 158–60
Elijah, 45, 78, 107–8
Elisha, 45, 109
Elohist tradition, 25–6, 44–6, 49
Elon, 73
Emmanuel, 121
Ephraim, 41, 52, 64–5, 67, 68, 71, 73, 78, 79, 81
Esau, 25, 30
Essenes, 10, 112, 149, 183, 187, 200, 201, 237–9
Esther, 155–6, 171, 174
Ezekiel, 70, 139, 143–4, 201, 235

F
Felix, 224–5
Festus, 225
flint, 13–4
Florus, 225

G
Gad, 9, 58–9, 65, 67, 68, 76, 78, 79
Gadara, 199, 205, 206
Galilee, 12, 94, 181, 188
Gamaliel I, 204, 242
Gamaliel II, 242, 246
Gath, 53, 89, 112, 118
Gaza, 8, 10, 36, 40, 53, 120, 124, 129,
    166, 187, 199, 206
Gerizim, 9, 132, 162, 166, 185, 212
Gezer, 10, 18, 34, 37, 41, 55, 56, 93,
    102, 182–3, 184
Gideon, 78–9
Gilead, 7, 9, 30, 58, 59, 72, 73, 76,
    120, 181, 187
Gilgal, 59, 62, 69, 78, 81
Golan, 188, 204
Goliath, 87
Gomorrah, 37

H
Habbakuk, 137–8, 240
Habiru, 23, 38, 41, 42, 44, 66, 68
Haggai, 150, 153
Hamath, 106, 113, 124, 139, 163
Hammurabi, 23–4, 48–9
Hanukah, 181
Haran, 26–7, 136, 147
Hasidim, 172, 180, 181, 184, 186, 191
Hasmoneans, 180–91
Hazor, 10, 30, 33, 34, 66, 76, 92, 93,
    104
Hebron, 8, 10, 56, 89, 97, 181
Herod Agrippa I, 213, 221–2
Herod Agrippa II, 222, 224–5
Herod Antipas, 204, 206–7
Herodian, 193, 203, 235
Herod Philip, 207
Herod the Great, 195–204

Hezekiah (king), 117, 124–9
Hezekiah (priest), 195, 224
Hiram, 92, 94
Hittite, 29, 39, 41, 42, 43, 50, 52, 68
Horace, 204, 247
Horeb, 46, 67
Hormah, 56
Hosea, 45, 120
Hyksos, 33–5, 38, 42, 43, 62, 79
Hyrcanus I, 185–6
Hyrcanus II, 188–9

I
Isaac, 24, 29–30, 45, 91
Isaiah (first), 119–21
    (second), 147–8
    (third), 152–3
Ishbaal, 89
Israel (patriarch), 30–1, 35
Issachar, 66–7, 68, 76

J
Jacob (patriarch), 24, 25, 30–1, 34, 58,
    67
Jaffa (Joppa), 7, 19, 185, 188
Jamnia, 177, 206, 240
Jehoram, 109
Jehoshaphat, 91
Jehu, 99
Jephthah, 72–3, 75
Jeremiah, 4, 136–41
Jericho, 9, 12, 14, 36, 51, 62, 77,
    168
Jeroboam I, 95, 100–1, 185, 199, 203,
    206, 236
Jeroboam II, 113–5
Jerubbaal, see Gideon
Jerusalem, 4, 10, 12, 32, 51, 55, 56,
    62, 90, 113, 118, 128, 131–3, 136–
    40, 156–7, 160, 168, 178–81, 183,
    196, 218, 221, 234–5, 244
Jesus ben Sirach, 171
Jesus Christ, 210–2, 238
Jethro, 44
Jezebel, 104–8

Jezreel, 8, 12, 33, 36, 37, 38, 53, 55, 59, 67, 76, 77, 109, 135
Joab, 89, 91–2
Joash of Israel, 113
Joash of Judah, 112
Job, 143, 163
John the Baptist, 207
Jonathan, 83, 87, 91
Joppa, see Jaffa
Joseph (patriarch), 34–5, 52, 64, 67, 68, 70, 71
Josephus, 33, 151, 157, 168, 169, 173, 188, 191, 207, 208, 213, 219
Joshua, 33, 51–70
Josiah, 130–6
judges, 71–85

K
Kadesh, 36, 42, 46, 58, 67
Karnak, 34, 36, 40, 102, 140
Kenites, 3–4, 44, 54–6, 58, 77
Kenizzites, 56, 58
King's Highway, 10, 33

L
Laban, 26, 30
Lachish, 4, 34, 37, 64, 101, 113, 139, 158
Laish, 64–5
law, 48–50, 68–9
Leah, 31, 67
Levi, 31, 35, 45, 58, 59, 67, 71
Libyans, 43, 52
Lot, 29–30

M
Maccabees, 6, 178–91, 193–4
Machaerus, 189, 194, 203, 235
Machir, 52, 59, 64, 65, 67, 76, 78
Machpelah, 25–6, 29
Madaba, 55, 105, 185
Malachi, 150, 156
Mamre, 26, 89, 200
Manasseh (king), 128–30

Manasseh (tribe), 52, 59, 64–5, 67, 68, 78
Manetho, 33
Mara, 48
Marc Antony, 196–9
Mari, 4, 23, 26, 29–30, 33, 41, 66
Mariamme, 196, 198, 206
Masada, 18, 198, 203, 228, 235
Medes, 146, 147
Medinet-Haba, 52–3
Megiddo, 4, 8, 10, 12, 21, 34, 36–7, 40, 55, 76, 93, 102, 104, 121, 136
Memphis, 42, 129, 140, 153, 182
Menahem, 120, 228–9
Meribah, 46
Meribbaal (Mephibosheth), 91
Mer-ne-ptah, 43, 52–3
Mesha, 58, 104–5
messiah, 87, 119, 123, 148, 153, 177, 191, 209–12, 224, 228, 238, 241–2
Micah, 123, 137
Micaiah, 106
Michal, 87
Miriam, 46, 48, 76
Mishnah, 240
Mitanni, 35, 36, 39, 40
Mizpah, 81, 103, 140
Moab/Moabites, 7, 9, 29, 43, 55, 58, 73, 77, 78, 90, 102, 138, 187
monarchy, 81–139
Moses, 3, 4, 6, 31, 43–50, 52, 55, 59, 62, 71, 78
Munhata, 16, 17

N
Nabateans, 8, 9, 10, 176, 182, 185–91, 200
Nabonidus, 147–9, 174
Nahum, 130, 136, 241
Nathan, 90, 92, 99
Nazareth, 209, 242
Nebuchadnezzar, 137–9, 147, 174, 177
Nebupolassar, 135, 137
Negeb, 8, 29, 54, 93
Nehemiah, 150, 157–8
Nephtali, 66, 67, 68, 76, 78

Nero, 210, 224–5
Nineveh, 129, 130
Nippur, 142, 150
Noth, Martin, 69–70
Nuzi, 36

O
Obadiah, 140
Octavian, 198–209
Og, 33, 59
Omri, 103–4
Othniel, 56, 75
Ovid, 247

P
Parthian, 181, 185, 196, 219–21, 243
Passover, 26, 45, 62
patriarchs, 24–41, 68, 78
Paul, 204, 221, 224, 240
Pekah, 120
Pella, 55, 241
Pentateuch, 43–4, 48–50, 144, 162, 240
Penuel, 57, 79, 100, 102
Petra, 9, 189–90, 194
Pharisees, 186–9, 244–6
Philip V, 172–3
Philistines, 7, 12, 25, 37, 41, 46, 64, 66, 71, 77, 81, 82, 89–90
Philo, 216–7, 237, 242, 247
Philostratus, 247
Phoenicians, 7, 12, 22, 38, 62, 81–2, 92–3, 104–5
Pompey, 189–95
Pontius Pilate, 209–12
Priestly Code, 49
Priestly tradition, 25–6, 28–9, 44–5
prophets (see also individual names), 45, 62, 73, 87
Proverbs, 163
Psalms, 86, 163
Ptolemais, see Acco
Purim, 156

Q
Quietus, 243–4

Quirinius, 207–8
Qumran, 4, 112, 201, 227, 236–9, 240, 244

R
Rachel, 31, 67
Ramah, 76, 81, 82, 103
Rameses II, 41–3
Rameses III, 4, 52, 54, 77
Rameses IV, 42
Red Sea, 4, 10, 54
Rehoboam, 99, 101–2
Reuben, 9, 58–9, 67, 71, 76
Ruth, 163

S
Sadducees, 186, 189, 198, 245
Samaria, 8, 12, 157, 178, 185, 191, 194, 199
Samaritans, 158, 162, 163, 164–5, 166
Samson, 80
Samuel, 80, 81–5, 87
Sanhedrin, 151, 189, 196, 204, 210, 240, 246
Sarah, 25
Sargon the Great, 22, 35, 44
Sargon II, 123, 141
Saul, 62, 82, 83, 85, 87, 91
schism, 97–115
Sea-Road (Via Maris), 10, 32, 36, 40, 102
Sennacherib, 124–8, 142
Sepphoris, 230, 246
Seti I, 40, 42
Shalmaneser III, 106–7
Shalmaneser V, 123
Shamgar, 58, 77
Shammai, 204
Shechem, 8, 12, 25, 26, 34, 41, 58, 59, 68, 79, 92, 99, 100, 132, 155, 185, 187
Shephelah, 7
Shiloh, 8, 12, 69, 81
Sidon, 7, 64, 83, 110, 113, 124–7, 171
Simeon, 31, 35, 58, 59, 67, 71

Sinai, 6, 8, 9, 21, 37, 46, 48–50, 67, 68, 223
Si-nuhe, 31–2, 44
Sirach, 171
Sisera, 76–7, 177
Sodom, 37
Solomon, 4, 6, 10, 24–5, 35, 66, 90, 92–5, 97
Sumer, 21–22, 41, 149
Suppiluliumas I, 40
synagogue, 145, 162, 169, 195, 240, 246

T
Taanach, 36, 37, 55, 66, 76, 102
Tabor, 67, 77, 188
Tacitus, 210, 247
Talmud, 164, 188, 210, 239–40, 244–5
Targum, 164, 238, 240
Tel-Abib (Tel-Aviv), 142–3
Teleiat Ghassul, 18
Tell el-Far'ah, 18, 34, 53
Temple of Jerusalem, 12, 112, 137, 139, 151, 153, 154, 157, 162, 168, 172, 178–82, 189, 194, 200–1, 230, 233, 239–40
    at Hazor, 66, 92
    at Shechem, 92
    Solomon's, 69, 92–3
Thutmose III, 36–7, 38, 42, 76
Tiglath-pileser I, 82–3
Tiglath-pileser III, 117–23, 141
Timnah, 9, 54
Titus, 216, 234, 239

Tobiads, 171–2
Tobias, 157, 171
Transjordan, 9, 10, 12, 18, 33, 58–9, 68, 79, 100, 187
twelve tribes, 67–9
Tyre, 7, 22, 92, 113, 120, 143, 158, 166

U
Ugarit, 24, 30–1, 35, 36, 37–8, 45, 49, 93
Ur, 21, 26–7
Uriah, 90
Uzziah, 118–9

V
Vespasian, 231–2, 239
Via Maris, see Sea-Road

X
Xerxes, 155

Y
Yahwist tradition, 24–5, 45–6, 49, 92

Z
Zadok, 90–1
Zealots, 223–4
Zebulun, 66, 67, 68, 73, 76, 78
Zechariah (first), 150, 154
Zechariah (second), 163
Zerubbabel, 153–4
Zilpah, 58, 67
Zipporah, 44